Theodore H. White writing in
"The New York Times" about
THE INCREDIBLE KRUPPS:

"Author Norbert Muhlen begins his account with the single-minded, grasping Alfred who, in the second quarter of the last century, transformed the little Essen iron works into Europe's finest steel processor. A totalitarian by instinct, who distrusted his workers, his associates, his family, his rivals. Alfred created one of the world's first industrial espionage systems. He constructed his home on the principles that the smell of horse manure stimulated creative thinking and open windows caused draft—(his) were forever sealed.

"Old Alfred left his industrial empire to his slightly-less repulsive son, Fritz. A suave and effective arms salesman, Fritz enjoyed the company of the mighty but enjoyed young boys more. He committed his wife to an insane asylum to silence her, but his remarkable orgies at Capri could not be silenced. Fritz was found dead under circumstances the family has never completely explained.

"Fritz' daughter Bertha, who inherited the family fortune, chose for marriage a man a full head shorter than she. Gustav Krupp von Bohlen und Halbach (he assumed the family name as well as its manners) was a gobbler of food, pompous, rude and scraped to only two people—his wife Bertha and a man he admired, Adolf Hitler."

Whether they were victims of history and genetics— whether they were active participants in the murder of innocents—they forged a personal and political chronicle unparalleled in fact or fiction!

Here is what the reviews said about
THE INCREDIBLE KRUPPS:

"Unusually competent writing, thoughtful historical research and the insight into men and events make this a fascinating story and a significant book. In a sense, this is the story of a significant segment of modern world history."   —*Chicago Tribune*

"Norbert Muhlen knows how to tell a story . . . The book should have wide reader appeal."
—*Library Journal*

"Mr. Muhlen's book makes all those dynastic novels about cynical and avaricious families seem pallid."
—*New Yorker*

"Author Muhlen livens his chronicle with a series of personality sketches of the lonely, driven eccentrics who lorded it over the steel works at Essen."
—*Time*

"An unusually readable book, highly personalized . . . it contains a great deal of fascinating information about the Krupp family."
—James Gavin, Lt. General, U.S.A. (ret.)

"Norbert Muhlen emerges as the master journalist, the impeccable student, the tireless researcher, the courageous analyst, and the natural storyteller. His book is not only exciting and suspenseful reading, but it is also an important contribution to understanding the dilemma of our times and the complex responsibility we all carry."
—Leo Cherne, Executive Director
The Research Institute of America, Inc.

ABOUT THE AUTHOR

Norbert Muhlen, a Bavarian by birth, has been a correspondent for American and European newspapers. The material for this book is based on years of scrupulous research which included several trips to Germany, where he had access to confidential files and scores of personal interviews with key figures. Mr. Muhlen is also a frequent contributor to such American magazines as *Reader's Digest* and *The Reporter*.

THE INCREDIBLE KRUPPS

The Rise, Fall, and Comeback
of Germany's Industrial Family

NORBERT MUHLEN

AWARD BOOKS
NEW YORK

TANDEM BOOKS
LONDON

FIRST AWARD PRINTING 1969

AWARD BOOKS are published by
Universal Publishing and Distributing Corporation
235 East Forty-fifth Street, New York, N. Y. 10017

TANDEM BOOKS are published by
Universal-Tandem Publishing Company Limited
14 Gloucester Road, London SW7, England

Manufactured in the United States of America

Contents

Foreword

For the past 160 years, the House of Krupp has worried, intimidated, occasionally shocked, and always puzzled the world at large. It continues to do so even today, although the reasons for our bewilderment have ceased to operate. Yet in the light of the rather rampant record and the many metaporphoses of the Krupps, it cannot come as a surprise that their fame and notoriety outlast their life.

The House of Krupp is a world-wide business empire, which was owned by one German family passing it on from one heir to the next, as if it were a small family farm. Over the past five generations it preserved this hereditary one-man rule as though this business empire were a feudal kingdom. Only yesterday, the world heard the announcement that "Krupp is dead!" But in the best monarchic fashion, there followed a call: "Long live Kruppdom!" Almost incredibly, the House of Krupp survived its own death. Today it is livelier than ever. Even this most recent revival followed the tradition of the House of Krupp, whose success story has been punctuated—and stimulated—by fall and failure over five generations.

Krupp is not a euphonious name. However you pronounce it, it sounds like the blast of a cannon, the explosion of a shell, a Tiger tank stopping in its track—in short, like all the deadly wares mass-produced on Krupp's assembly line for a century of conflict. Regardless of the sound of the name, the present-day Krupp—a member of

Armorers Anonymous, as it were—wouldn't touch a gun, let alone make one. The once leading armament manufacturers of Germany have gone on the wagon. That is, they have gone off the battle wagon, or so they have announced. Nevertheless, the old martial memories linger. On the rebound or not, Krupp still resounds in many ears with uncomfortable, enigmatic, if not dangerous, echoes and signals.

Over the past five generations Krupps have clicked glasses with the world's powerful—from the German Kaiser, to Adolf Hitler, to Nikita Khrushchev—and have done business with all of them. If, as many contemporaries assumed, this business concentrated great power in the hands of the Krupps, it certainly filled their cashbox made from their own heat-resistant, history-resistant Krupp steel. A penniless convict only twenty years ago, ten years later the ruling Krupp was once more one of the world's six wealthiest men, a worthy heir of his equally rich ancestors. He would not—or could not—tell me how much he owns in dollars and cents, but his personal wealth surpassed the billion-dollar mark, which seems impressive even in the years of the vanishing five-cent cigar.

But if the story of the House of Krupp were merely the story of its success in doing business and amassing wealth, it could be told on a few balance sheets and bank statements. The story of Krupp consists of considerably more and different chapters. Its heroes are the unusual men of the house—strange, often eccentric people caught in their private misfortunes, scandals, and failures. It deals with the powers and pitfalls of people whose billion-dollar fortunes did not free them of human bondage. It traces the growth of a unique private empire founded, preserved, and run along strictly dynastic lines. In the background of this story, and often enough in the center of the stage, we witness world politics, wars both hot and cold, and the great social changes of this century.

The Krupps can be fully seen and understood only against the background of modern German history. In fact, one can understand modern Germany better by a close look at the Krupps whose course reflected the course of their country. Therefore, the Krupp story is also one facet of the history of Germany.

Krupp history, like Soviet history, has been continuously rewritten. While contemporaries changed their views to denounce as crimes actions which only yesterday had been celebrated as meritorious feats, the public image of the Krupps changed and adapted accordingly. But as love is not love, history is not history "which alters when it alterations finds."

Only yesterday the Krupps appeared in many eyes as the demiurge who created war and wickedness throughout the world for personal gain, and their story was presented in this vein. "The men with the muckrakes are often indispensable to the well-being of society," Theodore Roosevelt once mused, "but only if they know when to stop raking the muck, and to look upward to the celestial crown above them, the crown of worthy endeavor." Muckrakers and other prosecutors of the Krupps have been preceded as well as followed by hero-worshipers and other propagandists of the House of Krupp, including its admirably industrious and pathetically cowed full-time-employed house chroniclers. Unhappily, they only looked upward to that "celestial crown of endeavor" until their necks were stiff and their eyes blinded to the less glittering, often outright dark facts that could be discerned on earth. But the facts about the Krupps, whether bright or sinister, are more fascinating than muckraking or stargazing fiction.

In the narrative that follows I have attempted to report meaningful, authenticated facts. Fortunately, many leaders, participants, and witnesses of the Krupp story are alive, and I have probed for their recollections. In Essen, Berlin, Hamburg, Munich, Stockholm, and New York, I talked with the head of the House of Krupp, its directors, employees, and workers, with its chauffeurs and butlers, some having served the Krupps for the past half century, and with its competitors, enemies, and disgruntled former associates, as well as its friends and relations.

Also fortunately, a wealth of material written by the

Krupps themselves, or their associates, has been carefully preserved since the house was founded. The father of the firm suffered from what psychoanalysts would have diagnosed as a writing compulsion (although I doubt whether he would ever have submitted to a psychoanalyst's probe, or accepted his diagnosis if he had). While his compulsion possibly reflected his personal unhappiness, it surely contributed to the happiness of this reporter in search of facts. Other valuable written material has been preserved in the files of the House of Krupp. I am grateful to its representatives who granted me access to some of these files.

From my personal interviews and from the documents there evolved a strange story, or rather, several strange stories intertwined and rolled into one. The rise, fall, and comeback of the House of Krupp and the fate of its heirs —forgers of their own fortunes upon whom "the iniquity of the fathers was visited unto the third and the fourth generation"—are part of our time, surely an adventurous part and perhaps a part of major consequence.

Unfortunately, I cannot enumerate all the names of those from whose personal information this book has benefited, and whom I should like to thank. Since I have foregone the use of footnotes my written sources are listed in the bibliography; I gratefully acknowledge my debt to those authors whose previous research has been used in this book.

The share which my editor, Beulah Harris, has had in the conception and making of this book seems to me far beyond and above the usual; hers was a most decisive contribution. I also want to convey my thanks to Dr. Bernd Hufschmid, Director of the Information Department of the Firm of Fried. Krupp in Essen, and to his staff for the coöperation in granting me access to the company and family archives and for arranging many interviews. I am deeply grateful to Dr. Ruth Berenson and Mr. Christopher Emmet of the American Council on Germany, Inc., for their friendship which helped me so much while I prepared this book.

—N.M.

PART I

The Foundation of Kruppdom

1587-1887

———

1

Roots and Fruits of a Family Tree

A penniless refugee—he called himself Arndt Krupp—
came to the town of Essen shortly before the year 1587.
A few years after his arrival he was a wealthy man.

The time was marked by turmoil and crisis. Germany
was divided into several parts ready to fight each other.
After Martin Luther proclaimed his ninety-five theses in
1517, some German lands were conquered by the Protestant reformation, while others remained faithful to the
Catholic Church. In an attempt to co-exist, Catholics and
Protestants arrived at a peace treaty in 1555: the Catholics gave up their goal to liberate by the sword the captives of the new order, and the Protestants surrendered
their aim of reforming the whole *Reich*. But throughout
the following decades, local limited wars continued to
rage.

Arndt Krupp, a convert to Protestantism, left his native
Lower Rhine River country where the Catholic faith remained in power. His exact place of origin and the year
of his emigration are unknown, despite the tireless labors
of latter-day Krupp historians to discover the roots of the
family tree. Neither do we know what led the emigrant to
settle in nearby Essen, unless we surmise that he was endowed with that fifth sense for the waves of the business
future which has characterized his offspring ever since.

With a population of less than 5000, Essen lacked the
beauty, wealth, and glory of German cities in the nearby
Rhine and Moselle river valleys. In fact, it was a rather
shabby place; for centuries the town had huddled in the

11

shadow of an old charterhouse for religious noblewomen whose abbess ruled the surrounding land with an efficient little army under her command. But the burghers of Essen grew restless in the middle of the sixteenth century, when the first promise of prosperity appeared on their horizon. As the forests which supplied them with charcoal were depleted, the ironmasters left the hills around Essen where they had exercised their modest craft and moved down to the Ruhr River Valley where coal was abundant under the ground.

With their advent, many poor burghers of Essen became ironmongers. Soon two dozen among them happily discovered a new and profitable use of iron when crossbows, the conventional weapon of warfare, were challenged by a new invention, the incomparably more destructive firearms. The manufacturers themselves fired the guns when the Essen burghers rebelled against their abbess-princess; they clamored for freedom from her rule, and won it as new adherents of the Protestant faith. Essen, with its Reformed and Lutheran population, became part of what was to be Prussia, and Arndt Krupp became part of Essen.

The refugee set up shop as a tradesman in his new community, and the register of the Town Merchants' Guild listed his name for the first time in the year 1587. Arndt Krupp bought and sold wine, liquor, spices, iron, cattle, in short, the main consumer commodities of his time.

He invested his profits, which were remarkably high, in real estate. Good luck was on his side. Twelve years after his arrival in Essen, the bubonic plague arrived. This Black Pest, as the murderous epidemic disease was called, made many Esseners believe that the end of the world had come. To enjoy their few last days on earth with a fistful of ready cash, they offered their land and gardens to the first buyer. Arndt Krupp, a cool-headed man, found profits rather than tragedy in the pest that threatened the townsfolk. In the panic, he bought all the real estate on which he could lay his hands, and, of course, at prices far below its value. The panic passed finally,

Krupp survived the plague, and thirteen years after his arrival in Essen, he was one of its wealthiest citizens.

After the plague Essen's artisans and tradesmen took over the city government from the impoverished patricians. The *nouveau-riche* newcomer Arndt Krupp was one of the leaders of the new class, which elected him to the city council. Rich and respected though he was at the time of his death in 1624, he would hardly be remembered today—as little as would the history of Essen itself —had not in the distant future, that is in our age, new Krupps succeeded on the trail which their ancestor had blazed.

The historian's hindsight tends to be color-blind; it often sees merely the purple thread of continuity in the sequence of generations. Whether it was such a significant thread, or merely seems so in hindsight, one of Arndt Krupp's sons, Anton, added guns made in Essen to the peaceful wares for sale in the store he inherited. The good luck which had helped his father to amass real estate favored the son, too. Three years after he went into the gun trade, war broke out. Luckily for him, it lasted thirty years and created an unheard-of demand for arms of any kind. This Thirty Years' War ended the dream of peaceful co-existence between Protestant and Catholic Germans. Foreign powers invaded Germany in the name of their religions and fought each other on German soil in a bitter, bloody struggle. According to the custom of the time, this second Krupp of Essen supplied both sides— the Catholics as well as the Protestants—with his wares, if and when they paid for them. An alert businessman, he also bought up quantities of iron as the raw material from which gun barrels were made, and sold the scarce commodity to the gunsmiths of Essen at good profits. Wine, beer, and schnapps enjoyed a tremendous wartime boom, as the mercenaries on both sides of the battle line were thirsty men; the best, if not the only way for the citizenry to keep them from raping their women, torturing their men, and sacking their cities was to regale them with potables until they fell asleep. While the war raged, the second Krupp of Essen expanded his wine trade in a big way. When the Thirty Years' War came to an end in 1648, Germany was in ruins, her unity destroyed, her economic strength thoroughly exhausted, and Krupp had waxed richer even than his father.

While this first Krupp heir concentrated on the martial trade in guns, iron, and wine, his sister Katharina, a widow who survived her husband by fifty-five years, tended her father's civilian store. Following his example, she also searched for bargains in real estate, and times of war favored this endeavor as much as times of plague. "While hundreds of Essen citizens were impoverished, and while the town itself was more than once forced to sell its valuables, we see her buying more and more lands in every year," Krupp's most devoted family chronicler, Wilhelm Berdrow, reports in admiration. "Throughout the thirty years of the war which ruined Essen, this woman amassed such a quantity of money, land, and interest claims that she probably became Essen's wealthiest woman." In 1675, she died at the age of eighty-eight, the first of a line of Krupp women who were to prove themselves outstandingly shrewd in business, a field in which career women made their mark a long time before they were "emancipated," or before it was discovered that there were careers for women.

The Krupps had become Essen's leading family by the time the grandchildren of the poor immigrant Arndt took over. As their family trade and real-estate businesses prospered, fellow citizens elected the head of the House of Krupp to the office of town clerk, a position rich in honors as well as in profits; only the victims objected to a municipal official who used his office as another private business opportunity. Town Clerk Krupp packed the city government with his relatives and hangers-on.

When, in the early eighteenth century, the fourth generation of Krupps took over, local chronicles called the family "Essen's uncrowned kings." Their rise to the summit coincided with the rise of Prussia, whose ruler was crowned King in 1701 when Prussia began to outgrow, or outgrab, its status as a poor and provincial fifth-rate power. By building up a strong military machine, Prussia's absolutist monarch forced the other, older, more civilized powers of Europe to take note of the newcomer state.

The fourth generation of Krupps ruled supreme in the Prussian town of Essen. One Arnold Krupp served as mayor, his brother—Georg Dietrich Krupp, the town's richest man—held the key position of town clerk, and other posts were occupied by their nephews and yes-men. Only one office—that of chairman of the Merchants' Guild—was held by an outsider, who according to custom was elected for lifetime. When, to the annoyance of the Krupps, who wanted no interference with their family rule, the chairman of the Merchants' Guild insisted on his independence, by personal decree Georg Dietrich Krupp removed him from his lifetime office and named as his successor another Krupp whose only qualification for the job was his name.

This was an open and unprovoked violation of law and custom, and a number of Essen citizens refused to accept it. They charged Krupp, their town clerk and uncrowned king, with arbitrary rule; they claimed that he had forged the election ballots, and soon they also accused him of fraud and graft. A delegation of citizens went to the town hall to ask for an accounting and for reinstatement of the illegally fired official. Town Clerk Krupp called his strongmen to beat up these advocates of a cleaner city government and throw them out. As a last resort, the rebels asked the Prussian government for help; the King dispatched two learned court councilors to his good town to investigate the disorders and try the culprits.

The first Krupp trial in history was held in 1707. The two investigating judges heard a long list of serious accusations against defendant Krupp: he did not pay any of the taxes which he imposed on his fellow citizens, he gave no accounting of the town finances, he hid the account books at his home, he appropriated building materials and other city property for his own personal use, he packed the town council with his followers and family, he decreed that the town pay him large honorariums and compensations for services never rendered and for dam-

ages never suffered—these were some of the charges leveled against him with facts and figures. After due investigation, Krupp was indicted on twelve counts. Rather than
deny his guilt, he tried to explain it away "with a show of
arrogance," as a contemporary chronicler wrote, and
asked that his accusers be prosecuted for smearing him,
slandering him, discriminating against him. A wild brawl
developed in the courtroom between accusers and accused, and the trial was adjourned. In the end, the judges
found most of the charges true. They ordered Krupp to
keep his city ledgers in a public place, to pay taxes like
his fellow citizens, and to cease persecuting his opponents; Krupp's countersuit against his alleged slanderers
was quashed. For his remaining years he succeeded in
holding on to his position of power and even to having
his nephew elected as his successor, before he died at
eighty-five. But he was hardly buried when the city
sequestered as much of his estate as was needed to satisfy
claims against his unlawful acquisitions.

Seven years after his death the Krupps of Essen—a
family of many branches by now—solemnly celebrated
the hundredth year in which the office of town clerk had
been held by one of their kin. But there was to be no second century of Krupp rule over Essen's town affairs.

With the fifth generation, the Krupps seemed to have
lost the drive and ambition of their ancestors. The scion
of the family lived quietly on the income which the store
and real estate brought him and made no effort to enlarge
his holdings. As often happens with late offspring of old
and wealthy families, the Krupps had arrived at a point
of stagnation, if not extinction. Like his brothers, the oldest Krupp of the fifth generation was childless on the
death of his wife. But he quickly married again. His bride
was a distant cousin who counted Arndt Krupp among
her forefathers; she was eighteen years old, her husband,
forty-six. He died five years later, leaving a son, an inherited fortune, and the family grocery.

The twenty-three-year-old woman carried on the business under the sign of the "Firm of the Widow Krupp,"
and she did so with all the energy, intelligence, and al-

most religious devotion in which Arndt Krupp, her ancestor, had excelled. She expanded the grocery, started a
prosperous trade in textiles and paints, and added a
butcher shop and a sales agency of lottery tickets.
Branching out into other new and promising fields, she
founded a snuff factory and bought at least six large
farms. If trade and real estate were traditional Krupp interests, she made a momentous new advance into heavy
industry—a new business field then—when she acquired
a bankrupt ironworks called the Forge of Good Hope. In
addition, she bought shares in four coal mines.

Once again a Krupp became one of Essen's richest citizens. Her son served as her bookkeeper and died at an
early age, leaving three children. Friedrich, the oldest, or-
phaned at seven, was the founder of the future Krupp
empire.

Friedrich Krupp was born in 1787, exactly two hundred years after his forefather was mentioned for the first
time in the annals of Essen. In those past two centuries,
the Krupp family had excelled in trade and business, but
in nothing else. Not a single clergyman, doctor, scholar,
or officer emerged from this family, as was customary
among other wealthy German families of the time. Nor
did the Krupps produce things as artisans did; their family tradition was trade, not manufacture. In strange sin-
gle-mindedness the Krupps pursued only the acquisition
of money and property. If for almost a century the family
had pursued this goal also by its hold on local political
power, the attempt had ended with rebellion, a public
trial, and a measure of disgrace. But as long as the
Krupps stuck to business and nothing else, they recovered
from trials and crises. Theirs was a family of purebred
capitalists, long before the term was invented, let alone
turned into a smear-word by Karl Marx and his followers. The Krupps were steeped in the Protestant ethics
which their ancestor had embraced and practiced; with
Calvin and Zwingli they believed in the godliness of secu-
lar success by hard work and the ingenious use of opportunity. "Blessed are those who make money." Wealth was
considered the tangible evidence of Divine Grace. To

prove one's blessedness, by the display of blessings, one
had to labor as hard as one could.

This new doctrine and the family tradition of financial
survival and growth, as well as a family fortune enormous
by the standards of his time, was the heritage handed
down to Friedrich Krupp. With him began the Krupp dynasty of our day.

2

Founded on Failure

The House of Krupp was founded on failure. While it grew to be a world-wide dynasty, it kept calling itself *Firma Fried. Krupp,* the "Firm of Friedrich Krupp," immortalizing the name of its founder. But Friedrich Krupp succeeded only in wasting away the reputation and fortune of his old, wealthy family. He died a powerless, penniless failure. The six generations of Krupps before him had been hit by misfortune, and the five generations to follow would meet with new, seemingly deadly, disasters, but invariably the Krupps recovered and rose to even prouder heights. The only exception to this family rule was the foundering founder of the dynasty, who not only did not rebound from his fall but was destroyed by his defeat.

But nothing succeeded like his failure. "There is the greatest practical benefit in making a few failures early in life," the British scientist Thomas Henry Huxley noted in 1870. If we are less hopeful today about this and other claims of that optimistic era, the House of Krupp proved Huxley's wishful pronouncement. The forces which led to the rise and triumphs of the Firm of Krupp were brought about by the defeat with which it began.

When Friedrich Krupp was young, his grandmother did her best to turn him into a good Krupp; she taught him the art and science of business in her retail store—the only business education he ever got—but this business of selling flour, salt, and snuff to his fellow citizens held

19

little appeal for the young heir. He dreamed of greater things.

"To get him a decent income," his rich grandmother presented to him on his twentieth birthday her Forge of Good Hope; he was to manage it, but she cautiously kept the title to the property in her name. Like most everything she owned, the little iron foundry had become a source of profit, particularly after she asked the Prussian government for subsidies and in response was given orders for several products, included cannon balls, to be produced in her forge.

The twenty-year-old new industrialist began immediately to transform the forge which had turned out pots, pans, and stoves for the local market. Friedrich Krupp discharged the old foreman, enlarged the forge, and set out to convert his industry to the production of machine parts, cylinders, and steam pipes.

The plan spoke well for his initiative and vision. The machine age was coming, and he recognized the wave of the future at an early moment. He erred in judgment, however, for the time had not yet come for him to plunge heavily into the new venture. Only decades later would the Ruhr Valley lose its predominantly rural character and develop into an industrial center. In addition, he himself lacked the technical and business experience which his plans required. He was not adverse to the enjoyment of wine, women, and song, which made him unique among the Krupps, but what he really loved, with an almost sensuous passion, were big contruction plans and great production projects. A playboy of the business world, he inherited from his ancestors his sense of future opportunities, but he lacked their cool judgment of present possibilities.

Under Friedrich Krupp's management, the profits of the forge dropped quickly and dangerously. Foreseeing further losses, his grandmother sold the Forge of Good Hope to a syndicate of Rhineland industrialists at a price several times higher than she had paid for it. At the time, her grandson Friedrich kept a diary whose first entry was

a ditty he had learned from an organ grinder, and which
wailed:

> *Oh, my fate is now to starve,*
> *My dear children, look at me,*
> *Distress, misery we carve*
> *From our tomfoolery.*

> Ach, mein Los is jetzt zu darben,
> Liebe Kinder, seht mich an,
> Jammer, Elend sind die Garben
> Die die Thorheit erndten kann.

Strange motto of a wealthy young heir-to-be! Did he
warn himself against, or rather foresee and call for, such a
fate?

After his first failure as an industrialist, Friedrich returned to the profitable family retail trade and, with his
young wife, moved back to Grandmother's house. But he
soon discovered a new business opportunity which to his
adventurous mind seemed more tempting than working in
the stolid store. Napoleon had decreed an economic blockade against England and its Continental allies, the purpose of which was to destroy, or at least fatally weaken,
the archenemy by economic warfare. Since English industry and trade dominated Europe, this was a serious threat.
But when trade in needed commodities is suppressed by
force, it is replaced by illegal exchanges through black
marketeers, blockade-runners, and smugglers, and this
battle of the wits began soon after Napoleon's decree.
Among the enterprising men who succeeded in their private war for profit was a young Frankfurt businessman by
the name of Nathan Rothschild. Leaving his French-occu-
pied home town, Nathan settled in London, and the gold
and textiles which he managed to smuggle back to his
brother on the continent laid the foundation on which the
House of Rothschild was built.

The young Essen businessman Friedrich Krupp also
went into this business. He made a contract with a company of Dutch wholesalers to send him coffee, indigo,

sugar, and soap across the blockaded border. As an advance, Krupp paid them a substantial sum, 10,000 thalers, for the clandestine operation. It brought him a small return until the border patrols became more effective, when some of the smugglers were killed en route and the Dutch partners could find no replacements. This ended Friedrich Krupp's second personal venture.

About the same time his grandmother died, leaving more than a hundred thousand thalers, at today's rates over a million dollars. For a private citizen, and a woman at that, to have amassed such a fortune was almost unheard-of in her time. His share in the inheritance made Friedrich Krupp a very wealthy young man, and he became even wealthier a year later when a great-aunt died and left him an additional fortune. He set about enlarging it all by himself.

He saw his great chance when the brothers Georg Karl Gottfried and Wilhelm Georg Ludwig von Kechel, two aging, pensioned army officers, arrived in Essen. Their wisdom seemed as imposing as their names; what they had discovered, they told the rich young man, was "the secret of casting steel." They were willing to share it, or at least its profits, with Krupp if he provided the money needed to translate their knowledge into a going operation. To know "the secret of casting steel" at that time held the same lure as had, say, a century before, the secret of making gold or the elixir of eternal life, and little more than a century later, the secret of splitting the atom, or making rain, or getting thin in a week.

The "secret of casting steel" stood exactly midway between alchemy and technology. This "secret" had been solved only in England where in Sheffield a watchmaker named Benjamin Huntsman had invented the process about 1740. His invention had been taken over, improved on, and used by several British factories which supplied the world's somewhat limited market, mainly makers of watches, precision tools, and dies for mints and engravings. But with the opening of the machine age in the nineteenth century the demand increased enormously. Cast steel could be mass-produced in large quantities of almost equal quality. It was hard, yet malleable. Pig iron, its main raw material, was available in abundance. In short, cast steel appeared as the matter from which the machine age itself could be forged. Again it was a credit to Friedrich Krupp's sense of business anticipation that he foresaw this tremendous future need for the then still relatively unimportant material. To master its production seemed to him an exciting adventure.

In order to break the British steelmaking monopoly and thus get a new strangle hold on his enemy, Napoleon offered an award of four thousand thalers to the first manufacturer on the Continent who would turn out cast steel of British quality. Several foundries in Belgium, Germany, and Switzerland were already working for this prize when Krupp joined the race. The rich coal and iron-ore reserves in the neighborhood of Essen supplied an excellent basis for industrial undertakings of this kind. The location became particularly favorable when the Prussian State turned the Ruhr River into a navigable waterway on which products could be cheaply transported. A few rich tradesmen in the Ruhr district, whose names still have a commanding sound in our day—Thyssen, Haniel, Poensgen—founded new iron- and coal-mining industries, and at the same time an almost illiterate cabinetmaker of technological genius built and installed the first steam engine in the Ruhr Valley. The age of industrialization was being born, and its first feeble heartbeat could be heard in the Ruhr district.

On November 20, 1811, Friedrich Krupp signed a contract with the two von Kechel brothers jointly to build and run "a factory making British cast steel and all products manufactured from it." This was the birth of the Firm of Friedrich Krupp. He himself would supply the capital, the plant, and all raw materials, while the two brothers were to contribute their knowledge of the production "secret." The profits would be shared equally by the three partners. Carried away by the prospects of the future, Krupp immediately hired more than fifty workers to construct smelting works, a forge, and other buildings, began to manufacture the crucibles in which the steel would be cast, and ordered large supplies of raw material, from coal to iron. One hundred elegant lists with the prices of Krupp's "Best British Steel" were printed by Messrs. Baedecker in Essen. He was in a rush to start the venture, the success of which he never doubted. As he triumphantly announced, he was ready "to supply all of Europe with his steel."

His hopes were upset, however, by the simple fact that his two partners were less ready than he. They were still searching for the "secret." While they kept his crucibles hot and sterile for three years, Krupp lost twenty times more than he earned, and his financial resources dwindled. He did not know—and only after World War II would an industrious historian discover—that the expert knowledge of his two partners was derived from a generally available textbook of chemistry, which described the process of casting steel as "a necessary and quintessential fusion which is handled in secret." Laymen easily misunderstood this clumsy description, and despite their long search, the two brothers remained laymen.

After some years, Friedrich Krupp's patience was as exhausted as his cashbox. He canceled his contract with the two brothers, and after a fight about the ownership of the Cast Steel Factory, which they lost, they disappeared from Essen. Friedrich Krupp was left the owner of an incomplete cast-steel foundry, poorer, perhaps somewhat sadder, and probably much wiser; watching his two partners at their experiments, he had acquired at least a smattering of knowledge about the use of crucibles and other machinery in his favorite industry.

But he was hardly much wiser when it came to the hard facts of business. A few months after the rule of Napoleon ended, a new steelmaking expert—again a retired officer, this time a former captain of the Prussian hussars by the name of Friedrich Nicolai—visited Krupp in Essen. The captain introduced himself and his abilities by a paid advertisement in the *Westfaelischer Anzeiger,* a newspaper widely read in the Ruhr Valley, as "a useful member of human society" who "has traveled widely throughout most of Germany, Holland, England, and

France to form his artistic talents, and has gathered on his travels a wealth of the most productive knowledge, notably about every kind of machine." In brief, he was looking for a job. When the job-hunting ex-officer confided to Krupp that he was thoroughly familiar with the secret art of casting steel and showed a letter from the Prussian authorities to prove it, Krupp signed a partnership agreement with him to revive his factory. But after the lesson of his previous fiasco, he tried to guard his financial interests more carefully. He made the initial investment, money newly inherited from his brother plus a loan from "the Jew Moses," as he noted in his ledger, but his partner was to pay all operating expenses. Once again Krupp started to build new plants, and sixty crucibles.

In a letter he described the "most pleasant sensation" which "beautiful and expensive construction plans" gave him. This sensation again carried him away before he discovered that his new partner was unable to pay the operating expenses. When Krupp tried at least to learn from him the "secret" of steelmaking, the partner confided that this was "classified and restricted" information; the state of Prussia had sworn him to secrecy for the sake of national security. Krupp believed him and was impressed. He enlarged his production schemes, but they were soon halted when his partner suddenly discovered that he could not use the coal available to the firm and that only coal from an abandoned mine close by would satisfy his needs. When Krupp attempted to purchase and reopen that mine, the Prussian government unexpectedly sent a commission of experts to the new foundry. They investigated, found the planned steelmaking technique unworkable, and so informed Krupp. Krupp furiously fired his partner who, after extended legal counterattacks, finally left. But if Krupp had been fooled twice by men who, though not charlatans, were surely swindlers, he had learned from their work, their frustrated experiments, their fruitless search for the "secret," that there was no magical secret to steelcasting. He had also learned the essential procedures of the craft.

Now sole owner of the five-year-old firm, Krupp began

producing steel for the first time in 1816. In an early and remarkable attempt at "public relations," he had an article about his work written by his bookkeeper and "planted" in an influential Frankfurt newspaper. Slowly he received and filled orders, mainly for artisans' and mechanics' tools and the more lucrative dies from which the Prussian Mint cast coins. The Prussian State also gave him a small order for cast steel for the manufacture of bayonets. His early ancestors had delivered iron for gun barrels, his grandmother iron for cannon balls, and this was the third, though rather insignificant, arms deal of a Krupp.

When the factory had been operating for four years, it looked as though Friedrich Krupp had finally succeeded in a modest way. But he was not the man to be content with limited success; it only stimulated him to anticipate a coming greater one. He branched out into the production of new products for which there was not yet a market, and at the same time started to build new and larger factories close to the town of Essen as well as to the coal mines. But his plans did not work out. He had overlooked the fact that he had built on a site which had only seasonal waterpower. This meant a severe loss, and he was able to keep going only by borrowing constantly from his family. His mother had to sell her land to help him pay his promissory notes and soon his inlaws had to lend him money to save the family reputation; bankruptcy was a crime in the eyes of nineteenth-century burghers. When his new factory finally was ready, he lacked the money to purchase proper raw materials and was forced to use cheap scrap iron, which in turn lowered the quality of his output. Although the general demand increased, his sales decreased, and he tottered precariously along the brink of failure.

His last resort was the State. He asked Prussia for subsidies, but his request was rejected. Forced to give up his independent operation, he applied for the job of manager in a new State-controlled steel foundry, but he was not hired. Next he offered his services to the Czar of Russia; he proposed that he set up the first steel mills in his empire. But Russia was no more interested in Krupp of Essen than was his native Prussia.

After all these disappointments, the gay and exuberant dreams of his youth faded away. He complained that he was tired and worn-out. He was in his mid-thirties. His sales—which had reached a few thousand thalers annually in his better years—dwindled to a few hundred thalers a year, mainly for small quantities of raw steel, tools, and scissors. He lost all interest in cast steel and other adventures of contemporary industry. He felt that the factory had failed him.

Like a disappointed lover, Friedrich Krupp turned his back to the firm and used the few sparks still alight under the ashes of his ambition to kindle fires other than those in his furnaces. With an energy which still appeared impressive, he entered Essen's local politics as a self-appointed city planner and town reformer. Public service was almost as close to his heart as the founding of new industries. As a young man of twenty-four, he had volunteered as billeting commissioner for the hated Napoleonic occupation troops in his town, an honorary position to which no other Essen citizen or Prussian patriot wished to be appointed. A year later he had served with the same enthusiasm as police commissioner for the Prussian liberation troops which ousted the French invaders. Now that he had lost his and his family's fortune in his factory ventures, he worked out new budget plans for his town. The Esseners found them much too grandiose for their rather sleepy country town of seven thousand. Next he dreamed up elaborate schemes for beautifying his town. According to his plan, Essen's main street was to be paved with cobblestones, to be supplied without cost by the demolition of the old city walls, which were to be replaced by a ring of greenery and landscaped gardens. In those years Essen was one of Germany's ugliest and most hazardous towns. "If one walks along its lanes in the evening, he risks his life in the most literal sense," a visiting Prussian official by the name of Justus Gruner wrote in his travelogue. Friedrich Krupp felt a civic challenge to make his backward town safe and beautiful, and his ideas, if not his qualifications, foreshadowed those of modern city planners.

While he busied himself in his community, his factory creditors pursued him through one law court after another. He transferred ownership of his household goods to his mother to remove them from the grip of the men to whom he was indebted, and his mother became entangled in his lawsuits. She, as well as the other members of the family, refused to throw any more money into the bottomless pit of his debt-ridden factory. Two years before his death the name of Friedrich Krupp was stricken from the register of Essen's taxable, which meant respectable businessmen. Disgraced as a citizen, penniless, and broken in health and spirit, he had to move from the old patrician family townhouse to the foreman's cottage on his factory grounds. Life had disappeared from these grounds on which he once had tried to produce steel and which he now tried to convert into gardens. The frustrated planner begged his old friends for trees and bushes from their parks and worked hard laying out flower beds around his furnaces. He managed to care for his wife and two youngest sons, but in the last year of his life, his daughter was forced to take a job as a governess and his son Alfred lived with relatives in town because he was unable to feed them. In 1826, at the age of thirty-nine, Friedrich Krupp died of dropsy. Perhaps he died also of failure.

Friedrich Krupp failed because he prematurely anticipated the triumph of steel and big business which was to come only a quarter of a century later. Even if he did succeed in solving several technological "secrets" of the new industry, he was bound to fail when it came to financing, marketing, and producing. Germany was not yet ready for the growth of industry he envisaged.

What was called Germany—that is, more than a dozen sovereign and independent kingdoms, archduchies, and duchies whose people happened to speak a similar language—was a "geographic conception" rather than a political, let alone an economic, reality. Contemptuous of power and aggrandizement, Germans then aspired to be "a people of poets and thinkers" rather than industrialists and soldiers. Prussia was still an agrarian state of feudal estates and garrisons. The pursuit of happiness still seemed life's desirable goal, rather than the pursuit of bigness and power. England moved into the industrial age with mighty strides, while Germany stood reluctantly at its entrance gate. In the year in which Friedrich Krupp died, Goethe complained to his friend Zelter that a new era was beginning in which "it is riches and speed that the world admires and strives for . . . ," an era which he denounced as "essentially the century of the able men, the practical, quickly comprehending heads who, equipped with a certain shrewdness, sense their superiority over the crowd, although they themselves are not of the highest character."

Friedrich Krupp lived the tragedy of the premature pioneer who is without honor in his time. But his children were rewarded with the benefits of his foolishness, or, if you prefer, his vision.

3

Essen to Empire

Alfred Krupp, Friedrich Krupp's oldest son, was an unhappy boy. Born with the silver spoon of Essen's richest family in his mouth, he spent his childhood in poverty brought about by his father. As his relatives and friends kept deploring, Alfred was *déclassé,* robbed of his rightful claims to wealth and rank, destined to a life far below his origins.

From the time he was eight, he had experienced only domestic disorders which grew worse with each year. At thirteen he was forced to quit school. In the eyes of his contemporaries, this marked him for the rest of his life as a nameless member of the lower classes, not so much because his education remained poor, but because custom required that the sons of "better families" attend school at least up to their eighteenth year.

His father could not afford even to send him to a master craftsman as an apprentice, as was customary for sons of lower-middle-class families. Since Friedrich Krupp could no longer afford to employ workers in his little factory, his thirteen-year-old boy took their place. At that time children of poor people worked in mines and mills before they reached puberty, sometimes for more than twelve hours a day, and, like them, Alfred Krupp became a juvenile worker. In the factory and at home, he watched the hopeless struggle and final surrender of his father. "I got my only schooling at an anvil," he used to reminisce later on, his bitterness posing as complacency.

The boy worked in the factory, at least sporadically,

30

when there was work, for half a year. He was barely fourteen when his father died. Friedrich Krupp, who had started his career with an inherited capital of more than 200,000 thalers, left an estate of 15,000, which, burdened by claims of 25,000, left a debt of 10,000 thalers.

Despite this debt-ridden inheritance and four minor children, the widow did not apply for bankruptcy, which would have entailed not only civic disgrace but also the loss of what remained of the factory and its machines. "Business will not suffer at all from my husband's passing away," she informed customers and suppliers eleven days after the event. "Providentially my husband taught the secret of casting steel to my eldest son, who has run the production and management of the factory all alone throughout his father's illness, and I shall carry on the business with his help."

She signed the announcement which was penned by her son. A rich peasant's daughter who had married Friedrich Krupp when she was sixteen, the widow, now thirty-six, was still hardly able "to speak her German mother-tongue correctly, let alone write it," as her brother-in-law had noted in a letter to her husband, with the suggestion he teach her these arts. But her husband never found time to follow this advice, and after his death she had to rely on her fourteen-year-old boy to write business letters, sell the products of the factory, and supervise their manufacture. A month after his father's death the youngster served a brief and tough notice of eviction on one of his father's oldest friends and fellow Freemasons, Chief Forester Griesenbeck, who had leased Krupp's old town house. Bitterly though the old gentleman complained to Alfred's mother about her rude, heartless child who "wants to lord it over the best friends of his father who has hardly been buried," and "who does not know the difference between a vagabond and a gentleman of rank," he had to move out. Forewarned by his father's failure, the boy had made up his mind he would be different: human feelings would not interfere with his business and he would make money in any way he could. These ideas held the makings of success and the foundations of an empire.

As was customary in poor Essen families, his mother kept a cow on the community pasture and a few pigs in the house, which saved her family from starving. But she looked to her eldest son, an extremely serious boy with no interest in play or the pleasures of his age, to succeed where his father had failed and be a good provider and a cool-headed businessman. Young Alfred himself desired nothing else, and accepted his new role with outward self-assurance. He felt contempt for the weakness of his father. "I learned a great deal more from my mother than from my father," he would later pointedly and publicly say. "I have inherited the industriousness by which she rescued the family." His entire life was a running battle against the memory of his father, while he tried to demonstrate that he himself was a different manner of man.

For this reason he chose to continue on the road on which his father had broken down, that is, in the making of cast steel. His grandmother and other relatives urged him to forget this failure-bound venture and join them in tending their prosperous stores. But the boy ignored their advice. If he succeeded where his father had failed, he would prove his superior worth and posthumously shame his father.

But as it looked to his doubting relatives, he only repeated the mistakes of his unfortunate father. With two to four occasional helpers who, he insisted, were to address him as *"Herr* Krupp," the youngster produced only the same pitifully small quantities of steel and the same rarely salable tools and dies as had his father. The greater part of his output he peddled to neighborhood customers. Despite his hard work, his turnover after four years was still lower than it had been in his father's best years.

The family supplied cash to keep him and his mother alive. Old friends of his likable, luckless father, pitying the young son, offered technological and commercial advice and often recommended his products to potential customers, or bought them themselves. From them he learned that profits were bigger if he manufactured and sold finished articles rather than partially completed products or the steel itself, as his father had done. This insight led to his first forward step.

But after several years of struggle, as soon as he saw the first ray of hope, young Krupp repeated to the letter the decisive mistake of his father. Before he could afford it he began to build a new machine shop in anticipation of future returns. Four years later, when it was completed, he discovered that he had built on a site that lacked water power for the greater part of the year. His loss threw him back to his beginnings. "Young Herr Krupp broods day and night over his business," his workers used to say.

The first real stroke of good luck came only after Alfred had brooded for eight years, struggling to turn his legacy into a going concern. Under Prussian pressure, in 1834, a German Customs Union was formed and the many independent German states agreed to tear down the customs barriers that divided them and unite in one large trade area. It was the first step toward Germany's political unification, a goal which some Germans feared because, with Goethe, they believed that their nation would remain truer to itself if it could avoid the drive toward bigness and its equalizing power; they preferred the division into small independent countries. But if they were right and German culture suffered, German commerce improved accordingly. For the first time a home market sufficient for the development of a modern German industry came into being.

Alfred Krupp was quick to see the opportunity, and to seize it. Immediately after the agreement was signed, Krupp left for his first business trip to distant parts of South and East Germany. On his return twelve weeks later, he had collected more orders than his little factory could fill. The following year his production tripled and his working force rose from nine to forty-five. Prussia's political and economic victory propelled his tiny factory to a middle-sized plant. At last he could afford to free himself from the vagaries and weaknesses of natural waterpower and buy his first steam engine. Ironically, it was from the Forge of Good Hope, which his grandmother had owned and his father had almost ruined, that he bought his machine. But Krupp's credit was still considered doubtful, and the steam engine was delivered to him only after a cousin had signed as guarantor. To install it and to enlarge the works required new credit, but, for the first time, he was rewarded by increased sales and profits.

Fired by this success, which provided both cash and confidence, he set out for bigger goals. As in his father's time, England still led in the making of cast steel; its plants turned out qualities and quantities incomparably superior to those of their German competitors. The best way to learn the "secret" of the British and to overtake them in the race was, it seemed to him, to go to England and watch the manufacturers at work—by a procedure which we would today call "industrial espionage." Alfred had taken as partners his two younger brothers, a brilliant technician and an able salesman, respectively, and they would take care of the factory in his absence. His passport introduced him as "A. Crup," and he introduced himself to the British as Herr Schropp, to hide his identity while he was snooping around the plants of his competitors.

He stayed abroad fifteen months. He had a pleasant time, in a very special way. "We called him the baron, he was very young, very tall and slim, of delicate, but good and interesting looks," Hermann von Mumm, a German diplomat who met Herr Schropp in England, reports in his memoirs. "He always wore small, long silver spurs and was quite a gentleman." The distinguished young foreigner was accepted with open arms by the unsuspecting British forgemasters; they would never have received him at all had they known that he was an aspiring competitor. "Yesterday I saw a new copper-plate rolling mill to which nobody is admitted. But I arrived on horseback with boots and spurs, and the owner was flattered that such a jolly gentleman stooped to pass by his shop," he wrote to his brothers from Sheffield. The main contents of his daily and lengthy letters were descriptions and drawings of what he had seen and advice on the business at Essen.

As he proudly wrote home, his British hosts taught him their language and fed him "at less than one-third of the costs." In the same letter he advised his brothers to cheat the mails by folding all enclosures into such small pieces that they would pass undetected at the post office. This would cost only half the legal postage.

But much space in his letters was taken up by his complaints, mainly about his health. On his twenty-seventh birthday he reported, "I celebrate my birthday in my own way, last year with cough medicine, this year with enemas." He sounded almost proud of his ailments, and he probably was.

After London, he went to Paris to sell some of his die cylinders to goldsmiths and jewelers. But after his arrival, the revolution of July, 1839, broke out, with the Liberals and Socialists trying to overthrow King Louis Philippe. "The revolution started here yesterday," Krupp informed his brothers, and added, "If it will improve business, they are free to bash in each other's heads. As far as I am concerned, I am satisfied. . . ."

What a sensation he would have created had the traveling salesman made this casual remark, say, twenty years later when he was trying hard to sell the weapons with which they could "bash in each other's heads," let alone fifty years later when he did supply the world with exactly these weapons. The world would have been shocked by the cynicism of the Cannon King and Merchant of Death, as the producers and traders of these arms were to be called. But when he wrote this, he did not yet even dream of that trade; his business was limited to such peaceful goods as tools for artisans and mints. The remark, however, revealed a basic and lasting axiom of Alfred Krupp and his firm. The axiom was simply that politics must not concern the businessman; he must remain indifferent to the course of human events, without participating in public affairs unless his business is directly affected. In brief, he must be *unpolitisch,* as the Germans call being apolitical.

This was a lesson he had learned from the failure of his father, who might have been more successful had he not spent so much time and energy in the service of his community. "We have no time for reading, politics, etc.," the son proudly described his prerequisite of success. What the "et cetera" stood for, we can only guess.

But if his paternal experience worked as a personal stimulus, Alfred Krupp was not alone among his countrymen with his *unpolitisch* view. On the contrary, in the eyes of the majority it seemed only right and good to steer clear of politics, not to participate in public life, to keep order in one's private house, and to leave the shaping of the common destiny to the government. In German usage, participants in government were called the *Obrigkeiten*, which literally and significantly means "the superiorities." Most Germans wholeheartedly agreed with Goethe, seeing "society, to whatever form of government it might be subject, as a state of nature which in its normal course alternates between rich and poor years, with occasional hailstorms, floods, and incendiary damages; the good is to be accepted and used, the evil to be avoided or tolerated."

Politics, as it appeared to Krupp, was a force not only to set apart from, but hostile to, the forces of business. With their passions and ideals the political men tended to disregard and disturb the "economic reason" of the businessmen.

Many businessmen of all nations have held similar views, and Alfred Krupp, one of Germany's first men of Big Business, was a businessman as much as a German in his belief that "business and politics don't mix." Over the next hundred years the history of the House of Krupp was to supply a case study in the advantages, dilemmas, and delusions which this attitude was bound to bring about.

Just as Krupp did not care about the revolution which he witnessed in Paris, or any other political happenings which did not influence his personal business, he showed little interest in the people and countries he encountered on his travels. The grandeur of Paris and London meant nothing to the young man from Essen. The only observations or experiences in the many and lengthy letters he wrote from his tour abroad concerned the manufacture and commerce of steel. "If a bride expected me at home, I couldn't return in a greater hurry," he replied to his brother's complaint that he was needed in the factory.

But he discovered in England what he had come to find out. "It is certain after what I've seen here," he reported to his brother, "that to make steel of good quality depends only on the iron." In brief, the famous "secret" boiled down to the quality of raw materials and workmanship. His second discovery in England was "how huge a market can be conquered by a good product." Rather than make steel, it now became his ambition to make "the best steel," and he pursued his goal with fanaticism. A steel cylinder to roll gold which he delivered to a manufacturer at Valbom, Portugal, in 1840, was still in use and in perfect shape as late as 1958.

On his return from the grand tour to Essen, he found "his bride," that is, his factory and business, waiting for him, but in much less attractive condition that he had expected. One of the economic recessions which occurred in the nineteenth century with regular frequency coincided with the disturbing political revolution in Paris. "Almost all the customers," Krupp complained in a letter, "who promised me orders for this year now won't give orders, saying they prefer to hold on to their money in the present unrest, since one doesn't know what may come of it." For several years after his trip the financial status of the factory was endangered, particularly since Alfred could no longer fall back on the family's real estate; all of it had already been sold to meet the obligations of the factory. Bank credits and a wealthy family friend, Fritz Soelling, who joined the firm as a silent partner, saved it again from ruin. The first thing Alfred did with his new partner's money, and against his protests, was to build a new smelting plant with fourteen furnaces, a three-story workshop, and a new house for himself and his family on the factory grounds. By that time, Alfred had been in command of the firm for fourteen years, exactly as long as his father had been and he was hardly more successful.

Since boyhood, Alfred Krupp had written down whatever came to his mind in connection with the business, and little else came to his mind, as his voluminous writings reveal. Proudly he reported from his foreign trip that he would stop on the street "twelve times a day" to jot down a new idea on the making and selling of steel. He kept a notebook near his bed and trained himself to write in the dark, and since he suffered from insomnia, he wrote as much by night as by day. His notes, carefully preserved, make dreary reading.

He continued his habit of mass-producing notes throughout his life, with an ever-increasing output of letters, memoranda, admonitions to his partners, and instructions to workers. His mania betrayed his loneliness; for him, the easiest way of communicating with other people was by the written rather than the spoken word. It deprived them of a chance of talking back.

This, he felt, was the way to deal with people. In his eyes they were merely means to his ends, not unlike machines, though less to be trusted. Insecurity haunted him all the time; he feared everybody with whom he had dealings.

"You know how easily a fire can break out, and a fire in the factory would destroy everything, everything!" he would complain in a typical letter from Paris to his brother, and continue, "We ought to have a second night watchman who could supervise the first, and a third one who would keep on eye on the second, but in the end all three would sleep. How unfortunate it is that there is no daylight at night, and one cannot know whether his most urgent instructions are being followed even in part. . . ." A little later, while he was busy spying out the "secrets" of his competitors, he suddenly suspected his night watchman of being in their service. "Even the role of the night watchman is not above suspicion," he warned his brother from the distance. "That man walks around too much in the factory by day." In countless other notes and letters Krupp set forth similar grave and groundless suspicions of his workers, his foremen, his customers, and his suppliers. Everybody, it seemed, was out to harm him.

His sickly distrust of other people led to a great change in the structure of the firm and to its new, lasting, and unique shape. In 1845 the period of prosperity came to an end. In the ensuing economic depression, Krupp's labor force dropped from 142 in 1845 to 76 in 1847. Alfred Krupp held his two brothers, rather than the strain of the general industrial crisis, responsible for this state. The firm was still owned by his mother, who planned to leave it to him and his two younger brothers. But Alfred suspected them of faithlessness, carelessness, and secret intrigues and insisted that his mother sell the factory to him alone. He acquired it at the extremely low price of 40,000 thalers, which was later further reduced to 25,000. The other children and heirs received only a modest settlement and were threatened with being disinherited altogether unless they agreed. Since they had no other choice, they accepted their shares, and left Essen forever. Alfred Krupp who would not trust a night watchman, or even his brothers, with the factory that was "his child" and "his bride," became its sole owner, or, as his favorite phrase had it, "master in his house."

Like his father, Alfred's brother Fritz had showed remarkable foresight in technological matters. He experimented with and came close to the invention of a modern vacuum cleaner, devised other new and valuable contrivances, for instance, bells of cast steel, and developed a new machine, a cast-steel die cylinder which could turn out a hundred and fifty spoons or forks a day. Displacing the master craftsmen who had made silverware by hand, this invention introduced industrial mass production of tableware and saved the Firm of Krupp from economic ruin. During the depression an Austrian company bought the license on the patent at a high price and set up the first spoon factory at Berndorf near Vienna. After the inventor had been forced to quit the firm and the factory, his invention was to save Alfred Krupp again from failure.

"On the twenty-fourth of February, 1848, on the same day on which the revolution broke out in France, my

mother handed over to me the wreck of the factory,"
Alfred Krupp proudly noted. With a little more interest in
politics he might have added that on the same day on
which a monarchy in France was overthrown in Paris,
Krupp's monarchy in Essen was established. The political revolution spread from Paris to Austria, Poland, Hungary, and also to Germany where, as Krupp's house historian Berdrow complains, "Not only the wrokers, but
also a great many of the manufacturers were caught up in
the political fever and forgot the main thing, that is, the
need for quiet and peace and employment."

Many industrialists of Prussia joined, and sometimes
led, the people in their demand for a constitution and liberty. In Berlin, for instance, Johann August Borsig, a
leading machine manufacturer, marched at the head of his
revolutionary workers to the royal castle. In the Rhine
and Ruhr districts, outstanding bankers and industrialists
—von Beckerath, Hansemann, Camphausen, Mevissen
—became spokesmen of the popular movement. But
Krupp took no part in it. His only action was to admon-
ish his workers to work harder and not get involved in any
goings-on outside the factory.

As his chronicler tells in innocent approval of his nonpolitical hero, "In the midst of the revolutionary days
Krupp gave less thought to the general riots than to all
the silver from the households of cautious citizens which
was now being smelted; as he saw it, it would soon
stream back into the mints and factories where his cylinders and dies would turn it again into new coins and jew-
elry, or into spoons and forks." Since the revolution
would later affect his business favorably, he was quite
pleased. "One must have patience now; the worse things
get today, the better it will be afterward," he wrote to his
customers. He himself brought his silver to the Düsseldorf
Mint. "Money," he explained to his managers, "was not
available on promissory notes, so I had my spoons, pitch-
ers, spurs, and medals melted down; miraculously, after
that very day orders again began to come in."

The miracle which he had foreseen came to pass when
the mints of Berlin and Utrecht reopened and gave him a

few small orders, and a larger order for his silverware-making machines came from Russia. After the revolution had been suppressed, a Russian grand-duke decided to establish a large spoon factory in St. Petersburg, and his price of 21,000 rubles for Krupp's machines was large enough to turn the "wrecked" firm again into a going company and to keep it prosperously afloat for awhile.

If the shot in the arm of Krupp's ailing business was given in Russian rubles, the defeat of the German revolution was to cure it in more lasting ways. The attempt of German democrats to end the absolute rule of Prussia's king, with his feudal estate-owners and army officers, miscarried under the fire of Prussian rifles. Power and freedom grew to be irreconcilable enemy forces in Germany. Otto von Bismarck, a young Prussian diplomat of political genius whose loyalty to the Prussian king equaled his contempt of civic freedom, came to the fore, while "the poets and thinkers" were pushed into a corner of their community, free only to reject the rulers in hopeless protest or to submit and serve as their camp-followers. Once Prussia had re-established the power of its king within its own frontiers, it set out to rule Germany.

Krupp went Prussia's way. In the "mad year" of 1848 his firm began to grow from a factory struggling for survival, and little different from other small or middle-sized enterprises, to a powerful industry in pursuit of bigness.

Business in general picked up after the revolution was defeated. The California Gold Rush had pleasant effects on the economy of every country, including Germany. More visible still were the effects of the speedy modern mass-transportation systems. Railroads and steamships created a new world. When the first railroads began running in his country, Alfred Krupp was jubilant. "A different future is before us," he wrote; "we live now in the steel age."

His beloved cast steel alone, he was to discover, would supply the material from which most new railroad parts could be reliably produced; the same was true of locomotives, wagons, wheels, and rails. At the time, Krupp's firm produced, and perhaps invented, seamless wheels, or ties,

which would not break under the stress of velocity and
weight, as the previously used old-style wagon wheels
often had done. Krupp was granted patents for this invention from many countries, although not from Prussia
which doubted his claim. Orders streamed in at the rate
of 30,000 pieces a year. Railway wares remained his
mainstay of production, and a profitable one, for the next
decade. The Jewish banking house of Salomon Oppen-
heim in Cologne gave him liberal credits to enlarge his
firm; his working force rose from 76 in 1847 to the first
thousand in 1857, despite strenuous competition and new
economic crises. A second new field of production
opened when the firm began to manufacture steel axles,
crankshafts, and screw propellers for steamships. The first
delivery went to the Viceroy of Egypt for his luxurious
yacht.

Proudly Krupp chose his seamless railway tires as the
trade-mark of his firm. With its three interlocking wheels
it resembled the symbol of the Olympics cut in half, or as
cynics were soon to find, the interlocking muzzles of three
cannons.

When Alfred Krupp finally arrived at success and recognition, he was forty years old. His failing father had
died at thirty-nine. Two milestones of his life, his marriage and his firm's breakthrough to the world scene,
were set in the three years after his fortieth birthday, and
also his mother's death. While his pursuit of happiness in
wedded life was to fail quickly and pitifully, as will be
told in the next chapter, his business advance abroad
began with a triumph.

In 1851 London held the first World's Fair. Leading
the world in power and production, Victorian England—
which had the ships, the men, and the money too, as Brit-
ons liked to sing—at first paid little notice to an unknown
firm named Krupp from an unknown place in that rather
ridiculous nation of Prussia, which was to show its wares
among the many exhibitors.

But the man and the firm from Essen won world-wide
attention and respect as soon as the Fair opened in London's Crystal Palace. Krupp exhibited a 4300-block of

steel, cast in one piece, which impressed people at that time as much as, say, atomic reactors would a century later. But Krupp also exhibited a second product which impressed the public even more. In a Prussian war tent under a playful canopy stood a six-pound field gun whose barrel, instead of being the usual bronze, was made of cast steel. Mounted on a carriage of ash, the wood from which the old Germans had made their lethal javelins, it was surrounded, "prettily and picturesquely," as the newspapers of the day reported, by half a dozen ten-pound cuirasses, also cast in Krupp's special steel. This armor could protect its wearer from the bullets of an infantry gun.

In terms of Victorian public relations—which were the purpose of the World's Fair—Krupp's steel stole the show from its competitors, including another newcomer to the world of steel, the United States. Rather than a cannon, this country exhibited a plowshare which was also a master-piece of steel casting, luxuriously outfitted and decorated with idyllic paintings. Alfred Krupp got no purchase orders for his remarkable cannon, but he was awarded the coveted gold medal for showing it. When he woke up the next morning he was famous. He was the man who had beaten England in its own steelmaking game on its homeground, and he taught a fascinated rather than scared world that his hands could beat the new steel into swords as well as plowshares. "Steel could the works of mortal pride confound, and hew triumphal arches to the ground," an Englishman named Alexander Pope had warned more than a century before.

It seemed strange that Alfred Krupp should enter the international contest with a cannon which held few profitable business prospects rather than with his peaceful and more profitable wares. Whether he just blundered into the arms business the way governments sometimes blunder into wars, or whether his fifth sense for the business of the future led him into this new field, has been answered in different ways by himself on different occasions. He had thought of this new market for a long time before he sold his first weapon. When he was twenty-four and still looking for first footholds for his firm, the idea was suggested by his brother who had been asked by an arms dealer in Munich whether it wouldn't be possible to make gun barrels from steel instead of bronze. With the detachment of a physicist experimenting with hydrogen bombs, Alfred set to work on the problem. "It was an interesting activity," he recalled thirty-five years later. It took seven years to forge the first steel gun, a remarkable and impressive technical achievement. That was in 1843, and he immediately sent samples to Prussian army officials and ordnance officers. Casually he told them that he could also forge a cannon of the same new, revolutionary kind, "if it were required and usable." But they were not interested. "The present way of manufacturing guns, and their quality, satisfies all fair needs and hardly leaves any room for improvement," the Prussian Minister of War informed him in reply to his offer. Alfred Krupp was not the first reformer and innovator of weapons who received such a cold-shouldering response from military authorities, nor would he be the last, whether the new weapons submitted to their judgment were airplanes, tanks, traditional or atomic-powered submarines, or missiles. While weaponry does change in continual "progress," the military mind which can see no need for, and only disadvantages, in, new weapons seems changelessly to survive.

Although he was rejected, Alfred Krupp did not give up easily when he sensed a good business prospect. Like his father he was endowed with vision, but his luck was better. When he sent his first sample of a steel cannon to Berlin in 1847, the tests were postponed for two years while the piece gathered dust in the corner of an arsenal. Only after Krupp had lobbied in many Prussian offices was it finally tested. The experts found that his steel cannon "surpassed cannons of every other known material in toughness and hardness," but it was too expensive. In addition, they said, there was "almost no need" for improving the conventional light and field cannons. But Krupp stuck to his "guns."

A little later, he sent his steel cannon to the King of

Prussia "as a personal present." Slightly embarrassed, the King placed the gift in the marble hall of his Potsdam Castle where he showed it to his guests. This was the best advance publicity Krupp could get, and he needed it. In contrast to his spoonmaking and gold-rolling machinery, military hardware could be sold only after the idea had been promoted by "public relations." Krupp was an early and accomplished master at this new art.

World exhibitions were then the most effective public-relations medium by which to reach an international audience. When, inspired by London, Paris held its great Exhibition in 1855, Krupp again sent a steel cannon, this time a twelve-pound muzzle-loader built like the bronze cannons then used by the French army, but two hundred pounds lighter and capable of firing three thousand shots without wear and tear. Was it also a device of public relations, or merely a mishap that the monster broke through the wooden floor of the hall in which it was shown? At any rate, this created in the public eye exactly that impressive image of its destructive power which Krupp sought. The name of Krupp, that "blasted Prussian squarehead of steel," as Paris newspapers called him, became as famous as that of his fellow-Prussian Otto von Bismarck, who was beginning to personify the new power and aspirations of Prussia.

After fourteen years of experiments and rejections, the first of Krupp's guns were sold to Egypt. Its Viceroy saw Krupp's model at the Paris World's Fair, liked it, and without much ado ordered six pieces, then more and heavier models, thirty-six altogether. Krupp's next cannon customer was Russia, which wanted a heavy gun for coastal defense, and received it. Neither the Khedive in Cairo nor the Czar in St. Petersburg had to ask their parliaments or bureaucracies about these purchases. Krupp concluded that you can do business with autocrats, perhaps only with autocrats, and the more autocratic, the better.

But Prussia continued to reject the offers of its native son, although Krupp tried in every way to come to terms with the military bureaucrats in Berlin. Furiously he blamed it on the control of parliament, on the social snobbishness of the aristocratic officers in the ordnance department, on personal enemies, some of whom were imaginary and some real.

Since the sale of his first cannons, he kept his assistants busy developing and testing improvements. Although his few sales did not cover the expenses of his experiments, with his earnings in civilian production he could well afford them. A second investment in the future was his carefully cultivated friendship with two high Prussian officers who showed more interest in his offerings than their colleagues. They belonged to a group led by Bismarck which aimed at the abolition of the last traces of democracy in their country, and at its quick and powerful rearmament. They were strongly backed by the King's brother, Prince Wilhelm of Prussia, whom Krupp also knew; he had visited Essen to thank the manufacturer for the gift of a steel cannon to his brother and to inspect the factory that produced it. Luckily for Krupp, mental disease forced the King to step down from the throne; his brother followed him, first as Prince-Regent, then as supreme ruler. When he appointed Bismarck as his Minister-President, a new era began, and Prussian rearmament, as well as suppression of parliamentary control, proceeded in earnest.

One of the first straws in the new wind was the personal decree of Prussia's new ruler that three hundred cannons be ordered from Krupp for the equipment of the Prussian field artillery. This was an enormous order. The director of the army's ordnance department cut it to a mere 72, still an impressive figure. But the ruler corrected his correction and without further discussion wrote out the final purchase order for three hundred pieces of artillery. This first big armament order marked the inception of two cannon kingdoms—Prussia's and Krupp's.

From 1815, when Napoleon was defeated, to the 1850's, Europe had been at peace. Cannons were made but not fired. "A long time of peace," Professor Leo, one of Prussia's leading writers, commented, "accumulates plenty of rotting ferments; therefore we need a fresh, jolly war to get the culture-bearing nations of Europe on the move again." Dictatorial France looked forward to a war with the same irresponsible expectations, though not necessarily for the same reasons of *weltanschauung* as autocratic Prussia. From 1859 on, Krupp was kept busy with Prussian artillery orders. "Neither speeches nor majority decisions resolve the great problems of the time, but blood and iron," Bismarck proclaimed. He honored his steel supplier in Essen with a formal visit; the two men found each other to their liking. The manufacturer added construction and research departments to his plants where his men, independent of the army ordnance department, could develop and improve the weapons. But at the same time Krupp also received and filled increasingly larger orders from other nations able to pay for a good cannon, German or otherwise. An armament race had begun. France, Prussia's prospective next enemy, bought gun barrels as well as steel from Krupp, Belgium —which saw its independence being threatened by France —in turn equipped its field artillery with Krupp guns. Holland, England, Switzerland, Spain, and Austria became cannon customers. The biggest customer was Russia, which bought one hundred and twenty cannons of a theretofore unheard of power from Krupp. This million-and-a-half thaler deal placed him in the ranks of Big Industry.

The weapon trade was only one section of his business, and in those years it was considered neither sinister nor disgraceful; it was an industry like any other. He made "tools of peace" and "tools of war," Krupp stated, and as far as he was concerned there was no difference between them. If Europe was armament bound under the impact of Prussia's growing power, of an ambitious dictator in France, of other powers readying themselves for war, it was a matter of "politics" which concerned him only as it boosted his business.

Was Alfred Krupp a Prussian patriot or perhaps a chauvinist who thought of little but the aggrandizement of his nation's power while he produced its firepower? This was what his patriotic and chauvinistic Prussian admirers and chroniclers said, while later on his German as well as foreign critics, let alone his Allied prosecutors, denounced him for the same thing. Or was he the very reverse, the international supersalesman delivering his weapons to friend and foe alike, without the slightest regard for his own nation? Other critics would bitterly attack him for this offense and his house chroniclers would just as bitterly deny it, until, when they were called to defend him against charges of chauvinism, they suddenly and proudly pointed to his internationalism. Only one of the two charges could be true. But if there seemed bases for both charges at the same time, the reason was that Krupp himself pretended to play sometimes the one and then again the other role.

While Prussia was and would remain his best cannon customer, he increased his trade by satisfying the artillery needs of foreign countries. This, in turn, strengthened him in his homeland, which was as dependent on him as he was on it. If Prussia hesitated to comply with his conditions, he had only to threaten to sell to other nations the produce his country needed; or he would pose as a martyr who in patriotic interest had foregone profitable orders from other countries. Whether he played the part of the blackmailer or of the patriot deserving to be rewarded for his sacrifices, he got what he wanted.

He used the same double-dealing tactics in his business with "tools of peace." A case in point was a multi-million-thaler sale of wagon wheels to the Spanish railroads which could, or would, pay him only with stock of their company. Krupp, who distrusted stock corporations, the stock exchange, and everything connected with it, insisted on cash. When the Spaniards did not accept his conditions, the deal fell through. A few weeks later the Prussian authorities were reluctant to extend his patent on the same wheels. Furiously he asserted that he had refused to sell his product to Spain only in order to reserve its use exclusively for his country; for this sacrifice in the service of Prussia he expected his due rewards. His patent was extended.

But his freedom of trade was one-sided. While he

claimed the right to supply everybody with his products, he deeply believed that Prussia was entitled to buy only from him. Under liberal pressures the Prussian War Ministry nevertheless ordered cannon specimens from other German steel-makers. When they proved to be of equal quality, the Minister decided to accept open bids. Alfred Krupp flew into a rage: "As soon as one other steel manufacturer shall get an order on one single cannon," he wrote, "I will deliver to the whole world what it wants." To make clear that "the whole world" included Napoleon and other enemies of Prussia, he explained that he was thinking of *"revanche"* against "the filthy clique in the War Department."

A Berlin newspaper, reporting his arrival in the capital on a business trip, called him *"le roi des cannons."* The new title pleased him so much that he sent clippings of the newspaper story to his family and customers. When he was anointed by printers' ink as Cannon King, he was nearly fifty years old. The title was to stick to his name.

In his way, he was a king, not only by the extent of his trade but by his absolutistic outlook. His firm was his realm; he believed that only he himself, by some sort of superior grace, could steer it on its way to power and glory. For this reason, he sputtered vulgar curses at the very suggestion that he transform it into a stockholders' corporation; stockholders, bankers, and brokers were dangerous outsiders whom he tried to hold at bay, or better still, ignore, as an absolute king tries to suppress parliaments, political parties, and a free press. Neither would he tolerate outside influences in his realm. When the other German rail producers concluded a cartel agreement, he refused to join the "cursed association," which was, as he put it, "below all dignity; it would humiliate me to commune with every little outfit. . . ." But neither did he believe in free competition; he took his monopoly for granted.

Although neither alliterations nor thought associations would lend it the same glamour, after the early 1860's the newly-anointed Cannon King was also a leader in the field of railway material and many other steel products.

But primarily he was and remained a manufacturer—by now the Continent's biggest manufacturer—of cast steel. The *Gusstahlfabrik,* which his father had founded, was still the center of his empire.

Two great new inventions in steelmaking revolutionized the industry in the decade of 1860. They were, in fact, the century's only two inventions to mark important progress over the "secret" in search of which his father had died and Alfred Krupp himself had spent his early manhood. But he did not have to run after these new "secrets"; they were brought to him. First, Sir Henry Bessemer invented his process of casting steel from liquid iron in converters rather than in closed furnaces. This could have turned Krupp's steel mills overnight into almost worthless antiques, but Henry Bessemer was a close friend of Frederick Longsdon, brother of Krupp's London representative and partner. Through him Krupp had advance knowledge of the new method, which enabled him secretly to build Germany's first Bessemer works.

Seven years later, Wilhelm Siemens, a German who had lived in England for a long time and learned the ways of steelmaking, invented a new method of casting steel from iron ore and scrap. It was superior to the Bessemer technique and Krupp bought Siemen's patent, although his multi-million-dollar changeover from his old furnaces to the Bessemer converters was not yet amortized. The new technique further strengthened his reputation of always being far ahead of his competitors.

With sales of "tools of peace and tools of war" multiplying, Krupp's working force jumped from 7 at his beginning in 1826 to 1500 in 1859, to 2000 in 1861, 4000 in 1863, and 8000 in 1865. It was then that Alfred Krupp perfected the shape of his empire. After he had branched out from the production of steel into the development, construction, and manufacture of finished steel products, he expanded in the reverse direction by adding to his holdings the sources of raw materials from which steel was made. Again with the assistance of Bismarck and the King, he bought from the Prussian State at the relatively cheap price of half a million thalers several first-rate iron-ore mines, and leased a coal mine. While the cast-steel factory remained the heart of his industrial empire, it now extended over the whole range of production. This made him not only independent of the whims and vagaries of the open market and outside influences, but it also brought about considerable savings. With this "vertical concentration" he was master over a combine which controlled the market.

In 1869 Alfred Krupp once more offered his newest cannons to French Emperor Napoleon III. A year later Napoleon appointed Krupp an officer of the *Légion d'Honneur,* and shortly thereafter war broke out between France and Prussia, which was joined by the other German states. Since way back, the military planners of autocratic France had opposed the introduction of modern weapons as rigidly and short-sightedly as the military planners of autocratic Prussia had done for more than a decade before their new ruler and Bismarck forced them to see the light. The French army was equipped mainly with traditional muzzle-loading bronze cannons and mitrailleuses—a breach-loading machine gun firing small projectiles rapidly from a number of barrels. French firepower was inferior by 30 per cent to Prussia's armor which consisted almost exclusively of Krupp's breachloading field guns and heavy steel mortars.

In this first great test and contest, Krupp won. His mortars and cannons pulverized the forts of Metz which, as grandparent of the Maginot Line, was expected to stop the invaders. They broke through Sedan where they won a decisive Prussian victory, and blasted their way to the suburbs of Paris. When the encircled Parisians kept in contact with the rest of France by balloons, Krupp hurriedly constructed a small-caliber special gun capable of firing straight up into the skies. It was the world's first anti-aircraft gun, and its very threat brought the Paris balloon airlift to a halt. Krupp, it seemed, had won his war while Prussia won hers. And Europe identified Krupp with the victory.

The final French defeat strengthened Germany's power immensely, but it also deprived it of the domestic happi-

ness which stems from a free and healthy society. While
Bismarck proclaimed the foundation of a new *Reich,* the
people had no part in it, least of all "the poets and thinkers." Founded on blood and iron, the new Prussian *Reich*
rested on the power of Potsdam and Essen, while the
spirit of Weimar and Munich was oppressed. The pursuit
of bigness won out over the pursuit of greatness.

United under Prussian hegemony, Germany had removed its main contestant for supremacy over Continental Europe. In the heavy industry of Prussian Germany
and the European continent, Krupp was the leader. His
working force reached the ten thousand mark at the war's
end. The technological and economic pattern along which
his firm would continue to rise had been perfected. It
controlled horizontally the production of many different
"tools of peace and war"; vertically it controlled production from raw materials to the final product; and all this
was controlled by one man, who at the moment of victory
neared his sixtieth birthday and his ultimate personal failure.

4

Master in His Mansion

In apparent anticipation of the coming victory of Germany and his firm, Alfred Krupp set the foundation stone of a new family dwelling exactly three months before war had even been declared. That stone was set in April, 1870, and while Krupp expected his new house to be completed in twelve months, the war lasted only a little more than six months. The timing was perfect.

What he called his house was really several palaces rolled into one, and it resembled a Victorian opera house to which a Victorian railroad station had been attached. Alfred Krupp himself designed it. The main building, with its façade of a renaissance castle, consisted of one hundred and sixty rooms, some larger than a city block. A gallery in neoclassic style connected this Main House with a second dwelling, the Little House, which contained a mere sixty rooms.

According to the designer's orders, not one piece of wood was used in construction or decoration. Wood can burn: Alfred Krupp, master of furnaces and forges whose flames lit the Ruhr Valley at night with their red-and-yellow fireworks, was obsessed by the fear of fire. For the same reason, gas and kerosene were unknown in his new house, although their use had become the rule in elegant and comfortable dwellings. Alfred Krupp shuddered at the imaginary fire hazards of those new-fangled contraptions and decreed that his house was to be lit only by candles. His only building materials were iron and stone. The first came from his own forge, while the second was

53

imported from France before and even during the first weeks of the war. Since books also burn easily, he decided that there would be no library in his home, and of course, no paintings, tapestries, or other inflammable nonsense.

His home was a monument to his fears, and Alfred Krupp was haunted by many strange ones. To forestall the danger of drafts which cause common colds, he invented windows which could not be opened. Only these perennially shut windows were installed in his house. Also in the interest of health, he designed an elaborate system of ventilators and shafts through which the fresh air and the "ozones" of the surrounding forests could be pumped into his rooms; their pipes towered weirdly above the iron roof. To keep the temperature at precisely the same level throughout his house he invented a kind of air-conditioning system which bore little resemblance to the air conditioners of our time (except, perhaps, those designed by cartoonist Rube Goldberg). Krupp's personal den was built over the stables; if the odor of manure, as his theory had it, permeated the house, he would be inspired to creative thinking. For this nightmare palace the Cannon King chose the name of Villa Hügel, or Hillside Villa. The mock-modest designation of the monstrous palace as a villa only underlined its bigness, a boast in disguise.

But from the beginning the villa seemed to stand under an unlucky star. Apparently it was easier and quicker to win a war than to build this house. First a hurricane destroyed its scaffolds, then cracks showed in its ill-founded walls, which had to be torn down and rebuilt; when the shell finally stood, neither the heating system nor the air-conditioning system worked. The only part quickly completed was the beautiful park which surrounded it. Too impatient to plant young trees and watch their growth, Krupp bought old wooden tracts, parks, and alleys wholesale and transplanted them on his grounds. Rather than one year, it was three years before Krupp and his family could move into their new palace.

Villa Hügel was the fourth house which Alfred Krupp

built, and the fifth in which he lived. His houses reflected the course of his business success as well as the sequence of his personal defeats. He began his career in the little foreman's cottage to which his impoverished father had been forced to move. The tiny wooden hut with its too small windows in front, under a steep and reassuring roof, recalled the traditional cottages of poor peasants from which the new class of workers had sprung. After Alfred had found a wealthy partner, he had erected a new, three-story house for his family and himself, again on the factory grounds where it almost disappeared among new halls and workshops.

His mother had died in this house; and after her death, he took a wife. Bertha Eichhoff, his bride, was the grand-daughter of the pastry cook of the Archbishop of Cologne, the daughter of a pensioned customs inspector, and a beautiful girl with blue eyes, blond hair, a sensuous mouth, and an easy smile. She was twenty years old while her groom was forty-one, but, according to contemporaries, he looked "twenty years older" than his age; his face showed deep lines, and he was almost bald. Bertha loved life and hoped for happiness; Alfred feared life, had no time to think of happiness, and was interested only in winning victories over men and materials. Immediately before his wedding, his voluminous correspondence was enriched by two or three love letters, the only ones he ever wrote in his life; they consisted of a few shabby cliches, his heart was not in them.

After a brief wedding trip to the nearby Rhine, he returned to the factory which was still "his bride," as he had once written, and "his child" too. No time for Bertha. In her first year of marriage she once shyly asked him to come with her to a concert to hear the famous violinist Wilhelmy; of course she could not go without him, and there were hardly more than two or three festive occasions of that kind in a year in Essen. "Sorry," he snorted, as a friend admiringly noted down, "it's impossible. I must see that my smokestacks continue to smoke, and when I shall hear my forge working away tomorrow, that'll be music more beautiful than the playing of all the

world's fiddles." When the same forges made the house
shake to its foundations and the chinaware fell from the
shelves and broke, as often happened, he consoled his
frightened wife with a grin. "It's only a few porcelain
plates," he laughed. "I'll make the customers pay for
them."

But to please his wife he set out to build a new house.
Again he chose the factory grounds, although they had
become almost unbearably noisy and dirty with the recent
growth of business. He could not tear himself away from
his true love. Yet this new, third house was made after a
woman's heart as he understood it. A large glass-encased
winter garden and an orangery were attached; tiny, carefully laid out French gardens surrounded it; peacocks
stalked over the lawns, which were embellished with
grottoes, lily ponds, and fountains. True, the flowers
could not bloom in the smoke and the peacocks did not
survive the soot that covered this little Versailles among
the blast furnaces and iron hammers. Crowded between
workshops and machines, the Garden House, as it was
called, seemed pathetic rather than pleasing.

The only child of Alfred and Bertha Krupp, called
Fritz, the name which was also given to "the world's
greatest iron hammer" which Krupp built shortly after the
birth of his son, was born in the Garden House. Afterward, Bertha Krupp preferred spas and resort places to
Essen, where she came to live only at infrequent inter-
vals; she complained that the factory destroyed her and
her son's health. Big Fritz, the hammer, seemed to crush
little Fritz.

Only four years after the Garden House was completed,
his doctors told him that it was not good for his own
health to live on the factory grounds, and Alfred Krupp
decided to move again. He went castle-hunting in the
neighborhood. But the scions of old and noble families
who still lived in their ancestral homes in the Ruhr Valley
would rather have torn them down than sell them to
Krupp. The Baron von Fürstenberg, whose Borbeck Castle near Essen was for sale, refused to receive Krupp
when he wanted to inspect the property. As Count Nes-

selrode, a guest at the castle, remembered, when explosions were heard in the distance the lord of the manor explained in contempt: "There goes that blacksmith in Essen again, a man named Krupp or something." If the world had anointed him Cannon King, in the eyes of true aristocrats he remained a *nouveau-riche* blacksmith. It was to spite them as well as to impress the rest of the world with his riches that Alfred Krupp built his hilltop palace and called it Villa Hügel.

At the same time, he erected another—his last and newest, as well as his first—house when he rebuilt the foreman's cottage in which he and his father had lived. It had almost sunk into the ground.

After the old building was restored exactly as it had once been, he decorated it with a steel plaque which pronounced: "Fifty years ago this former workingman's house was the refuge of my parents. May all of our workers be spared the sorrows which the founding of the factory fated onto us. For twenty-five years success remained doubtful, until it has slowly rewarded our past frustrations, efforts, confidence, and perseverance in such wonderful ways." The plaque was signed in his "personal signature by his own hand."

In the following years, he wrote and published new pronouncements to glorify his triumphal rise of which this restored cottage was to remind his contemporaries. But if it was a monument to his personal victory, it was also a monument of spite against his father, whose defeat it tried to immortalize. He could not often enough repeat that he grew up in this house because his "father lost a considerable fortune, and also his vitality and health, without success. . . ." The triumph of the son over his father could be measured by a comparison of the father's four-room refuge with the son's 220-room residence. The comparison also helped to demonstrate to his workingmen that they could have risen as high as he himself from a modest cottage, had they only been as hard-working, thrifty, inventive, and persevering as Alfred Krupp.

But if he restored the cottage next to his palace as a stage prop for his own success drama, the setting could impress only his audience, not the hero himself. Even after his victorious rise from the hut to the hilltop, he was haunted by lethal fears of a fall.

As soon as he saw his success threatened by dangers and difficulties, the man of steel broke down; he had a lifelong habit of becoming ill and hiding out in his sickbed to escape responsibility when the going got rough. This happened several times a year, and always coincided with disappointments in the firm. Doctor Kuester, his personal physician, diagnosed his sickness as "hypochondria bordering on insanity."

When an expected contract was not concluded, or when his products seem to fail—for instance in Prussia's war with Austria in 1866, when his steel guns did not show up very well in their first crucial test—he fled into bed and stayed there in complete lethargy for a week or more. At fifty, as his doctor noted, "He was a strange-looking, conspicuous man of unusual length, and terribly lean; his face, which had once been very regular and handsome, betrayed premature marks of old age, being dull, pale, wrinkled all over, the little remaining gray hairs hidden under a wig. Rarely was it enlivened by a smile and mostly [it was] motionless as stone. . . ."

A favorite place for Krupp to become ill was far from home; to travel and to become ill on his travels were Krupp's two ways of escape. In his younger years, his partners kept complaining that he "rushed around the world like the Wandering Jew," instead of staying at work in Essen. When he had ridded himself of partners and critics, he dropped altogether the pretense that his travels were necessitated by business, and simply ran away. On these trips—always accompanied by his personal physician, less frequently also by his family—he aimlessly hurried from one place to another. When he was fifty-nine and a crisis threatened his firm, he stayed away for almost three years. Most of the time he spent in bed, speaking only to complain of his ailments, which, his doctor found, were imaginary. If he heard of another guest's illness, let alone death, he left the hotel and the town in panic.

But even from his faraway sickbed, Alfred Krupp ran his firm by a stream of written communications to the home office. More than thirty thousand have been preserved. Many consisted merely of denunciations which betrayed his general misanthropism. Informed that a water pipe had broken in Essen, he dispatched a furious letter in which he declared that "every mishap results from indolence, from lack of precaution, and from basic laziness —in short, it results from qualities which are called trust and confidence."

Faithful to this principle, he suspected everybody of weakness or wickedness. The less he himself was in Essen, the more signs of "laxness" and "betrayal" did he discover among his employees.

What manner of man he wanted for subjects was clearly defined when he set forth: "Intelligence does not help, without morality it is more dangerous than mediocrity." He would conclude: "Only moral men deserve to and can belong to our organization; immoral men must be driven out without regard to their personalities or positions." Morality, in Alfred Krupp's language, meant submission to the leader and no other aim, interest, or activity in life but the progress of the firm. Krupp's ideas seemed to foreshadow the age of the Organization Man.

Since he had won his victory with the victory of Prussia, a new idea began to interest Krupp more than the current business of the firm. He brooded about a system which would safeguard the firm's continued prosperity "for a hundred years or more," as he put it, and even "for times perennial." Fearful of his own life, he wanted to assure the lasting life of his firm. In his distrust of all his associates and workers, he wished to keep them in line and lead them during his protracted absences, and even after his permanent absence, that is, after his death. "The cast iron factory," he foresaw, "has the ability and the vocation to grow with increasing strength for centuries." To keep the firm alive without its czar, he finally decided he would write down the rules to be followed in and after his lifetime; in this way, his voice would still be heard and obeyed, giving its commands from the grave.

These written rules, he declared, "must show what to do in any and every case, must foresee everything, must outline the rights and duties of everyone in the firm."

This was no mere figure of speech. Shortly after the victory of 1871 he left Essen once again for a health cure, in the British spa of Torquay. From far away he informed the management in Essen of his plan to draft a *General-Reglement,* a term taken from the language of Prussian bureaucracy to describe a set of binding rules. Like the constitution and laws of a country, it would regulate the life of the firm. While his managers worked in Essen, he brooded on these basic laws, which would foresee every possible future situation as well as prescribe every necessary future action. "No emergency shall occur in years or in a century," he communicated to his executives, "which is not taken care of in this collection of laws; there must be nobody from the director-general down to the worker who does not find succinct information on how to perform his duties in this collection of laws." It took more than a year, and the help of experienced jurists, to complete this Magna Charta of the House of Krupp. Signed by five Krupp executives and countersigned by Alfred Krupp, its closely printed twenty-two pages laid down the laws of the Firm of Krupp.

The *Generalregulativ* as it was called in the end—to soothe the sensibilities of Krupp's managers who objected to a *Reglement* with its boot-camp connotations—was clearly the outcome of its author's almost psychotic belief that his, and only his, written word could save his firm "in eternity." Nevertheless, it was adopted to the letter, and to the surprise of everybody it worked. A cross between the laws of an absolute monarchy and the rules of a Prussian army barracks, it made no mention of rights or duties of "the owner"; as such, he towered above the law. But the duties, without equivalent rights, of his subjects were narrowly defined. They had to belong to the firm with their whole person, as though the firm owned them. Everybody, the *Generalregulativ* stated, was "under obligation" to give himself completely and exclusively to his job; if once in a while current business "does not take up all his time and energies, he must find some other way to use them in the interest of the firm." From managers to office boys, the subjects of Krupp were not permitted to have outside interests, were granted no leave of absence even for a few minutes without written request and permission, and if they had any complaints, they were to go "through channels." The majority of the seventy-two paragraphs delineated specific duties of and relations between the members of Krupp's industrial hierarchy.

The strange idea of preparing a written set of laws to govern the firm according to his wishes had not come to Krupp overnight. From his earliest years in the factory he had thought of "precautions that would protect it from laxness for all eternity." Since those early years, he had written tens of thousands of orders, commands, and admonitions which, as he saw it, had only to be compiled into a work of lasting validity. Before he traveled to England, on his first absence from the firm, he had issued his first "Rulings for the Workers," with carefully spelled-out laws and by-laws; every ten years or so, he revised and published them anew, until they became part and parcel of the *Generalregulativ*.

As early as 1838, when he was only twenty-six years old, his first rules proclaimed with the bark of a Prussian drill sergeant: "He who wants to defy me, or do less than this duty, will be discharged when caught, ditto he who makes repeated mistakes. . . . Showoffs must expect to be dismissed at the first opportunity. . . . Impudence is punished by immediate dismissal. . . ." To arrive late at work by five minutes was punished with the loss of one hour's wages. Workers who showed a lack of "discipline or morality" were liable to "punitive fines," and these fines went into a fund from which, in turn, hard-working, punctual, and good workers were rewarded with a "gift" payable on their retirement. If workers did not earn such a premium for their punctual, obedient, and hard work every few years, it indicated a "lack of morality and discipline," and they were discharged. If they earned it, there was still the threat that it would be taken away again together with their jobs, unless they kept on being "good."

In short, to get their due they had to work hard and obediently to the very last day of their "service."

They were also to be fired, young Krupp elaborately
set forth, if they ran up debts at the grocery store or the
saloon. "How could they ever pay their debts except by
stealing the money from me?" he explained. Later in life
he detailed in a lengthy letter to his managers his plan of
uniforms for his workers, which they were to wear even
in their leisure time; it included wooden clogs rather than
the comfortable shoes which they preferred, but of which
he disapproved. He distrusted the private life of his
workingmen which he could not control; again and again
he ordered his managers "to appoint supervisors and supervisors of supervisors to watch what our men are
doing." When he learned that a poster with his admonish-
ments to the workers had been torn down, he flew into a
rage. "Regardless of the costs," he said, "all workers
must always be supervised by experienced, energetic men
who will be paid a premium for everybody they catch."
And he added, "I don't care at all whether he be a
worker or a foreman, or whether we have to pay high sal-
aries to twenty more men for snooping."

As Alfred Krupp got older, his unquestioned position
as "master of his house" began to be shaken. New, stir-
ring voices proclaimed that the workers had rights of their
own; the Socialists, the fledgling trade unions, Catholic
and Protestant clergymen, challenged the absolute rule of
employers. In reply Krupp published in 1877 "A Word to
the Members of My Industrial Works," in which he
briefly informed his men that for them to be interested in
politics of any kind was *verboten*. "Serious concern with
the politics of the country requires more time and better
understanding of difficult questions than you have," he
told them, and announced that he would fire any man
"who does not march on our side with devotion in his
heart." But even if they remained as "unpolitical" as he
demanded, they could not be trusted in other directions.
On his last visit to the factory, on Easter Sunday of 1887,
he noticed that a few workers had attached sheds to their
cottages in which they kept goats. Since, as he reasoned,

these animals probably fed on the grass growing on his grounds and therefore were stealing his property, he put up a large sign; it was *verboten* also for his men to keep goats.

According to the Cannon King's convictions, workers were to be treated as children, following the pattern set by military leaders and colonizers of the time with soldiers and natives. Kindly but sternly, the boss had to look after their health, housing, and working conditions, and their discipline; they were denied a voice in public affairs, or even in their own private affairs. "Father knows best," and Krupp was the father of the firm, just as in German eyes a sovereign was the father of the country and its people. His labor force, as the aging Cannon King proclaimed in a remarkable statement, must "supply many faithful subjects to the State, and workers of a special race to the firm." His spelling of "race" was English, the word had not yet been Germanized as *Rasse,* but what Krupp meant did not differ very much from its later usage. To cultivate this new "race" required much more concern for the welfare of his workers than was customary at the time. As he came to understand early in his life and never forgot, a "race" of workers with a modicum of wage and job security was highly advantageous, if not necessary, to the progress of his business, in which high skills were needed. The longer a man worked for Krupp and the more contented he was with his work, the better the results. This was a revolutionary and beneficial insight at the time, whatever its motivation.

Alfred Krupp was ingenious in forging ties between his firm and his workers, who would develop their special and superior abilities and hand them down to their offspring. He tried to free them from the most pressing worries and provide them with animal comforts, thereby enabling them to work harder and better. What he attempted to establish, almost a century before modern corporations started their programs of Industrial Relations, was a "welfare firm." Of course, its benefits could be enjoyed only by those workers whose performance, obedience and usability came up to Alfred Krupp's standards.

Proudly they were called *die Kruppianer,* or the Kruppians, as if they were a distinct German tribe. Just as,
say, Bavarians owed allegiance to their king, their country, and Germany, Kruppians owed it to their boss, their
firm, and their state, in that order.

The subjects of Krupp's welfare firm had a better
chance of keeping their jobs even at times of economic
decline than most of their fellow workers elsewhere. Since
they were going to be needed again as soon as business
would improve, to keep them constantly employed was a
capital investment that paid dividends in the long run. To
save their know-how for his firm, Alfred Krupp discharged few of his men even in bad times. Moreover, he
suggested that "in times of unemployment, it is very important to find ways of providing the workers with work
which will turn out to be productive, though only belatedly—work in forests, for instance, or meadows, or soil cul-
tivation and road-building." Only in the next century
would the Works Progress Administration and similar
projects express this idea; Krupp, as his father before
him, deserves credit as a premature pioneer.

In many other trail-blazing ways, Krupp cared for the
welfare of those workers who repaid him with performance and devotion. Early in his career he thought of low-
cost, low-rent housing facilities for Kruppian families.
This was necessitated by the growth of the firm. Its working force increased by leaps and bounds, inundating the
town of Essen. There was not enough room for the influx
of newcomers, who were often immigrants from the rural
parts of East Germany in search of industrial employment. Essen's population had risen from 7200 in 1850 to
over 20,000 in 1860, and to over 50,000 in 1870. "Un-
healthy housing conditions, regrettable exploitation of the
workers by retail and liquor stores" resulted, as a historian reported. Further results were epidemics of cholera
which scared Alfred Krupp so badly that he would leave
town the moment they broke out.

The danger of a labor shortage in Essen was serious
until Krupp built barracks in which unmarried workers
were fed and sheltered by the firm, and had his factory

architects draw plans of housing settlements in which his married workers could live with their families. "I believe that a great sacrifice must be made," he explained, "or we will lack what is needed most, that is, men." In the postwar boom of 1871, the first Krupp houses quickly grew until thousands of Kruppians lived as tenants in three full-fledged settlements, or Krupp colonies, as they were called. Ugly and primitive though they were, the settlements were embellished with playgrounds and greenery; a church and a school were built in their midst. While construction of these settlements on Essen's outskirts was under way, construction of Krupp's palace on the hilltop was also in progress; it cost only slightly less than the new settlements for thousands of families.

Hardly any financial risk, let alone sacrifices, were involved in Krupp's social housing program (which was financed with bank credits). Since only a few thousand company houses were available for the tens of thousands of families eager to move in, there were never any vacancies, and rents were paid promptly, for if a tenant was delinquent, the firm would deduct the rent from his wages. If he lost his job, he was evicted. In addition, the increase in the value of real estate turned Krupp's original outlay into a highly profitable investment.

But the firm drew other advantages from its housing program. The tenants of its "colonies" or "workers' villages" were subject to complete and continuous control by Krupp's "supervision officers," even in their personal relations. The private housing policemen "could check at any time to see whether all regulations are being strictly followed," as T. Kellen, one of Alfred Krupp's contemporary chroniclers, reported. They inspected even the newspapers read by the tenants and the leaflets found in their trash baskets. In accordance with Alfred Krupp's wishes, his housing projects contributed greatly to the breeding of his "pure race of Kruppians." A long time before 1984 Alfred Krupp pioneered also the image of Big Brother.

Similarly, Krupp's other and memorable innovations were at least as beneficial to the firm as to the workers. To free the men from their bondage to storekeepers

and innkeepers, he established his own cheap soup kitch-
ens. Nevertheless many of his workers founded and
joined independent consumers' cooperatives following the
model of the British industrialist and Socialist Robert
Owen, which Herman Schulze-Delitzsch, a German liberal, introduced to the poor of his country. Alfred Krupp
resented his workers going "into business for themselves,"
as he called this cooperative effort at self-help. Sternly he
warned his managers to watch out for these transgressors.
"We must make sure that every worker's first thought is
of the firm and the interests of the factory and that he is
not tempted to mull over speculations in coffee, tobacco,
sugar, and raisins." Three years later he took over these
consumers' cooperatives, renamed them Consumers' Institutions, and ran them according to the principles of free
enterprise. As he had foreseen, the new venture developed into a highly rewarding million-dollar department
store. Again, as in his industrial works, he expanded in
both horizontal and vertical directions, adding a bread
factory, a wine store, a butcher plant, and new retail outlets. But he abolished the original cooperative principle
according to which the consumers, as members of their
association, discussed their joint enterprise in general
meeting and voted dividends for themselves from the
profits at the end of the business year. "The master in the
house" did not tolerate partners.

Krupp's welfare firm combined modern ideas with ar-
chaic paternalism. Surely his pension and insurance funds
for old and needy workers were helpful to the recipients.
The bigger share of these funds was contributed by the
workers—originally from fines for misdemeanors, later
from wage deductions—while a smaller share was contributed by the firm. But if a worker lost his job, he lost
also all his claims, and with them all his contributions.
Only after Alfred Krupp's death was this modern bondage changed by court order.

"I am very tired, nervous, *kaputt,* and cannot go on
like this," he wrote in 1877. He was sixty-five years old.
The victory of 1871 had catapulted him and the new
Imperial Germany into superior power. Krupp's steel pro-

duction doubled. In the flush of victory, with French reparation payments flooding into Germany, an unheard-of expansion took place. According to Wilhelm Berdrow, Krupp's most devoted chronicler, "he saw his whole life's work and future connected with German rearmament." The reason, he explained in almost disarming innocence, was self-protection: "Who would protect Krupp's Works, which are located so close to the border, against the French in a new *revanche* war if the ratio of artillery firepower were reversed?"

To protect himself, he frantically bought mines and raw material sources to secure the largest supply reserves possible. He purchased hundreds of iron mines in West Germany, and across the border he bought the rich Spanish ore fields near Bilbao; he also acquired one of Germany's largest coal mines, the "Hannover," at a price of a million dollars, and two big smelting works. The prices he paid to lay his hands on as much property as possible seemed fantastic to his fellow industrialists.

In his moves toward vertical and horizontal concentration, Alfred Krupp was motivated by his old wish to be independent of any and all outsiders and partners. He built four steamships in Holland to transport his iron ore to Essen. He prepared to build a private firing range on which the firm could test its new cannons. Up to then these tests had been made in cooperation with the Prussian army on the state testing range, but Krupp distrusted even this partner. His own testing range was to be larger than any owned by the army, and the Prussian military leaders, highly as they regarded the Cannon King, shook their heads over his show of ignorance and fantasy. But hardly had he completed his range and started testing his cannons when the army and navy ordnance officers themselves asked permission to use it—it was superior to theirs in every way. For the privilege of using his testing grounds, Alfred Krupp demanded and received substantial payments from his best customer, the Fatherland. "Krupp tells governments what they must buy," the old German Kaiser said in a jest which was quite close to the facts.

But in the midst of its new power and glory, the firm which Alfred Krupp built was not so strong and secure as it seemed. In fact, while it basked in triumphs, it was threatened by bankruptcy. This had happened often in the past, but now the stakes were more than a hundred times higher. The new sudden danger arose in 1873 when a large economic crisis ended the German postwar boom in which industrial, banking, transportation companies, and fortunes had feverishly been founded. In the flush of victory, Krupp had badly overexpanded, as had the majority of German industrialists. When the bubble burst, his wealth was frozen in real estate and industrial long-term investments. Short of working capital, he was unable to continue production. Shades of his father's failure! And like his father, as well as he himself in the darker days of his youth, he called on the Prussian State for help; he needed ten million marks at once, in the new currency of the new *Reich*. Despite the recommendations of the Kaiser and Bismarck, the State refused to give him that much. Krupp, in turn, refused to accept credit from the big commercial banks, whose influence on his monarchic rule he feared. The delay quadrupled his immediate needs. The end of his empire seemed near. After personal audiences with the Kaiser, he finally was granted a ten-year loan of forty million marks, a gigantic amount at that time, from a syndicate of commercial banks headed by the Prussian State Bank. It saved him from absorption by private interests, but he had to mortgage all his industrial investments to the syndicate. This included all the factories, mines, mills, railroads, and ships which the largest firm in Germany owned. His independence seemed lost again. Krupp was, as he himself admitted, "exhausted by insomnia and feverish fears" and "close to insanity."

In the next years, he succeeded in selling steel guns to many foreign countries, including enemies of the new Germany such as Austria, despite the protests of German military and political leaders. "We cannot live from Prussia alone. In the next ten years we need orders of at least fifty million marks, and when foreign states place orders,

I cannot supply bad stuff to them," he told the complaining Kaiser. And the Kaiser submitted to Krupp.

In reverse, he successfully insisted that Prussia place its orders only with Krupp. If any orders were given to his competitors, he threatened in a memorandum to the Government, "the question arises whether I shall not act fittingly if I sell my whole establishment and emigrate abroad." Prussia complied with Krupp's wishes.

The third, and probably decisive source of income which saved Krupp was the United States of America. His relations here had begun as early as 1849 when he sold two steel car axles to the Pennsylvania Railroad, which in the first five years of use ran over 80,000 miles and showed almost no signs of wear and tear. This was good publicity. Since 1851 his American sales agency, the House of Prosser & Son in New York City, had sold Krupp's steel cylinders, axles, and railroad-car wheels to American companies. But Krupp's big American business began in earnest only with the extension of the American railroad system over the continent. After the Civil War, additional lines were built, old lines improved, and short lines consolidated, so that between 1865 and 1880 the mileage was more than doubled. Quantities of steel tracks were ordered from Krupp by America's new lines, from the Atchison, Topeka and Sante Fe to the New York Central & Hudson River railroad companies.

At Philadelphia's Centennial Exhibition of 1876, seven cannons—among them the world's biggest, a 35.5 cm.-caliber cannon geared to 1000 pound-shells—were Krupp's main exhibit. American visitors called it "the killing machine." The largest cannon Krupp had ever built, it was to be given later to the Turkish Sultan as a personal present from the Cannon King. Krupp's other great showpiece at America's first world exhibition was a heavy steel shaft for a German warship. Although impressed, America showed little enthusiasm for these martial monsters. The military demands of this country were modest at the time; the year of the Philadelphia Exhibition was also the year of General Custer's last stand. But America continued to buy railroad material and other "tools of peace" from the Essen firm until the 1880's, when the domestic steel industry made the country less dependent on foreign supplies. With remarkable foresight, Alfred Krupp had already sent some of his technicians and engineers to Pittsburgh to study American methods of work and production. In this, too, he was a pioneer. By 1890 the young steel industry of the United States began to lead the other steel-producing countries of the world.

As if to compensate for America's disinterest in Krupp's "tools of war," other countries needed them in growing quantities. In addition to Prussia and Russia, orders for "killing machines" of many kinds for use on ground and sea came from Italy, Denmark, Spain, the Balkan States, Sweden, Portugal, the Netherlands, and Greece. His most antiquated and outdated models were still salable in Japan, Turkey, and other militarily "underdeveloped countries."

In 1887, a year before the large loan was due, the firm was able to repay it. Recovered from its fall, it continued on an uninterrupted rise. It had a working force of 20,000, a total of 23,000 cannons delivered all over the world from Switzerland to China, from Japan to Montenegro, and a daily production of 1,000 shells, 500 steel wheels, axles, and springs, and almost 20,000 rails, impressive figures which established Krupp again as the greatest industrialist on the Continent. He kept expanding his empire, buying a metal cartridge factory here, a gun and pistol parts plant there. When Alfred Nobel invented his smokeless powder, he rushed to Essen to offer it to Krupp, who bought the license at once.

But with his empire finally and firmly established, the Cannon King faced personal failure. He carefully kept away from the factory, as if he had come to fear his former "bride." From the distance and seclusion of his villa, he watched its progress and scolded the managers in daily missives. On the rare occasions on which he met them face to face, he showered them with curses and accusations.

His wife was his favorite victim. When he was sixty-five, she left him after an argument which shook the walls of Villa Hügel. According to family friends, their last quarrel concerned their son. Bertha objected to the spiteful manner in which her husband treated him; when she saw that she could not win a measure of freedom for her child, she chose freedom for herself. This version seems more trustworthy than the Essen gossip which claimed that Alfred Krupp was jealous of a young family physician who had been seen escorting Bertha Krupp on her daily coach-rides. So much is certain: Alfred Krupp's last words, yelled at his wife as she left the room, were: "Bertha, consider what you are doing!" She had considered it for many years. And she never returned.

Since their brief honeymoon, the couple had grown apart and lived separate lives. But the final break was hard to bear for Alfred Krupp, who could rule an empire but not a wife. As though to prove to himself and to the world that he was able to love and be loved, he suddenly and almost ostentatiously showed interest in the opposite sex. "I enjoy now only nature and—a real achievement! —women. After evading them throughout my life I now have quite intimate relationships with the noblest ladies I can find," he wrote in a letter. Was this the boastful, wishful thinking of a senile man posing as a teen-ager, or an act of revenge against his wife?

Gossip linked him with a young pianist and a young actress whom he invited as house guests to the villa. But after a few months this brief amorous intermezzo ended as quickly as it had begun, and he stopped talking to people of either sex altogether. On the rare occasions when guests still came to the hilltop palace, he would tack little sheets of paper to the doors of their rooms with scribbled instructions, including the hours and minutes which they could devote to this or that activity and the dress they were to wear. If he had criticisms to make of his guests' behavior, he also tacked notes of these to their doors. In his last years he ceased writing instructions to his factory, but he still wrote notes and plans for himself. These were mainly technical schemes of a somewhat fantastic character, such as an armored gun which could turn itself around and fire away under a protective wall of impenetrable armor plate. Could this seemingly crackpot idea have been a forerunner of the tank? In another flight of imagination, he wished for "a highly talented somebody to start a counterrevolution for the best of the people." Did this dream perhaps contain a vision of the coming totalitarian dictators?

"Millionaires who laugh are rare," that other great steelmaker of his time, Andrew Carnegie, noted a little later (in his book, *Problems of Today*), and elaborated: "The most miserable of men, as old age approaches, are those who have made money-making their god; like flies bound to the wheel, these unfortunates fondly believe they were really driving it, only to find when tired and craving rest that it is impossible for them to get off, and they are lost, plenty to retire upon but nothing to retire to."

In contrast to Carnegie, Alfred Krupp never understood the sadness of soulless success. Nor did he in his secret last will and testament, let alone in his lifetime, try to escape the solitary despair to which he had sentenced himself and "give away" what he had "made." He did not part with a single pfennig to help the arts, science, the poor, his church, his community, or anybody or anything.

He never looked above himself and his firm. Success was his goddess, and he knew no God. As he once put it, and as Kruppians have piously quoted ever since, work was his prayer. His "prayer" was answered; he succeeded in making more and better steel than anyone in his time.

In 1887, alone but for his valet, Alfred Krupp died of a heart attack in the seventy-fifth year of his powerful, pitiful life.

PART II

The Haunting Heritage

1887-1933

5

Sons and Lovers

It should not come as a surprise to anyone that Alfred Krupp's only son grew up to be a strange man. But it came as a surprise to his father, who knew more about business than about human beings. Alfred Krupp believed he could shape and toughen his son the way he cast his steel, and he fancied it possible to decree what kind of a life his son would lead after his own death, just as he more successfully did with his firm.

The heir was born the year after his parents' wedding. Baptized with his father's and grandfather's names as Friedrich Alfred, he was called only by the abbreviated name of Fritz. This, we remember, was also the name his father gave to "the world's greatest iron hammer," which he built shortly after the birth of his son. But if the hammer fulfilled all the hopes of Alfred Krupp, the boy did not. He suffered poor health from his early childhood in the Garden House on the factory grounds, in the shadow of the giant hammer; the noise, soot, smoke, and fog affected him like poison. That not merely his physical health was twisted and ruined would be shown only later when his secret life was to scandalize Europe.

Little Fritz could not attend school with other children because he suffered from asthma and rheumatism of the joints; tutors educated him at home. Switzerland's Alpine climate was expected to repair some of the damages to his health caused by the atmosphere of Essen and the factory. But once abroad he came down with scarlet fever, while the attacks of rheumatism persisted and his tutor

—according to custom, a gifted student—cared for him. "Will Fritz ever be an upright man?" his distraught father wondered in a letter.

In his late teens, young Fritz served as confidential secretary to his father, took his dictation and transcribed his night-time notes. He wanted to enroll at a university and study natural science, but his father violently denied this wish. "Leave science to the employees who get paid for it," he said, and that settled the question. Self-educated, hardly educated, Alfred Krupp had little respect for education. "More inventors work themselves from the best flat in the house to a garret than the other way round," he remarked. "Let's leave inventing to other people since it's much better and cheaper to buy and use their thoughts." What Fritz had to learn, he wrote him, was "to judge the knowledge and abilities of others whom you will have to hire and to pay."

Fritz was educated as a crown prince who would succeed his father as ruler of the firm, and his father went to great pains to teach him his art; according to his habit, he did so by scribbling daily letters and notes. "The best I can hope . . . for Fritz is to advise him to collect and file all my writings, so that he will always know where to find them," he said. Often the advice to his son consisted only of grandiloquent generalities. For instance, he ordered him "to gain insight into everything that happens in the firm, with a view over the whole and into the future, in space and time." He also taught him to distrust people. "Nobody must be able to fool you," he wrote, "or you won't be safe from what I want to warn you against, that is, that egotism and schemers could force you to abandon your domain."

When the boy was twenty, a serious attack of rheumatic fever invalided him. His father sent him to Egypt, this time accompanied by a young doctor rather than a tutor. As if it were a business trip, the father chased the sick boy all over the country with urgent orders to find out all the facts about a railroad line the Egyptians were alleged to be planning, to bag this special business for Krupp, and, after succeeding in this, to supervise the con-

struction. To rescue his friend's and patient's health from
the demands of the father, the doctor took young Krupp
on a three months' cruise on the Nile. There was no mail
service aboard, Fritz was safely secluded from his father's letters, and his health improved considerably. When
the cruise was over, a batch of angry epistles from Essen
was waiting for him; they contained the usual long-
winded pieces of advice on how to be a Krupp and rule
an empire.

The moment inevitably came when the boy tried to
make a decision of his own. At the age of twenty-five he
told his father he wanted to get married; his choice was
Margarethe von Ende, daughter of a high Prussian
official. The elder Krupp refused permission; he did not
explain his reasons. Was it, as one of the Krupp chroniclers suggests, out of pride, to snub the aristocrats who
only a short while ago had snubbed "the blacksmith
Krupp"? Marga von Ende hailed from this group. Or was
his reason the reverse: did he reject her because her family, though titled and ancient, was poor?

Marga herself was something of an outcast. After helping to bring up eight younger brothers and sisters, she escaped from the drudgery and discipline of her home to
work as a governess in a British admiral's family. For this
show of rebellion her parents denounced her. On her next
visit home they made her sleep in the servants' quarters;
as her mother explained, "You are a wage-earner, and
therefore no better than a servant." Perhaps the Cannon
King shared these views.

In addition, Marga was rather plain-looking, and a little forbidding. Even the Krupp chroniclers with their gift
of singing panegyrics to each and every member of the
family could find nothing better to say in her praise than
that she was "energetic and motherly"; but then, it must
have been precisely these two traits which impressed and
captivated Fritz. No deep affection, let alone passion,
bound Fritz to Marga, or vice versa.

Alfred Krupp continued to object to his son's marriage
for the next eight years, and Fritz obediently remained a
bachelor. But hardly had Alfred Krupp been deserted by

his wife when he gave permission, if not an order, to his
son to marry Marga right away. He did not attend their
wedding; nor, when he received the newlyweds on their
first formal visit, did he address his daughter-in-law. He
pretended not to hear what she said, and, in brief, ignored her. It turned out that he had encouraged the marriage in order to have a new victim in place of his wife to
humiliate and hurt. Perhaps the only joy of his last years
were the petty insults which he carefully planned to punish
his daughter-in-law and his son.

While the old gentleman resided in the lonely splendor
of his 160-room mansion of Villa Hügel, he banished the
young couple to the "Little House"—only 60 rooms—as
if he wanted to avoid close contact with them. He advised
his head gardener not to supply them with the flowers
and vegetables that abounded in his gardens; young Frau
Krupp had to buy them at the public market like a common Essen housewife. He watched her movements behind
his drawn curtains; when she left her house, he sent her a
note scolding her for going out while he needed her. He
was as inventive in these tortures as in his business ways,
but daughter-in-law and son submitted and suffered in
patience.

Four years after the wedding their first child was born,
a daughter whom they named Bertha. Perhaps in a subtle
protest against Life with Father, they gave her the name
of the wife who had left Alfred Krupp. Only a few
months before the birth of his granddaughter, Old
Krupp had removed his wife's furniture from her rooms
and turned them into store-rooms, as if to extinguish her
memory. A second grandchild was named Barbara after
the patron saint of the artillery, and this name was closer
to the grandfather's heart. A few weeks after her birth,
however, the old despot died, and Fritz and Marga moved
across the lawn to the palace.

As soon as he returned from exile in the Little House
to the official residence of Kruppdom in Villa Hügel,
Fritz Krupp gave orders to remove the old windows and
replace them with new ones that could be opened; to do
away with the complicated, cranky air-conditioner, venti-

lator, and other gadgets that never worked; to collect books and paintings and sculptures to relieve the bare fire-proof walls. Was a new wind blowing in the House of Krupp?

The thirty-three-year-old heir seemed like a study in contrast to his tall, haggard father, who had worn no glasses even in his old age. Fritz was short and fat, with a gold-rimmed pince-nez dangling on his slightly crooked nose, a bushy dark mustache above his sensual lips. Unlike his father's commanding figure, Fritz seemed patterned after the middle-class Germans of his time. If it did not require much imagination to compare his father to a steel ingot, Fritz rather recalled a potato dumpling as they are turned out by the housewives of the Ruhr Valley.

But Alfred Krupp had seen to it that his firm would continue to rise, whoever headed it, even if only his son and heir. When Fritz took over sole ownership, according to the General Regulations and the secret last will and testament of his father, he found the accumulation of mills, forges, factories, fleets, and other enterprises going full blast. All he had to do was to assert his leadership, and by acting according to his father's regulations keep them going in the same direction, at the same speed, with the same power and success. *Le roi est mort, vive le roi.*

Satraps often see their chance in the moment of succession and try to extend their own power when the crown prince mounts the throne. Krupp's directors attempted this stratagem and drafted amendments to the old man's General Regulations which would have restrained the new owner's absolute rule over the firm; but Fritz put his foot down and in few words rejected any change. Although he depended on his able directors, he aborted their revolt before it had begun. His only concession was that the five leading underlings were to be addressed as "directors" instead of "confidential clerks," which had been their previous title. This did not cost him anything in power or money, yet it seemed to indicate a more pliable new ruler. After his father's absolute dictatorship, Fritz wished to appear accessible to "collective leader-

ship" without giving up one inch of his might. Apparently
he was quite shrewd.

As the next step in his first year of rule the young sec-
ond Cannon King introduced himself to the world. Fritz
Krupp also proved to be a master of "public relations."
With a large entourage consisting of two directors, several
employees, and his brother-in-law, he set out to pay courtesy calls on the German Kaiser in Berlin, the King of
Belgium in Bruxelles, the King of Saxony in Dresden, the
King of Rumania in Bucharest, and finally the Turkish
Sultan in Constantinople—great potentates in the world
of their day as well as great customers of the House of
Krupp. On this business trip, turned into a visit of state,
the head of the House of Krupp visited the monarchs like
a new king greeting his crowned cousins. There was no
talk of business. Fritz Krupp showed Sultan Abdul
Hamid pictures of his hillside palace and its parks, and
the Sultan held forth on gardening which, he said, tends
to keep people from doing things they would regret later
on. He himself had many gardens and enjoyed gardening.
He also enjoyed, although he did not mention it in his
talks with Krupp, drowning his domestic opponents in the
Bosporus and exterminating his captive peoples—Alba-
nians, Greeks, Yemenites, and Armenians.

Hardly had the new Cannon King returned to his
Essen capital when a new Kaiser mounted the thrones of
Prussia and Germany, and set out on a new course of history. In the preceding era, French supremacy over the
Continent had been victoriously overcome and the division of Germany into many independent countries had
been ended by their final submission to Prussia. The new
course aimed at greater victories; the new *Reich* saw as its
goal the destruction of the naval and economic superiority
of Great Britain throughout the world. Bismarck, a no-
bleman of the old Prussian school, wise in the ways of di-
plomacy and the whims of the world, satisfied with Prussia's hegemony over Germany, was fired by his young,
new monarch. "The pilot has left the ship," as *Punch* in
London commented in distress. On its new course, the
ship followed different directions. In one sentence, they

were summed up by Prince Bernhard Bülow, a later successor to Bismarck in the Reich Chancellery, who proclaimed: "The King of Prussia first, Prussia first in Germany, Germany first in the world!"

Old Alfred Krupp had understood the common destiny of Prussia and his firm which he purposely patterned after the Prussian model. "If the State can annex and rule a lot of other states in one year," he had written after Prussia's successful expansion in 1871, "we, the House of Krupp, shall also be able to introduce and safely rule a dozen new industries." With Krupp first in his firm and the firm first in Germany, the third condition—Krupp's firm first in the world—was to follow under his heir. By symbolic coincidence, Fritz Krupp inherited his firm at the same time that the new Kaiser inherited his *Reich*. Eager to build up his power of arms and ships, to reach out across the seas and end British superiority, the new Kaiser depended as much on his leading armorer, shipbuilder, and industrialist, as Krupp depended on his Kaiser. Krupp's and Germany's interests, prospects, and ambitions ran along parallel lines until eventually they became two sides of the same coin.

As Prussia remained the center of strength and purpose in the new *Reich,* the "cast iron factory" remained the basis and driving force in the new Krupp combine, but under its new head and in the new *Reich* the firm was expanded to a "colossal" extent, as the era's favorite phrase expressed it. New sources of raw materials were acquired with the enthusiasm of a collector, from rich coal mines in Germany, French Lorraine, and Luxembourg to iron-ore fields in Spain and Sweden. At Rheinhausen near Essen, the firm began to construct Europe's largest iron-works, the Friedrich Alfred Forge. It was based on the Thomas process which, supplanting the Bessemer process, permitted the smelting and forging of phosphorous ores with which Fritz Krupp was richly supplied. His aging father had postponed the introduction of this new process because he had come to distrust the technical progress in which he had believed in his youth. Now new smelting works and factories, several to produce cannons, grew up around the old cast-steel plants.

Moreover, young Krupp branched out into entirely new fields of production by acquiring well-established corporations. This was a striking departure from the ways of his father. In his hatred of stock-exchange deals and modern corporations, Alfred Krupp had carefully abstained from the activities that characterized most other industrial success stories in his age, that is, the stock-exchange piracy and corporation brigandage so dear to the hearts of the "robber barons." But his son had not inherited this aversion, and took to this method of aggrandizement without scruples.

Fritz Krupp's first acquisition was the Grusonwerk, an arms factory in the Saxonian city of Magdeburg which in the last years of Alfred Krupp had begun to threaten his firm's hegemony in the field. It had developed new shells, armored towers and other fortifications parts, and armored plates, as well as new light cannons, spitfire howitzers, and revolver cannons. With this production the Gruson Works became the first big-time competitor to threaten Krupp in Germany. If you can't lick 'em, trap 'em into joining you, was Krupp's answer to the threat, although he did not try to lick 'em in open competition. His secret go-betweens bought up shares of his competitor over three years until he controlled a majority. Then he surprised the stockholders of the Gruson Works with the news that he had leased the corporation, and a year later he bought it outright. To the detriment of its stockholders, he acquired the corporation at a fraction of its value, turned it into an auxiliary of his private empire, and strengthened it by constructing two additional armor-plate works. Through this maneuver, his monopoly in the artillery field was restored and expanded.

By similar methods Krupp also took over the Germaniawerft in Kiel, a struggling shipyard on Germany's North Sea coast. After the shareholders had sold a controlling majority to his financial undercover agents at low prices, he "leased," then bought, the company, and immediately started to modernize the "Fried. Krupp-Germania Shipyards" with multimillion-dollar investments.

With these new acquisitions, Krupp was ready for all demands. The firm could supply a man-of-war from the ship itself to its guns, armor plates, machines, and boilers without outside help. Two years after Krupp took over the Germania Yards and became a navy-builder, the Kaiser won his campaign to build a German battle fleet which could challenge Great Britain's sea power in trade or war, and also serve as the link to a new, world-wide German colonial empire. In its drive for colonies, Germany was a Wilhelm-come-lately; the older colonizing nations of Europe had already conquered their own and little was left for the Germans to acquire without intruding into spheres which other European nations, England in particular, already controlled. When the Kaiser proclaimed that "our future lies on water," neither Germans nor Britishers misunderstood his challenge, although for a decade many German liberals and some conservatives unsuccessfully resisted it. Germany spent billions of dollars on its navy as the new plaything of its new power, a plaything, it is true, bound to kill either its owner or his enemies in the end. The Firm of Krupp was its main manufacturer.

The armament business which Krupp controlled had a built-in mechanism of increasing profits, unlike any other business. Every new offensive weapon was a challenge to be eventually answered by the invention, development, and production of a new defensive weapon, which then, and in turn, was bound to be overcome by the invention and production of a new offensive weapon, against which a new defensive weapon had to be constructed.

The firm demonstrated by impressive example the working of this vicious circle in perpetual motion. Since the 1890's Krupp produced gun barrels from an alloy of steel and nickel which the American H. A. Harvey had invented. Less rigid than pure steel, it was therefore more efficient when used in armor plate. Its resistance was further increased when Krupp added oil. While Krupp manufactured and sold this special armor in quantities, his research department was busy developing a new missile which would pierce this special armor. It succeeded in inventing such a missile by alloying that metal with chromium. Of course, Krupp sold great quantities of this miracle missile which took the miracle out of his miracle armor. Then Krupp's research department was ordered to find a new steel armor which would give protection against the new shells, and in a few years it accomplished this assignment. The new steel, enriched with carbon under high pressure and called simply "Krupp steel," was one of the sensations of the Chicago World's Fair and made Krupp's armor even more world-famous than his cannons. Orders for it kept the firm busy until it developed a new shell that contained in its cap an explosive which could perforate the formerly shell-proof plates of Krupp steel. This entire exploit took less than twenty years.

But a threat to disturb, if not to stop, this built-in, self-perpetuating business in weaponry came from the opposition of German Socialists, liberals, and some conservatives to the overly massive armament of their nation. This political danger could be resisted only by political means, and this forced Fritz Krupp to give up to some degree the parental aloofness from politics. The firm had grown too big, and its business had become too closely intertwined with public events.

Fritz Krupp was not the man to stand up and fight in the open political arena. When in his youth he had run twice as a candidate to represent Essen in the *Reichstag,* he was defeated both times, although the foremen in his factories and the supervisors in his housing developments threatened with dire consequences all those "Kruppians" who dared to vote for his adversary, a former metal-turner in Krupp's steel plant who had founded a Christian Workers' Association as a moderate trade union. Only on his third try, in 1893, did Fritz Krupp win the election as Essen's representative to the German parliament. He won because his Social Democrat and Christian adversaries could not agree on a joint candidate. A torch parade was organized in honor of his victory. When he appeared on the balcony of the hilltop palace to thank his electorate, he could only stammer a few unintelligible words. Nor did Fritz Krupp ever speak while he held his parliamentary seat.

If there were more effective weapons available to Krupp in the fight for public opinion than his own voice and mind, he was rather inept in their use, too. In the year of his election to parliament a daily newspaper was founded in Berlin to defend the interests of the firm. But the *Berliner Neueste Nachrichten*, as this paper was called, was attacked and rejected by the public as Fritz Krupp's personal voice. In a confidential letter to the Prussian Minister of Education, Konrad von Studt, which was found later, he explained that he had severed his official connection with the paper. But this was only a blind. "Quite *entre nous*," he underlined this confidential opening, "I decided, after I gave my shares in the paper to industrial corporations, to contribute the necessary means to this venture for the next years as an *outsider*," the last word also underlined. But the public was not deceived or the paper ever taken seriously. He kept it for thirteen years, until in 1919 the German revolution ended its publication.

In secret, he also financed a news service, as he confided to the Kaiser and his chief of cabinet. Its aim was to supply the South German press with "news on the activities of Your Majesty, Navy, Army, financial, and foreign affairs," and to offset the influence of liberal and Catholic, or anti-Kaiser and anti-Krupp, opinion. Although the fact that it was edited in Berlin and Essen, the knowledge of which would have made it worthless from the beginning, was carefully camouflaged, the venture failed.

The most influential weapon forged by the Firm of Krupp to win public opinion was the German Navy League, which it financed at the rate of several hundred thousand dollars a year. This organization tried to stir up enthusiastic support for far-reaching German Navy plans and policies, edited and distributed a monthly publication with one million circulation, and lobbied extensively in parliament and elsewhere. But when the German public continued to object to the Navy budget despite all this expensive propaganda, Krupp stopped his subsidies.

Fritz Krupp was more successful in personally influencing leaders of German politics when they visited his hilltop palace. He was quite able at quiet persuasion over a bottle of wine. Among Fritz Krupp's guests and friends, Kaiser Wilhelm II held the place of honor.

Only once did the Cannon King and the German Kaiser clash. During his first years of rule the Kaiser tried to introduce social legislation which, he hoped, would reconcile the Socialist opposition and unite his people behind him. Labor arbitration courts, restrictions on child labor and women's work, general rest on Sundays, and elected spokesmen to represent the workers to management were on the Kaiser's program, against which Fritz Krupp protested first in a memorandum, then in a personal audience. If the Kaiser proclaimed that "only one man is master over the land and that is I," Krupp upheld his claim to remain "master in his own house." Not even the Kaiser could interfere with it. In the end, the erratic Kaiser himself renounced most of his plans when he saw that German labor was not won over by them. While the conflict left no ill feelings between the rulers of the firm and the *Reich*, Fritz Krupp continued to influence the Kaiser against a more favorable and flexible labor policy. In a secret memoranda preserved in German government files, he informed the Kaiser that he ruthlessly punished striking workers, that this procedure worked well, and that leniency was bound to backfire.

If two-thirds of Krupp's production had gone abroad before the era of Kaiser Wilhelm II, only one-third, and sometimes only one-fourth, now found its way into foreign countries. But this resulted from an increased demand of the home market rather than from a decrease in foreign demand. In addition, the equally prospering armaments industries of other countries began to produce for their own consumption on licenses and patents acquired from Krupp. His famous new armor-plate steel was an example of this. After its value was demonstrated to American producers at the Indianhead firing range,

Bethlehem Steel and Carnegie bought the patent, and royalties of forty-five dollars on every ton produced in America were paid to Krupp. France and England, Russia, Austria and Italy, in short, friend and foe alike, paid similar tribute to Krupp. The main foreign income of the firm, however, still stemmed from direct deliveries of its "tools of peace and war." In the Chinese-Japanese War of 1894 both sides were privileged to kill each other with the same Krupp guns. This was another peculiarity of the weapon trade in Fritz Krupp's time: it stood above warring nations. Rather than get entangled in alien quarrels, the firm upheld its proud and prosperous neutrality and impartially sold its goods to every buyer. In this happy era Fritz Krupp's personal fortune rose from 119 million marks in 1895 to 187 million marks in 1902; his personal income in the same period, from 7 to 21 million marks a year. Smoothly running and rising on the tracks which his father had laid out, helped along by the course of German politics and his own ability, his firm moved on in seemingly self-perpetuating success.

Rather than live the drab life of dreary Essen, and in the forbidding Villa Hügel, Fritz Krupp spent more and more of his time in the distant, elegant spas of Southern France and Italy. The island of Capri, his favorite refuge, came to be his second home. Since the first century A.D., when the Roman Emperor Tiberius had chosen this island near Naples as the favorite scene of his orgies, it had preserved its reputation for debauchery as well as beauty. Escaping from the world of his father in which "work was prayer," in Capri Fritz Krupp found an island without work, or prayer either.

Krupp's health was still weak and he had to undergo many different cures. One eye-witness recalls that his physician, *"Professor Doktor* Schweninger, ordered him to stretch on his belly for an hour after every meal . . . while the other gentlemen of his entourage joined him in this exercise in order to keep him from being bored."

To escape the boredom of the firm and Essen, Fritz Krupp, whose scientific interests had been frustrated by his father, took up studies in deep-sea life and oceanography. He found crustaceans more interesting than Kruppians, and he fancied himself quite a scholar in the field. But when Anton Dohrn, the celebrated creator of the Zoological Research Station at Naples, invited him to join in its researches, he refused. "He wanted to fish as it pleased him," one of his friends reported; in other words, he wanted to be master of the house even below the sea. Instead of working with a team of serious scientists, the multimillionaire bought his own yacht, named her the *Puritan,* outfitted her with elaborate scientific instruments and gadgets, and carried on his personal explorations; for his friends and himself, this sufficed to establish his role as a great scientist.

But more pleasure awaited the Cannon King abroad, and they were of a different kind. Fritz Krupp bought the Grotto of Fra Felice, a cave above the ocean near Capri and inaccessible by land. Originally, a pious hermit had chosen it as his dwelling place. Krupp had a private road blasted to the grotto through the rocks of the Marina Piccola, and gave golden keys to its gate to his Caprese friends, among whom were young fishermen, barbers, and beggars. The grotto, he announced in mock solemnity, was the inner sanctum of a mysterious order of holy men; he himself was its founder and leader. A golden medal with two crossed forks, which he designed himself and distributed among his friends, was the membership badge. Caprese boys dressed as Franciscan Friars guarded the grotto when the members of the order met at night. Germany's biggest industrialist chose to entertain himself and others in ways which seemed to many somewhat eccentric, and to Catholics blasphemous. But the natives of Capri, accustomed to eccentrics, tolerated him with a shrug; he had his pockets filled with golden coins, and he gave them away on the slightest provocation. Once he passed the shop of a local craftsman who was just finishing a life-sized bronze bust of Dante. Krupp looked at the craftsman, who was young and strong, then at the bust, and ordered one hundred and fifty life-sized Dantes. He paid twice the price their maker asked and sent them to Essen to decorate his factory.

These seemingly harmless amusements ended overnight when that ugly and unhappy affair which came to be called "the Krupp scandal" broke into the open. It shook the House of Krupp to its foundations. The world learned, in details which were shocking and which would have better remained unknown, that the heir of one of the world's greatest fortunes was a criminal according to the law of his land. Equally upsetting was the sudden revelation that the powerful little man—not at all the morally lily-pure, mediocre, work-obsessed Organization Man whose image his father had conjured—lived a secret double life.

Naples newspapers, then other Italian publications, and finally the German press began to publish local rumors of Capri's famous guest, and soon backed them with facts. As they revealed, and as had been common knowledge on Capri for some time, Fritz Krupp indulged in homosexual practices. While this was a crime according to German law, it was not in Italy. But Italian law considered the corruption of minors, whether of the opposite or the same sex, a crime, and according to the reports, Krupp had committed it with a number of young native boys. Lewd snapshots of orgies in which Krupp and his friends participated were sold under the counter in Capri's taverns to anybody interested in pictures of perversion.

Krupp left Capri overnight. It has been claimed, but never proved, that the Italian government discreetly asked him to depart. It seems probable however, in view of the admission of a Krupp house chronicler that the Kaiser "let Krupp know that he wanted to see him in Germany, and therefore Krupp returned." A declaration of Krupp as *persona non grata* was apparently communicated from Rome to Berlin by diplomatic channels.

But while the Italian press published the sensational story, Krupp remained silent. And the Kaiser's orders manifestly exiled Krupp only from Capri, not from foreign countries altogether. In October he was in London "to recover from the rather great strains of the last weeks," as he wrote in a business letter to Friedrich Karl

Hermann von Lucanus, Chief of the Prussian Secret Civilian Cabinet.

Ten days later Fritz Krupp was back in Germany, committing his wife to an asylum for the mentally disturbed. As he explained to his embarrassed friends, "she voluntarily consented to a thorough-going treatment."

In his absence his wife had learned of his scandalous adventures in Capri and Berlin, and asked the Kaiser for help. The Kaiser was furious with the wife for bothering him with her stories, rather than with her husband; in the eyes of the potentate, the lady was a troublemaker. In marked anger, he sent her away with an order to keep silent. But instead of obeying the order, she implored her friends and acquaintances for help and advice. "The rumors which she is circulating are spreading through wider circles," an adviser of the Kaiser warned Fritz Krupp in a confidential letter, and suggested that he see to it that his wife could not reach the public with her dangerous knowledge.

The Cannon King had his wife declared temporarily insane; while she was immured in a private asylum, her charges would not be heard, or at least, not taken seriously. In a letter to the Kaiser, he thanked "His Majesty for the gracious proof of most benevolent kindness." Power was on his side, and nothing much could happen to Fritz Krupp.

But in the same week the silence was broken when the *Augsburger Postzeitung,* a highly respected Bavarian conservative newspaper, alluded to Italian reports of the case without naming names, referring only to "a big industrialist of the best reputation, whose close relationships to the Kaiser's court are well known." And one month after Marga Krupp's commitment to silence, a Berlin newspaper, the Social-Democratic *Vorwärts,* campaigning against the German laws on homosexuality, published a news story on "Krupp in Capri," which presented names as well as facts.

The exposé came as a shock to the German public but not to the German leaders, least of all to the Kaiser himself. Even before Marga Krupp had asked for help against her husband's irresponsible ways, the matter had been known in Berlin where Krupp had indulged in similar perversions. As Hans von Tresckow, Commissioner of Criminal Police in the Prussian capital, revealed later on —after the German revolution gave the signal that "now it can be told"—a secret dossier on homosexual blackmail cases of prominent personalities was kept in his office and the file on Fritz Krupp had been growing in volume over the years. Krupp found himself in what he considered good company, from Philipp Prince Eulenburg, personal aide-de-camp of the Kaiser, to the Chief of Cabinet of the Empress, the Berlin city commandant, and even one of the Kaiser's brothers; many "personalities of the highest rank at the Court" shared Fritz Krupp's distaste of women. Youngsters from Capri used to introduce themselves to the owner of Berlin's Bristol Hotel, where Fritz Krupp was a frequent guest, with a letter from the Cannon King asking that he give them employment. The hotel keeper kept a running correspondence with his distinguished guest who inquired about the well-being of his young protégés. When he came to Berlin for a stay at the Bristol, while his wife stayed in a different hotel, he enjoyed their room service. At least one valet of Fritz Krupp received from his master a valuable diamond ring as a present because, as he told the police, "Krupp was my friend." But the police as well as the court succeeded in keeping such affairs from the public eye; the vice was widespread in a society which boasted of its virility and morality. And the public—in the year 1902 when polite society did not discuss, let alone explain, matters connected with sex—wavered between disbelief and horror when the allegations concerning the leading industrialist of the nation were published. Sigmund Freud's name was still unknown, and nobody wondered what made Fritz Krupp the person he was alleged to be. Nobody recalled that his childhood was dominated by a father who taught him contempt for women and forced him to seem stronger than he was.

Fritz Krupp sued the editors of the German newspaper which published the story of his Capri adventures for

libel several hours after the article hit the streets. Spokesmen of the House of Krupp presented harmless-sounding
tales in defense of their master (which are still rehashed
today by devoted chroniclers). One argument was that
Krupp had been so generous with his money, as well as
with his show of good will toward everyone, that the Ital-
ians misunderstood it. This was also what Norman Douglas, British author of *South Wind* and of a cookbook of
aphrodisiacs, and a long-time resident of Capri, has told
in his autobiographical memoirs, *Looking Back*. His
lengthy, chatty testimony to the fact that Fritz Krupp
must have been innocent because in his Capri years he
was "of advanced age, over sixty. . . . an old gentleman . . . ," in short, harmless and impotent, was less
than convincing. In fact, Krupp was then only forty-nine,
an age at which few men have lost the power of love-
making. Norman Douglas himself was not a detached
observer. As his friend and admirer Richard Aldington
wrote in 1954, and as Aubrey Menen recalled, he himself
had also been asked by the local police to leave Capri,
and for the same reason as Fritz Krupp.

Three days after publication of the *Vorwärts* article,
Fritz Krupp requested a personal audience with the Kaiser. He did not keep his appointment. The next morning
Krupp was found unconscious in bed by his physician.
Despite immediate treatment by his doctor and other physicians, Krupp's condition deteriorated quickly; in the afternoon he died of a cerebral stroke. At least this was
what his doctors—among them the psychiatrist to whose
clinic Krupp's wife was committed—reported in their
communiqué. Rumors that Fritz Krupp's life had ended
by suicide were immediately heard, and are still being
whispered today in Essen, even among the most devoted
and trusted of his old servants. In contrast to custom his
coffin was closed and its lid sealed only a few hours after
his death.

The funeral of Fritz Krupp was held with all the pomp
of national mourning. From less than a dozen Kruppian
workers with whom his father had begun, and who num-
bered 20,000 at the time of his death, the Kruppians had

now grown to 43,000. Like people on the death of their dictator, they lined the streets. Fritz Krupp's wife, who had been released from the psychiatric clinic, attended, and the Kaiser himself walked behind the coffin, "to keep the shield of the German Emperor over [sic] the house and the memory of Krupp." After the funeral he addressed the leading men of Essen and the firm in a speech to be remembered in German history. He put the blame for Krupp's death on the Social Democrats whose newspaper, he said, had "murdered" his friend. "He who does not cut the tablecloth between himself and those scoundrels," he cried out against the men of Germany's labor party, "shares the moral guilt for this deed."

The widow, Marga Krupp, requested that the authorities quash her husband's libel suit; to continue the fight for her husband's honor, she wrote, was "against her innermost feelings." The request was quickly obeyed.

We shall never know whether the second heir of the House of Krupp died by his own hand or not. But this much is certain: his life was haunted by his heritage until it overwhelmed him.

6

Daughter and Prince Consort

The fourth generation of the House of Krupp entered the scene against the background of the firm's success and the father's personal failure. According to Fritz Krupp's last will and testament—which was modeled after his own father's will—his firstborn child, the older daughter, was his sole heiress. This made sixteen-year-old Bertha Krupp owner of Germany's largest fortune, queen of the most powerful industrial empire of her time, ruler over almost 50,000 workers, and head of the "armory of the Reich," as the German cliché had come to call Krupp's cannon kingdom. Her first step in the new role was a letter to the Kaiser to tell him that "in my thoughts, I most submissively kiss Your Majesty's hand," and to ask him to "continue Your merciful protection on my road of life which will be filled with responsibilities."

To prepare for these responsibilities, before she reached the legal age to assume them fully, Bertha was sent to a fashionable boarding school at Baden-Baden which groomed future housewives of the upper classes. For her to receive a more serious education would not have been proper in an age in which women were excluded from German universities. Bertha learned how to supervise a staff of household servants and how to be a gracious hostess; horseback riding and French language courses rounded out her curriculum. In her boarding school she was secluded from the waves of scandal that broke high after her father's distressing death and her mother's stay in an asylum. With her tall and lanky

figure, her bony face, and her cold eyes, Bertha Krupp
closely resembled her grandfather Alfred. But the same
features that lend an air of striking distinction to a man
do not tend to make a woman attractive.

Until Bertha Krupp reached her majority, her mother
served as acting head of the house. For a woman stepping
from a psychiatric ward directly onto the temporary
throne of an empire, she showed remarkably little weakness. "Our mother," Bertha later recalled, "seemed infal-
lible to us [her two children] in every respect, and we
clung to her in deepest devotion, not quite without certain
feelings of inferiority, since we children as well as our
whole entourage were always scared we might not completely satisfy her demands." Tender affections were not
mentioned in this daughterly eulogy which sounded more
like the eulogy of a Prussian soldier on his sergeant. But
then, this was the style of the Krupps.

Bertha's mother was a lady, not a business leader. "I
was little prepared for the tasks awaiting me after my
spouse's death, since he held the principle that business
matters were a male domain," Marga Krupp reported of
her five-year legal custodianship of the firm. Neither did
she learn to master business matters. Jokingly she would
declare that she was and would remain "a goose" when it
came to the mysteries of accounts and balances; what she
meant was that she stood above these lowlands of common life, as a lady of noble birth and a dowager queen
should.

In anticipation, her husband had left a will by which
the government of the firm was reformed. Krupp finally
became a corporation, but its shares would be held only
by the family's oldest heir. This continued the order decreed by the will of Alfred Krupp, and the dynastic principle remained in power, since one single person, and
only a Krupp, was to continue to own and rule the firm.
Its constitution alone was reformed; legislation regulated
all corporations and required a Board of Directors and a
Board of Trustees to share in some responsibilities. The
House of Krupp adjusted its rule to the new times; as it
had grown too big, and its heirs had shrunk to too small

a size, it was better to limit the absolute autocratic government with which Alfred Krupp had run it. The gigantic new organization drew its strength from the teamwork of mediocre, yet devoted, employees rather than from aggressive leaders. Krupp's executives came frequently from high bureaucratic posts in the civilian and military administration of Germany to their new industrial jobs and held no proprietary share in the industry.

The firm was incorporated at the transparently undercapitalized value of $40,000,000; the entire capital, with the exception of $1000 distributed among the members of the board to comply with the law, was held exclusively by Bertha Krupp. Actually the heiress in her sailor suit was worth many times more, and she had directors and managers to take care of her interests.

In the new order, her mother devoted herself in the main to those tasks which are reserved to queens in a modern monarchy, that is, to the welfare tasks of the welfare firm. "Giving," which had held no lure for Alfred Krupp, had been practiced by his son after the old man's death. Fritz Krupp had donated $250,000 to a new foundation to take care of workers in cases of sickness or emergencies which were not "their fault." A year later he founded a housing settlement for the families of 850 old, pensioned Kruppians, a hospital for Kruppians and a library, but his main interests had been in sponsoring fencing, glee, and boating clubs for white-collar Kruppians. His widow added hospitals for the wives and daughters, donated $750,000 to needy families, and organized a visiting nurse service. She, herself, often visited the homes of old and sick Kruppians, to brighten their lives with a few kind and gracious words, again the fashion of a dowager queen. If her donations amounted only to a small percentage of the firm's income, they established her in the new image of the Mother of the Country who cared for her subjects, or an "angel of charity," as Krupp's public-relations rhetoric dubbed her. The rule of the business empire remained in the hands of Krupp men, while the welfare of the subjects was personified by a *Frau* Krupp.

Bertha's education was completed when she went with

her mother, her sister, and a staff of servants on a sight-seeing tour of Europe. In Rome, at a reception given by the Royal Prussian Embassy to the Holy See, she met a young and undistinguished attaché named Gustav von Bohlen und Halbach. According to some contemporary observers, he had been selected by the Kaiser himself as the consort of Germany's most eligible heiress.

In spite of his resounding family name, Bertha Krupp's future husband was not of noble descent. His family origins seemed strangely similar to those of the Krupps; in fact, nobody would have been surprised if one of Gustav's forefathers had married one of Bertha's foremothers two or three hundred years before Gustav and Bertha met. That was after the Halbachs, at the beginning of the sixteenth century, settled at Remscheid, a town on the outskirts of the Ruhr district and not far from Essen, where for the next two hundred years they would make iron and steel. As early as 1666 one Peter Halbach had received a patent to run an iron mine and produce iron bullets for cannons, which he lost twenty years later only because he was, as a contemporary chronicle reported, "a quite dissolute man who was very addicted to drinking." But the Halbachs continued as ironsmiths, and by the end of the eighteenth century they had become prosperous manufacturers with their own ironworks, where they produced scythes which since 1791 they had sold under a trade-mark advertising them (in English) as "Very best German steel." The owner of the family enterprise sent his son Arnold—born in the same year as Alfred Krupp —to America to sell steel in the young republic.

As if by a magnet, the young immigrant from the Ruhr Valley was quickly attracted to the Commonwealth of Pennsylvania. He felt at ease amid all its coal and iron, and went quickly into the coal industry. "My father's mines are now worth $45,000 and their prices climb every day," Arnold Halbach's son Gustav noted in his diary after his father took him to the coal mines of Scranton, Pennsylvania, which he owned and developed. The Halbachs settled in Philadelphia where the German element played a large part in city life. Among the leading

Philadelphians of German descent were the Bohlens, who traced their family back to German Frisia and claimed relationship with England's Queen Anne Boleyn; two Bohlen brothers also had left their native farm at the end of the eighteenth century and emigrated to America. The older brother, Bohl Bohlen, also opened an import business in Philadelphia which prospered for many years on North Water Street, later on South Fourth Street. A daughter of "Beau Bohlen," as he was dubbed in Philadelphia, and his third wife, a daughter of Dutch immigrants, married the steel importer and coal-mine owner Halbach in Philadelphia.

As his years advanced, the well-to-do businessman retired with his wife and his son Henry to Amsterdam in the Netherlands, but Henry Bohlen returned to Philadelphia at sixteen. If he became a prosperous Quaker City merchant by vocation, he was by avocation a soldier of fortune who volunteered his services wherever war was waged—from the Mexican campaign, in which he participated as an American, to the Crimean War, in which he fought on the French side. After the bombardment of Fort Sumter, Henry Bohlen immediately organized a German regiment in his home town—the 75th Pennsylvania Volunteers—paid the recruiting costs himself and even had a book of regimental battle songs printed at his own expense. He was also the author of its contents, including the regimental anthem:

And if as a sacrifice you are slain,
No man of honor dies in vain.

Und opferst du dich auch, wohlan,
Vergebens stirbt kein Ehrenmann.

Under General Frémont and General Franz Sigel, Colonel Henry Bohlen fought his way bravely through many of the Civil War's major battles, from the Shenandoah Valley and Cross Keys back to Cedar Creek and Bull Run, where he was killed. The city of Philadelphia ordered thirty days of public mourning for its hero. He left

a wife of French and British descent and thirteen children. One of his daughters married her cousin, Gustav
Halbach, who added his wife's well-known name to his
own; in the historian's hindsight, this seems a strange pattern of repetition, for this Bohlen-Halbach was the father
of the future "prince consort" who would also add his
wife's famous name to his own, as Krupp von Bohlen und
Halbach.

In a meandering life unusual for prospering new Americans of German descent, Gustav Bohlen-Halbach returned to Germany. Apparently he felt no ties to the
country which his family had adopted but had a strong
ambition to partake of the monarchic splendor of Germany. With his inherited wealth, it was not difficult for
him to be appointed a minor diplomat at a minor German
court; the Grand Duke of Baden nominated Bohlen-Halbach his Chief of Protocol, and in 1871 raised him to the
nobility. This gave him the right to change his name to a
more resounding "von Bohlen und Halbach," but except
for this right coveted by snobs, the honor was meaning-
less. Genuine nobility based its title on the traditions,
privileges, and obligations of an order which had become
extinct; now titles could be bought from the rulers at high
prices, or went almost automatically with appointments to
the higher diplomatic, bureaucratic, and military positions. The Krupps, who completed their hilltop residence
in the year Bohlen-Halbach acquired his title, consistently
refused to embellish their family name with aristocratic
prefixes.

The new aristocrat, a descendant of Ruhr craftsmen
and Philadelphia merchants of mixed German, American,
Dutch, and French stock, saw to it that his son—also
named Gustav von Bohlen und Halbach—started a career
befitting a true-born German aristocrat. But while he proceeded on this career, it showed all the telltale signs of
mediocrity. Everything in it went exactly according to
plan and revealed the carefully controlled ambition of a
mediocre climber. After his military service in a fashionable regiment, he joined the Prussian Foreign Service
where he was slowly and silently promoted, until he met

twenty-year-old Bertha Krupp in Rome. The attaché was
sixteen years older than the heiress and shorter by at least
a head. While she had grown to impressive proportions
which she carried with the dignity of a matron, he almost
disappeared in her shadow, though he carried himself
with exaggerated erectness. A picture of the correctitude
valued by Prussian officers and officials, this thin-lipped,
piercing-eyed, subaltern-minded little man in his corset
would have made a perfect aide-de-camp to any general,
a splendid attaché to any ambassador, an excellent second-in-command to any domineering, strong-willed wife.
It was this last post which he chose when he wed the firm
of Krupp, or more precisely, Bertha Krupp. As the prince
consort of either, he was an excellent choice. His personality seemed a safeguard against the eccentricities of the
degenerating Krupps. His social background wed the
Krupps to the officialdom of the Prussian Establishment;
his own family lineage reflected the ascent from the
smithy to the *salon*. While the firm had grown to be an almost autonomous oversized organization, it found in him
its proper, leading Organization Man. The new, great ambition of Bertha Krupp's husband was to fit into this organization and "to be a real Krupp." (In their strange
destiny the Krupps always met, wed, and were rescued by
"a real Krupp" from outside their family ranks when the
vital strength of their own offspring was exhausted.)

Three months after Gustav had been introduced to
Bertha, the wedding was celebrated at Villa Hügel. The
Kaiser himself attended to demonstrate his joyful approval. It was the first time that he had favored the
Krupps with his friendship since Fritz Krupp had died; in
the following four years he had not visited Essen or the
hilltop palace, urgently though the widow had entreated
him to come. "Such a sign of grace would give to me and
my daughters the consoling assurance that Your Majesty's benevolence toward, and interest in, the Firm of
Krupp continues without a change," she wrote him. But
he avoided the widow and any gesture of good will toward the woman whom he did not forgive for her role in

"that Capri affair." But things were different with Bertha and her consort.

At the wedding dinner in the great hall of Hügel, the Kaiser first addressed "My dear Bertha," in a formal speech, full of respect for the bride: "When you stride through the factory, may the worker take off his cap before you in grateful love." But when he turned to the groom, whom he addressed only by his last name, it sounded rather like a pep talk of an advertising-agency account man to a junior executive: "My dear Bohlen" was admonished by the monarch "to keep supplying our German fatherland with those *Schutz-und Trutzwaffen,* those defensive and offensive weapons, whose production and efficiency cannot be attained by any other nation."

After dinner, a reception was held. According to protocol, nobody was permitted to sit down or speak while the Kaiser stood. Wilhelm II kept standing, talking, and laughing for two hours while the guests stood in silence. Before he departed he made a solemn announcement. Gustav von Bohlen und Halbach and his heirs were granted the personal privilege to call themselves Krupp von Bohlen und Halbach. The Imperial edict was correctly interpreted throughout Germany as a unique proof of grace toward the House of Krupp which, with its new American ancestry and its new nobility, would preserve its heritage.

At the same time, Bertha's younger sister married a scion of authentic Prussian nobility. Thilo Baron von Wilmowsky, her groom, was the son of the Chief Civilian Adviser to the first German Kaiser, who had supported Alfred Krupp in his struggles to establish his autocratic and uncontested rule as the Cannon King. As is customary among dynasties, marriages became an instrument by which the House of Krupp strengthened its ties to other spheres of power.

Marga Krupp, the dowager queen, moved to the Little House in which she had spent her first unhappy years of marriage. Bertha and Gustav Krupp von Bohlen und Halbach settled down in the palace as the new rulers.

A Victorian rather than an Elizabethan age opened for

the House of Krupp under Queen Bertha, no Virgin Queen she. The old Krupp spirit of dangerous expansion disappeared under her rule. The firm ran almost automatically, according to the solid, self-assured laws of its overpowering bigness and importance. The rise of German prosperity before World War I and the European armament race of those years were bound to carry the House of Krupp to new heights. If Great Britain looked in anger at the growing German world competition, German politics, which were handled as a personal business of the erratic, often irresponsible Kaiser, seemed set on provoking the British. To make things worse, Germany also alienated the other nations of Europe until they forgot their previous bitter antagonisms against each other and joined in an anti-German alliance. In more boastful moments the Kaiser quoted the old German proverb, "Many enemies, much honor," but then again, he bitterly denounced the "encirclement." While German liberals, Socialists, Catholics, and thoughtful people in general fought a losing battle against their government, and while pacifists from Berlin to New York clamored for peace congresses and international arbitration courts, armament budgets of all European nations grew to unprecedented heights. With these demands, plus the peaceful needs of industry and transportation, employment figures, production output, and profits of the Firm of Krupp rose steadily and steeply, year after year.

The colossus was reorganized in this new era. The original cast-steel factory had grown into a labyrinth of more than a hundred factories interspersed with furnaces, workshops, and other industrial establishments connected by a maze of private railroad tracks. Under the rule of Bertha and Gustav Krupp, this outcome of a haphazard growth was rebuilt and modernized in rational order by a systematic plan. The work of consolidation was accompanied by new expansion of production facilities, supplies, and capacity. While more coal and iron fields at home and abroad were purchased and added, the Friedrich-Alfred Steel Mill at Rheinhausen, which Fritz Krupp had begun to construct, began to produce. Steel was still

Krupp's mainstay, with new uses being developed as Krupp specialties. The most important, perhaps, was the revolutionary motor which Rudolf Diesel built from steel. He offered his invention to the Firm of Krupp which soon became and remained the leading Diesel motor plant.

In 1906 Krupp's Germania Shipyards completed the first modern submarine. It provided Germany with a revolutionary new weapon. Packs of submarines could weaken, if not shatter, the might of the British fleet. But the German Navy, commanded by Admiral Alfred von Tirpitz, thought little of this new-fangled idea and preferred to concentrate on conventional battleships. Until World War I broke out in 1914, Krupp produced only nine submarines.

The decisive weapons of the prewar naval race were the "dreadnoughts," named after a 17,000-ton battleship which Britain completed in 1907 equipped with ten 12-inch guns and twenty-four 12-pound quick-fire guns. These swimming fortresses became the symbol of sea power, and Germany built up its own battle fleet to match the British. All its armor plates and guns were made from Krupp steel.

The technicians of Krupp's arms construction and research departments showed considerably more foresight and imagination than the military leaders. Since Count Ferdinand Zeppelin had risen in his dirigible to greet the new century, followed by the Wright brothers in their airplane, Krupp's experts worked hard at a new weapon to fire at the new flying machines whose military potential they quickly understood. As early as 1909 Krupp introduced its anti-Zeppelin guns to the world at the International Aircraft Fair in Frankfurt, and sold many of them. Since dirigibles were considered a special German weapon, most purchasers of Krupp's defense guns were enemy nations of Germany.

Although the Firm of Krupp was anchored to the home market, it continued to supply foreign customers with military hardware in large quantities. Before World War I, for instance, Krupp sold 24,000 guns to Prussian Germany and 26,000 to fifty-two other nations—twenty-three in Europe, eighteen in the Western hemisphere, six in Asia, five in Africa. Czarist Russia, defeated in its war with Japan and anxious to recover its martial strength, offered the largest plum in this foreign business. It rearmed from scratch, buying everything from guns to fortresses, factories, and fleets. Sometimes jointly with and then again competing against British and French arms-makers, Krupp shared in the Russian billion-dollar orders.

The armament industry, a business like any other in many ways, yet unlike any other in its dependence on political tensions and governments, was profitably caught between nationalism and internationalism. On the one hand it was inextricably tied to the politics of its home country, while on the other its strength increased by unrestricted exports which were often controlled by cartels and gentlemen's agreements between the cosmopolitan competitors. This paradoxical, though transitory, and in the long run, self-terminating, situation led to many charges against, and myths about, the "bloody International of the Merchants of Death." Krupp tried to counter these charges by setting up a publicity department which fed fewer news items than presents to spokesmen of the public. The main assignment of this publicity department, however, was to see to it that no information on the firm reached the world outside the factory walls. In short, it was an anti-publicity department.

True to the tradition of the house to which he wanted to belong as a "real Kruppian," Gustav Krupp von Bohlen gave little thought to the implications and uses of the arms which his firm produced. As Gert von Klass, his benevolent biographer, reports, he felt that "politics was a matter for the professionals, and bowed to their authority." As Krupp himself explained in a personal letter to Rudolf von Valentini, the Kaiser's Chief of Cabinet, he doggedly stuck to this nonpolitical principle. "Neither the Firm of Krupp nor its owner must be shoved to the forefront of political struggles," he proclaimed. "Complete aloofness from political life is not possible any more nowadays for myself or the executives of the firm, but to do more than the most necessary minimum would only damage the particular position of the firm."

Rather than dreaming up and carrying through dangerous conspiracies behind the wings of domestic and foreign politics as romantic critics have suspected, Gustav Krupp was content to study the files and listen to the reports of such goings-on if and when they took place. The dominating passions in his dream world of a Prussian Organization Man were austerity and discipline. His only departure from "Krupp tradition" was when he ordered that the windows of Villa Hügel—which Alfred had kept shut and Fritz had opened occasionally—were always to remain open, except on especially cold winter nights. The temperature in his own office was kept as near to the freezing point as possible. This, he thought, would force visitors to be brief and not to waste one superfluous word.

The prince consort at the head of the firm created a temperature below freezing in less literal ways. He ordered his secretary to clock the exact length of every long-distance telephone call he made and check it with the operator; if there was a minute's discrepancy, he would insist that the bill be corrected and the operator reprimanded or fired. At night his chauffeur and his valet had to account to him for every pfennig spent during the day. Whether he approved or criticized their expenses, he never addressed them on any other subject; he treated them as sternly as a feudal landlord treated his serfs.

In his home the husband of Europe's richest heiress introduced the rules of a model prison, too. Not only were the one hundred and twenty servants of Villa Hügel treated as prison inmates, but also his wife and he himself, as well as their children. Their periods of "togetherness" were also clocked—every day for fifteen minutes at breakfast, for fifty minutes at dinner, neither more nor less. According to the master's rule, the waiters took everybody's plate away the moment he finished his. Since he devoured his meals in record time—to enjoy them would have been a sin against the spirit of the house—guests and children rarely got a chance to eat as much as they wished. There was hardly any table talk. The children were not permitted to speak, and the grownups themselves rarely spoke. When once a week, for one whole hour, the father would play with his offspring, loud laughter or unseemly movements were strictly *verboten*. The children's hour at Krupps' was devoted to running in togetherness an elaborate toy electric train. A number of servants performed as secret house police. They were ordered to keep track of the children's activities during the day, and to submit a detailed report every evening. Driven by his sense of duty and discipline, the prince consort seemed more of a Krupp than the Krupps themselves.

Since Gustav Krupp insisted on going to bed at ten o'clock sharp every night, he took no chances with guests who might stay a little longer and keep him up. When he gave a party, his butlers were instructed to approach every guest a few minutes before ten and discreetly say, "Sir, your car is waiting at the front gate." The guests left at once, and the perfect host could retire on time.

Bertha Krupp fitted well into this picture of order and obedience in her double role as mistress of the house and angel of charity in the firm. One of her favorite self-chosen duties was to hide at night near the servants' sleeping quarters. The long rows of tiny cubicles were located in two different wings separated according to sex and connected only by an iron bridge. If she saw a servant in the corridor leading from one wing to the other, she fired him on the spot. Everybody on the staff feared her, even if he or she kept chastely off the forbidden bridge. She kept the only set of keys to the household closets and once a week carefully counted the linen and silverware. If even one piece was missing, she conducted an investigation with the methods and ingeniousness of a Scotland Yard detective until the culprit was found.

Yet those who knew her well knew also that her influence exceeded by far these *hausfrau* antics. When she believed herself unobserved, she told her husband in a commanding voice what his next orders were to be, or what business decision he had to make as "a real Krupp." He would answer with a snappy *"Jawohl,* Bertha," and act accordingly. While she appeared to the outside world in the image of a gracious lady, she remained the steely queen of Kruppdom over whose regent she reigned.

Her memory was preserved when the chief of the development section of the firm, Professor Rausenberger, constructed a 420-mm. gun able to fire its 930 kilogram shells over a distance of six to eight miles, an unheard of show of firepower. In thoroughly unintentional irony, he named this frightening new weapon *"die dicke Bertha,"* in honor of the owner and heiress of the House of Krupp. Fat Bertha, or as it came to be known in English, Big Bertha, was the first and probably only cannon ever to be named for a living woman. But, then, the "gun" itself is believed to owe its name to a woman—an otherwise forgotten Lady Gunhilda, whose pet name was Gunna. One of the world's first cannons was named in her memory when guns, like ships, were given names by their owners.

Nobody in Essen recalled on the twenty-ninth of November, 1911, that a century had passed since Friedrich Krupp founded the steel factory from which the Krupp empire had grown. But one year later, the Krupps planned a celebration as "colossal" and triumphant as their rise since the year 1812 when Alfred Krupp was born. They preferred to remember his spectacular victory rather than the failure of his father. With her husband and her managers, Bertha Krupp prepared to celebrate this centenary of her house with a three-day festival. Once again Kaiser Wilhelm II came as the guest of honor with ranking members of his court and his cabinet to mingle with Germany's biggest industrialists and bankers, a few Krupp relatives, and some foreign military-purchase commission heads. At the dinner with sixty guests, Bertha sat between the Kaiser and his Chancellor.

The great surprise and highlight was scheduled for the third day of the celebration. In a tent specially set up for the occasion, one thousand Kruppians who had served the firm for more than fifty years were honored with gold watches. After the social conscience was put at ease by this "particularly solemn act," as the Krupps' chroniclers called it, the guests of honor were to be regaled with a medieval pageant and a knightly tournament, exactly as it had been held the last time, *circa* 1500, when Emperor Maximilian ruled the *Reich* and the Krupps were still unknown in Essen, let alone at more distant points. Although this was the year 1912, the fantasy amidst the forges was to be "authentic" from the armor worn by the knights to the joust they were to engage in, at the risk of one or more knights being pierced to death by his adversary's lance. Precisely because death often ended these tilts, they had been outlawed since the sixteenth century. Bertha Krupp was to hand the prize to the winner. The Kaiser looked forward to the tournament, as excited as a teen-age boy.

Several hundred costumed people stood ready to march in a festive procession before the tournament began. A company of lansquenets under their ensign headed the pageant, followed by Kruppians outfitted as members of the nobility, the priesthood, and burghers and peasants, and by many medieval maidens on loan from nearby Düsseldorf's Art Academy. Their costumes had been designed by professors of history and art. Had an honest historian remarked that knighthood held little in common with the firm's one-hundred-year history and that the spirit of chivalry seemed somewhat alien to the spirit of Kruppdom, neither the Kaiser nor the Krupps would have understood him. To misuse the German past as a false face and a fancy front behind which the brutal present hid and justified itself was typical of Kaiser Wilhelm II's era, and therefore the expensive masquerade did not completely lack significance concerning the centenary history of the House of Krupp.

But a few minutes before the tilt was to begin a messenger brought a letter. It announced that a disaster had occurred in the Lorraine coal mine and eight hundred miners had lost their lives. The festivities were canceled, the costumes of the pageant and the armor of the tilt were put aside, while the House of Krupp, rising ever higher, entered its second century.

7

The Power and the Poverty

"It is a thing blameworthy, shameful, and barbarous, worthy of severe punishment before God and man, to wish to bring to perfection an art that damages one's neighbor and destroys the human race," wrote a citizen of Verona named Niccolo Tartaglia in the year 1531 (before the first Krupp arrived in Essen). The "art" to which Tartaglia alluded, and which he had founded, was the science of hurling missile weapons by the use of an engine, and the related science of the motion of projectiles, in brief, the science by which guns, cannons, howitzers, and mortars have been developed and fired ever since. But Tartaglia abandoned his treatise entitled *L'Art de Jecter Les Bombes* (The Art of Throwing Bombs), declared that he was "ashamed and remorseful of his past devotion to these matters which are a grave sin and which shipwreck the soul," and burned his work.

A few years later the Turkist "ferocious wolf" prepared to invade Italy, or so it was feared. In the face of this threat, Tartaglia revived, revised, and finally published his work from which gunnery and cannonry have developed. The father of modern ballistics, it would seem, was also the father of the moral dilemma likely to torture men in search of new and better, that is, deadlier, arms.

No such scruples delayed or even troubled the men of the House of Krupp while they developed, produced, and sold their arms. In the summer of 1914, Dr. Wilhelm Mühlon, one of Krupp's directors, resigned from the firm, left for Switzerland, and began in that neutral country to denounce the German government for war preparations. He based his alleged revelations not on special information gathered in the firm, but on one conversation with high government officials and the study of official documents.

When World War I broke out in September, 1914, the Firm of Krupp lost control over its fate and its owner lost absolute rule over the firm. For the first time in a century it was forced to cut down on the production of "tools of peace" and even more so on those "tools of war" which it sold abroad. To a high degree the war subordinated the firm to the plans of the military, who would give the orders, orders to be filled as well as orders to be obeyed. If in the last prewar years less than one-third of Krupp's total production had gone to the German army and navy, during the war almost 100 per cent went to these purveyors. But as Krupp confidently calculated, victory would pay for the large conversion and expansion costs of the war. In this expectation Krupp did not differ from the armament industrialists in France, England, and elsewhere, with the possible exception of Andrew Carnegie whose pacifist objections to arms production were only overcome (yet thoroughly overcome) by urgent admonitions of the United States government. With a slight switch on Karl von Clausewitz's famous dictum, "War is a continuation of politics by other means," Krupp considered war as a continuation of the weapon business by other means.

For at least one small group of Germans the war meant more. "Now it has come, the holy hour! The world's breath stops, and every nation shows its true nature," wrote Heinrich Class when he learned that war had been declared. He was a lawyer and the founder of the Pan-German Movement, which since 1891 had propagandized an imperialist anti-Semitic policy for Germany. (If it had little success in Germany, its ideas were heard and embraced in Austria by at least one follower by the name of Adolf Hitler.) A co-founder of that movement, Class' close friend Alfred Hugenberg had served since 1908 as chairman of Krupp's Board of Directors. Members of the Prussian administration had recommended him for the job after he had resigned as a government official when his ultranationalist program to Germanize the Polish-settled eastern parts of Prussia had been rejected. "It is a wasted labor of love to give one's self to that kind of State," Hugenberg had complained, before he moved to Krupp where he saw higher rewards. The Pan-German Movement remained his and Class' sounding board while they beat the drum for the annexation and Germanization of many parts of Europe against the will of the majority of the German people.

In the first months of the war, Herr Class was invited to a Villa Hügel dinner with Gustav and Bertha Krupp. As Class reported in his memoirs, Gustav agreed with him about his expansionist war aims "in a cautious way," while Frau Bertha showed herself as "a passionately German woman," that is, she wholeheartedly applauded the visitor's program. Krupp promised to support the Pan-German proposals in Berlin, but when Class met him several months later, Krupp seemed "a changed person." Krupp had learned that the government opposed these plans and refused to participate in the political dispute, pointing out that Hugenberg did not speak for Krupp in politics; the Firm of Krupp remained "nonpolitical."

But Gustav Krupp wrote in a letter to the Prussian government (according to an East German historian who claimed to have found it in a Prussian archive) that he, "like every thinking German, had his ideas of what will be necessary for the future security and development of the German people as the result of this horrible war." The outcome of his thinking appeared in an enclosed confidential memorandum in which he set forth that "the possibility of a 'Peace Conference' as American and other circle want it will be excluded, and that the peace can and must be dictated to the enemies." This German-dictated peace, as Gustav Krupp wished it, would safeguard the annexation of northern and eastern France where rich iron and coal reserves were located, as well as of most of Poland and Lithuania; the foreign population of these parts should not be granted voting rights in Germany, and their coal, iron, and steelmaking plants should be given to Germany as reparations. Economic domination of the West European countries by Germany and a new, big German colonial empire in Africa rounded out Krupp's proposals of 1915. "To fight for such aims, and win, is worth the blood of the best," his memorandum ended. If the letter is authentic—and it seems to be— Gustav Krupp's war aims closely resembled the plans which the Pan-Germans had prepared and the reverse of the plans of men in France and England for their victory over Germany.

As the firm entered the war, it seemed well-prepared to arm the *Reich*. With its 82,000 workers, the biggest European industrial combine included 9 steelworks, 181 power hammers, and 7,160 other major machines. But the firm was little prepared for the war to come, for the stockpiles of raw materials which could be supplied only by imports from abroad were so insignificant as to be soon exhausted. The German General Staff counted on a quick German victory.

Five months after the beginning of the war Admiral Tirpitz visited Krupp's Germania Shipyard to inspect the submarines under construction. "Ha!" he snorted, "they won't be completed by the time we'll have won the war." The submarines were completed two months later; in three war years to follow, two hundred more submarines were produced in Germany, more than eighty of them by Krupp.

The German M-Day Plan which the General Staff planners had prepared in great detail, ordered Krupp to produce and supply two hundred artillery guns and howitzers, one hundred and forty torpedo-boat guns, and six submarines. An order of a dozen pails in preparation of a Mississippi River flood would have revealed equal prescience. In the first two war years more than nine hundred heavy cannons, as well as thousands of lighter cannons, were purveyed from Krupp. Its output in the course of the war amounted to fifteen times more guns and twenty times more shells than the mobilization plan had foreseen.

Not only quantities, but also the types of military hardware were badly miscalculated by Krupp's great customer. True, "Big Bertha" was an effective new weapon ready for this war. It helped to crash the walls of the fortified city of Liége in Belgium as well as other Belgian and French strongholds, to support the German advance into France, and to augment the fame—or notoriety, depending on where you stood—of the House of Krupp. In appreciation of his performance with Big Bertha, Bertha's husband was awarded the Iron Cross from the Kaiser and the honorary degree of doctor of philosophy from Bonn University. Big Bertha was the only superior new weapon Krupp's constructors and the General Staff planners held in readiness. Other guns, such as the 10-cm. cannon and a specially potent 15-cm. cannon—which according to some experts could have changed the course of the war had it been available in time—were not completed. The heavy field howitzer 13, which was superior to all corresponding enemy guns, was still in the testing stage. Despite Krupp's previous experiments practically no anti-aircraft guns had reached the production stage.

German preparedness was even poorer when it came to weapons other than guns. Nobody in Berlin or Essen foresaw the role which motorization—and with it, tanks—would play in the war. When news of Allied tank production first reached German army headquarters, General Field-Marshal Paul von Hindenburg, the chief commander whose oversized mustache almost hid his undersized intelligence, snorted: "The German infantry can get along quite well without those peculiar motorcars," and Krupp was ordered to concentrate on artillery rather than such outlandish battle-wagons. But when the first British tanks appeared at the front, panic broke out among the defenseless German forces. While France and Britain set out to mass produce armored cars, a German ordnance colonel named Bauer took it on his own responsibility to order from Krupp twenty-five light, fast models. But Krupp did not fill the order in time, and only in March, 1918, shortly before the end of the war, were a few heavy tanks produced. The German war effort failed also in the new field of planes, and it was the same with every other modern weapon.

True, the main fault was with the Prussian military bureaucracy which had resisted innovation and ridiculed new weapons ever since Alfred Krupp had offered his first cannon cast from steel. But then the old Krupp had the stamina, the vision, and the inventiveness to fight for his new weapons until he could push them over the bureaucratic hurdle. A century later the Firm of Krupp itself had become a bureaucracy, burdened by tradition, paralyzed by bigness, and petrified as an organization in which "mediocre men" were more desirable than brilliant men. It had lost its initial vital drive toward progress.

The same failings also held back the enemy powers of Germany in the beginning of the war, but only in its beginning. At first Great Britain was short of artillery and planes were looked upon as military playthings, while France had to mobilize the battered taxis of Paris for lack of motorized military vehicles. But when the short-sightedness of the professional military planners revealed itself, a French Premier who was a physician and a politician decided that war was "too serious a business to be left to the generals," and took over the leadership. In a similar way Britain's Lloyd George, rather than let his generals continue to fumble with the production and purchase of armament, set up an ammunitions ministry under civilian command. The military leaders of the Allies were closely supervised and led by the people's elected civilian representatives, even in their purely strategic planning. In Germany however, the military continued holding the reins, since the social and political system was intertwined with, if not based on, their power. As it proceeded, the war became less and less of the "fresh, jolly war" of which the Kaiser and his friends had dreamed. More and more it turned into a "war of materials" in which the greater mass of weapons, bullets, and shells decided the outcome, and in which even men were counted under the horrible heading of "human material." If the enemies of Germany had stronger material reserves, they also organized them in better, more efficient ways.

Undoubtedly Krupp produced fast and successfully as far as mere quantities went. The production figures climbed to fantastic heights, while the new works, factories, and machines constructed by Krupp during the war grew into a statistician's nightmare. Besides submarines, battleships, and armor plate, the firm made production records with 14,000 tons of explosives, 9 million artilley shells, and 3000 field pieces a month.

But as for weapons, only two really new and valiant achievements came out of the Krupp works during the war, and in a quite literal sense both backfired badly. The first was the sensational gun officially dubbed—as a companion piece to "Big Bertha"—"Big Gustav." It took almost four years to complete it. It was developed from a heavy naval gun which Krupp had tested in the fall of 1914, and which fired at a greater distance than its constructors had expected. By the fall of 1918 the longest long-distance cannon, able to send its missiles over almost ninety miles, was ready for use. Paris was selected as its target. Its first shot from Crépy Forest exploded on the Place de la Republique, followed by 452 more shots from the eight similar guns which Krupp built. One-hundred and eighty shots hit Paris, 140 others its suburbs, killing at least 1000 people. Ninety-one victims were killed at Good Friday services in the old Church of Saint Gervais. Other than that "Big Gustav" had no impact on the course of the war, which ended one month after it fired its last shot. What it did accomplish was to stir up hatred against Germany as well as against the House of Krupp.

Considerably more unfortunate consequences resulted from the second new masterpiece made in Essen, the submarine. With the bad turn the war was taking for Germany, Admiral Tirpitz took recourse to that wonder weapon and decided to gamble on its ability to blockade England and starve it into submission. But the German announcement that submarines would fire at, and sink, all foreign merchant marine vessels sailing in certain areas led America to enter the war. In a war that had become a war of materials, that side was bound to win on which America stood.

When Germans had argued whether to resort to this unrestrained submarine warfare, Krupp took no part in the debate. Whatever the authorities decided, he would do. After his brief and unfortunate outing into politics early in the war, he had kept aloof. To head the organization took up his energies. His labor force grew from 82,000 in 1914 to 150,000 in 1918, including 20,000 women who were paid only half the wage rates of the men they replaced. On the basis of figures of production, new properties, and profits, the House of Krupp had reached its summit after a century-long ascent, or so it seemed.

But Krupp was only as strong as Germany's military position, and by 1918, German defeat was in the offing. The German armies were beating a hasty retreat and the German home front had begun to crumble. In September, 1918, Kaiser Wilhelm sent out a call for a last stand. At Krupp's Essen works, he climbed on a machine in the cast-steel mill to address the workers with words that sounded hollow against the background of retreat and defeat: "Be strong as steel, my dear friends," he shouted. "Hold out like a block of steel." With his carefully coiffured mustachio, his permanent wave, his personal uniform modeled after the British army battle dress, his cane, and his nasal, artificial voice, he recalled an aged actor touring the hinterland in the role of the young hero. The audience was not impressed. Few workers applauded. There were some who answered him with a shout of "Hunger!" With Krupp's machines, cranes, carts, and tools framing their Kaiser, the Kruppians thought of shortages of food and material, and an end to all this.

Sixty days later the war came to an end. The Kaiser fled. His rule, of which the House of Krupp was part and parcel, was overthrown by a handful of angry sailors, eccentric intellectuals, and well-meaning politicians who were themselves surprised. Would Krupp go down and disappear with the *Reich*, as the Allies and the domestic Left had foresworn for the day of their victory? Gustav and Bertha believed in the survival of Kruppdom.

On November 8, 1918, a labor force of 170,000—

more people than live today in, say Hartford, Connecticut, or Grand Rapids, Michigan—left Krupp's Essen cast-steel factory after a day as busy as any other in the making of steel, arms, and ammunition. But on the next morning, nobody showed up for work, and for the first time in more than a century, Krupp stood still. Elsewhere in Germany people marched in anger, and, although they had little hope for the future, cheered the revolution. In Essen they merely ceased to work, and a delegation of workers who called themselves Soviets asked to see the Chief. Gustav Krupp von Bohlen received them with correct coolness. They told him that his business belonged now to the people, and that they would show the masters who was master. "It is the tradition of the House of Krupp," answered the master-to-be-dethroned, "that the leader act in the interests of his workers first and foremost." Since neither Krupp nor the revolutionaries knew who was to rule their country, or what the next day would bring, they found little else to tell each other. That night the servants at Villa Hügel were armed to defend the palace against mobs and a red flag was hastily fashioned to be hoisted on their arrival. But no mobs marched toward the hill. The armament workers of all Germany held an orderly congress at the Thuringian industrial town of Erfurt where they discussed the socialization of the arms industries and voted resolutions to dispossess their owners at the earliest possible moment.

Rather than let this moment come, Krupp dismissed the threat by dismissing the threatening workers. The firm announced that, owing to events and lack of new work, it unfortunately could keep only those workers in its employ who had been Kruppians on the day the war started. By this edict, over 100,000 workers were fired. If they left Essen within three days to look for jobs elsewhere, the firm offered to pay their trainfare. Since there was a shortage of trains, many left on foot. Fewer than 50,000 Kruppians remained, and most of them were too pleased about keeping their jobs to think of revolution and expropriation. The former bustling Essen seemed a ghost town.

But if the firm of Krupp was quickly saved from its

workers, no such quick and easy remedies were available to defend it against foreign enemies. In French and British eyes, the House of Krupp appeared as Samson's hair. Germany, that dangerous giant, would be emasculated if the Essen firm, the center of its power, were razed. This was the other side of the image which the Firm of Krupp itself had worked hard and successfully to create.

A peace treaty was "dictated" to Germany, not unlike the peace treaty which, in reverse, Gustav Krupp had suggested be "dictated" to the Allies after a German victory. It was motivated by a desire for revenge, rather than a desire for reconstruction. The Germans had no choice but to accept it. American delegates to the Peace Meeting in Versailles shuddered at the perversion which President Wilson's ideas of a just and lasting peace suffered under the hate-driven hands of European chauvinists.

Even without special measures against the House of Krupp, the Versailles Treaty was bound to dismember, if not kill, the firm. As its purpose was to disarm and impoverish Germany and to keep it in a state of disarmament and impoverishment for times to come, there seemed little hope for the future of Krupp. So-called "reparation payments"—which many Germans soon called tribute payments, a hardly less accurate designation—to be made by Germany to the victor nations (with the exception of the United States which refused to sign the Treaty) would forestall Germany's economic recovery. The monetary value and the time over which these payments were to be made were left to the discretion of the victors. What the victors themselves ignored was the fact that, given the economic interdependence of Western Europe, they were damaging themselves as badly as the Germans. Detached experts such as the British economist John Maynard Keynes warned against these economic consequences of the Peace Treaty, but in the flush of victory, the peacemakers did not listen to the voices of reason. Little wonder that many Germans, including those who had fought a lifelong battle against the nationalism and militarism of their own rulers, were unhappy. After the overthrow of their old order, they wanted to build a new, peaceful Germany, but it seemed doubtful that this could be achieved while Germany was impoverished and disgraced. They agreed with the disarmament of their nation if and when it was part of a more general disarmament, but while Germany was forced to disarm, its neighbors rearmed and had a defenseless Germany at their mercy.

According to the Treaty Germany was to have no defense forces except an army of one hundred thousand soldiers, and a token fleet of fifteen thousand sailors. German arms, and all the factories and machines that produced them, were to be extradited or demolished, under the supervision of Allied control officers. Under the impact of these provisions, which endangered the security of every single German, the people paid little notice to a third provision which decreed that 859 individual Germans were to be tried as war criminals. The list of the defendants began with the Kaiser; Gustav Krupp von Bohlen was also named.

Paradoxically, German disarmament began with an order for new weapons to be produced by the Firm of Krupp. In their effort to disarm Germany, the Allies demanded the extradition of greater amounts of German war equipment than there were in German arsenals. To live up to the Treaty, Krupp had to turn out these additional weapons in a hurry for prompt delivery to the Allies, who just as promptly destroyed them.

But after these last orders had been filled, the Allies saw to it that no new ones would be placed with the Essen armorer. On Allied orders and under Allied supervision, the workers of Krupp dismantled and destroyed 9000 machines, 800,000 tools, and 22,000 cubic meters of masonry, which had been used for Krupp's production of cannons and other weapons. Samson was forced at pistol-point to shear his hair himself.

No longer allowed to produce "tools of war," Krupp also had difficulty producing "tools of peace." During the war, foreign concerns had learned to make many products which had been Krupp specialties, and the Firm of Krupp had lost its competitive position. Gustav Hugen-

berg, the Pan-German manager, left the firm to lead a
new nationalist party. Several executives suggested that
Krupp close down and liquidate, but Bertha and Gustav
Krupp emphatically vetoed this. Whatever the difficulties,
the will of Alfred Krupp bound his heirs to keep his work
alive "for eternity."

At least one threat to the firm and its head disappeared
when it became clear that Gustav Krupp and the other
"war criminals" would not be tried. Whatever their sins,
the legal grounds on which to try and sentence them were
too shaky, as the Germans who had been commissioned
to hold these trials quickly discovered. Had a prophet
then told Gustav Krupp that he was going to be charged
again with war crimes in the distant future, he would
have considered the idea fantasy.

The fallen giant tried hard to get back on his feet, or at
least to keep breathing. The firm offered prizes to its
workers and employees for the submission of acceptable
ideas on new goods which it could produce, "tools of
peace," of course. After all, the steel mill, the cell from
which the giant had been born, and its auxiliary works
were still intact and the war had speeded up the firm's
technical progress. Only a few months after the end of
the war, Krupp's conversion to peacetime work began.
Along with railroad parts, which had been the mainstay
of Alfred Krupp before he ever sold a steel cannon, the
Firm of Krupp began to produce locomotives and freight
cars. In the first postwar year, the Prussian State Railroads Administration promised to buy 100 locomotives
and 2000 freight cars over the next five years. Soon
Krupp could boast that its capacity approached 300 locomotives a year. A few were exported, mainly to Soviet
Russia.

In search of new business, the firm tried its hand at numerous other products—hydraulic installations, roller
bearings, movie projectors, textile and agricultural machines, trucks, cash registers, calendars, typewriters, combination locks, printing presses, motor scooters. With few
exceptions, these products sold poorly or only at a loss.
More promising was the new production of stainless steel

and stainless-steel products, which dated from the war when the firm had developed a rust-resistant steel alloy for use in submarines whose steel gun locks and armor plate deteriorated from salt water. Hardened by additional processing, the new stainless V2A Steel, as it was called, was desirable material for such peaceful goods as surgical instruments, tableware—shades of the spoonmaking cylinders that had kept the firm alive a century before—and dentures; stainless-steel teeth found a good market in Soviet Russia.

Besides its Soviet sales of dentures and locomotives, the House of Krupp concluded another more adventurous contract with the leaders of the Kremlin. Lenin himself, as Krupp's chairman of the board proudly remembered, had decreed: "The steppe must be turned into a bread factory, and Krupp must help us." Accordingly, the Firm of Krupp and the Communists made an interesting deal in 1922; Krupp would transform 25,000 hectares of wasteland in the Don district into wheat-growing, mechanized farm lands. While the Soviets supplied the men and the soil, the firm supplied the tractors, technicians, and capital. But three years later, only one twenty-fifth of the area was put to agricultural use and no crops were harvested. Belatedly the experts discovered that the yearly spring storms frustrated their efforts and transformed the new fields back into dust bowls. For the next two years, Krupp tried to turn the steppe at least into pastures on which sheep could graze. This experiment also failed, and ended the first attempt at cooperation between Krupp and the Communists. As both were to learn later in the 1950's, it had, however, set the pattern for successive, more successful joint ventures.

Krupp's experiments in survival were brave but barely profitable. Four years after the end of the war, the firm was in a critical state. With its old reserves almost exhausted, and burdened by new debts, it was weaker from its attempts to recover than it had been immediately after the lost war.

In this moment of need, the firm, for the first and only time in its history, deviated from its principle of sole fam-

ily ownership. In a revolutionary move, it invited its
Kruppians to buy shares in the organization. But only
one-fifth, 100,000,000 marks out of a capital of
500,000,000 were offered for sale. Shareholders were
limited to one share of 100 marks and deprived of all the
rights which customarily go with corporation shares. They
were not permitted to attend let alone vote at, company
meetings, but could be present by proxy, the proxy being
a fiduciary appointed by the owner. In brief, Krupp's
offer of "workers' shares" was merely a grab for workers'
savings. Fewer than three dozen, out of 50,000, Kruppians responded to the offer, and they did not dare admit
to their colleagues that they had invested their money in
the firm. Soon the experiment was ended, and the firm remained as exclusively in the hands of the heiress as before.

Despite its general decline, Krupp, in true tradition,
began again investing its capital in new ventures. Even in
the worst postwar years, it bought new real estate for future works, leased coal mines, and acquired shares in met-
allurgical plants at home and abroad.

It seems that the House of Krupp had become accustomed to automatic growth and prosperity in the half century of rise that preceded its fall. With its bureaucratic
bigness, led and staffed by mediocre organization men, it
had lost its capacity to respond quickly and profitably
with technological or business advances to the new and
serious challenge. But then, in the Germany of those first
postwar years, it took either a genius or an unscrupulous
speculator to run a profitable concern, and Bertha Krupp,
Gustav Krupp, and their managers were neither. Inflation
was running wild, and upset all long-term plans. The Nazi
and Communist movements, enemy brothers who fought
as well as fed on each other, exploited and promoted the
general chaos, and the forces of order found no encour-
agement from the nations of the West.

Germany was driven even further on its road to chaos
when in 1922 France announced, against the protest of
the other Allied powers, that it would take its own security for future German reparation payments, and occupied

the Ruhr district in which the industry of Germany was centered. Immediately after the French announcement, Gustav Krupp called several young employees of established "trustworthiness" into his office. In great secrecy he told them to smuggle big stacks of correspondence, blueprints, and files to safe hiding places in Berlin and East Germany, and promised to reward them later with job promotions, a promise he kept. We will soon see what that secret material contained.

In a policy of passive resistance, which Gandhi was to use in similar ways, the people of the Ruhr were asked by the government not to work for, or cooperate with, the French invasion troops. When this passive resistance proved effective, the French proclaimed the death sentence against noncooperators. In turn, the Germans threatened all cooperators with hard-labor sentences.

The Firm of Krupp ordered its workers to keep calm if and when the French occupation troops arrived. They came to Krupp two months after the invasion of the Ruhr. One lieutenant with eleven men, one armed with a machine-gun, made up their force. The small detachment had orders to occupy a garage near the office building where trucks and cars were parked. Later that day, a French confiscation commission was expected to arrive and to seize a few trucks.

Hardly had the French soldiers reached the Krupp site when all its factory sirens, several hundred altogether, began to scream. The tocsin called the workers to quit their work in protest. At least ten thousand Kruppians heeded the call, hurried to the garage and the neighboring alleys, and blocked off the main street. The workers were excited; some of the trucks under confiscation orders were used to supply them with food and to transport them to work. The chairman of their workers' council, a respectable old trade unionist, explained this to the officer and asked him to leave. The officer answered in elegant French that he "would never harm poor people," which was translated into less elegant German by one of his men with a poor command of the language. But the French did not move. Some workers grew angry, but the majority, as snapshots of laughing crowds taken by the ever busy publicity department of the firm showed, were in good spirits. When agitators tried to incite them to sing patriotic songs, the Kruppians did not respond. A man threw leaflets to the crowd from a window in the administration building, but the workers hardly stooped to pick them up, let alone read them. At the time, the proto-Nazi nationalists and the Communists were allied in the Ruhr in their fight against "French and German capitalism." Moscow tried to turn the resistance of the Ruhr Germans into a revolution, but as Ruth Fischer, a Communist leader, reported, the Kruppians, even the Communist Kruppians, were "Right-wingers" and averse to a battle. Their workers' council chairman went twice more to the French officer with the request to depart. After their second discussion, the Kruppian thought he had persuaded the invaders to leave and informed the workers accordingly.

While the Kruppians resisted the invasion by their walkout, Gustav Krupp himself sat high above them in his office and listened to the report of a director just returned from financial negotiations in Berlin. Krupp was not distracted. The idea of joining his workers on the street did not occur to him, but he spoke to the garage guardian over the telephone to make sure that his private car was not damaged or confiscated. The sirens kept screaming, and the workers kept protesting while their head shut himself up in his office.

More and more workers from outlying plants joined their protesting fellow Kruppians and the crowd, now numbering over 15,000, began to press against the garage in which the twelve French soldiers stood like captives. Suddenly the officer ordered his men to fire, whether at the crowd in self-defense or into the air as warning shots has not been established. They fired one volley; it killed thirteen Kruppian workers, among them five teen-age apprentices, and wounded forty more, fifteen seriously. Some workers carried them away, and others fled, while the French patrol marched off.

Gustav Krupp, nine of the directors of the firm, and

the chairman of the workers' council were arrested by the French occupation authorities and charged with instigating the massacre. A drumhead court was held against them in a courtroom filled with steel-helmeted, battle-ready poilus. Five French army officers served as judges. Although no evidence was presented to prove that Gustav Krupp or his colleagues had anything to do with the tragic events—in fact, the proceedings showed the very opposite—he was sentenced to fifteen years in prison and fined one hundred million marks. His directors and the spokesman for the workers got off with slightly lighter sentences.

Krupp, who wanted to keep his firm busy, French occupation or not, deserved this sentence as little as he deserved the aura of a national resistance hero, but in German eyes he was glorified for a feat he had not committed. An innocent bystander rather than a wicked wire-puller, he was surely no martyr, either.

He did not consider himself a hero of the German passive resistance in his prison, where he was treated well by the French. What he felt was revealed when his wife, Bertha, and his brother-in-law first visited him in his cell. As the latter reports, Krupp's first words to his wife were: "Now I may really call myself a Kruppian, may I not?" Proudly, he felt himself a martyr to the service of Krupp, rather than to his fatherland. The hatred which led to his conviction, as he sensed quite correctly, was aimed at Krupp rather than at Germany. In tears, his wife told him that he had become worthy of her forebears.

After Gustav Krupp had been in prison seven months the Ruhr occupation ended and he was released. The firm had gone down very rapidly during the occupation and it was now in a critical state. To a high degree, it was saved from bankruptcy only by government subsidies. Besides a fifty-million-mark credit, it received substantial payments from the *Reich* as restitution and indemnification for damages suffered in the war and post war years. It was compensated for government weapon orders filled and not paid for after the war, for its losses in foreign holdings, for the destruction of its arms machinery, and even for damages suffered by its passive resistance. It has been estimated by an expert that the firm received from the German government in those years at least three hundred million marks. With this help, its fall was broken, but the firm still hovered precariously over the abyss.

Only after long quarrels was Krupp compensated from abroad for a wartime claim of a special kind. Before the war, it had leased its patents on shell fuses to the British arms trust of Vickers, against a license fee of one shilling three pence per fuse. Since the British had in the war used, and fired at German troops, hundreds of thousands of these fuses, Krupp asked Vickers to pay him 123 million shillings. After several lawsuits, a secret settlement was reached and Krupp received his pay for the bullets which had killed his countrymen.

Six years after the end of the war, hope showed again on the German horizon. The government succeeded in putting an end to the runaway inflation and stabilized its currency. Industry had a firmer basis on which to work. With decreased unemployment, the Communists and Nazis lost followers. The majority of the people united in the middle of the road to recovery. America supported this effort. Under its auspices the amount of reparations to be paid in the foreseeable future was settled, which, while leaving Germany still with a heavy burden, removed at least the previous uncertainty about its future obligations. America helped with large credits, and among the first to partake of these dollar blessings was the Firm of Krupp. At that time, Otto Wiedfeldt, Krupp's chief manager after the war, was in Washington as Ambassador of the young German Republic, and his influence may have favorably affected the grant of credits from America to Krupp.

Toward the end of 1926 German banks helped the firm with new credits on the condition that it close all production units which were not working at a profit. This surgical operation, accompanied by new blood transfusions in the form of more dollar credits from America, strengthened the patient considerably. By 1928 Krupp's employment figures had risen again from 50,000 to

80,000, still far below the better years of the past yet pleasantly above the low point of the crisis. It seemed that the House of Krupp was able to adjust itself to new, peaceful business, to beat swords into plow shares and spears into pruning hooks, or, literally, stainless-steel armor plate into dental plates.

Metallurgy was improving throughout the world, with harder and better steels being developed by new chemical processes. Krupp was the first, though not the only industry, to mass produce a tungsten-carbide alloy which it called Widia. As hard as diamonds, though considerably cheaper, Widia, which was used in tools and machine parts, was Krupp's only important technological innovation in the twenties.

One of the more important business deals Krupp hoped to conclude at that time was frustrated by a man whose name was Konrad Adenauer. He was Lord Mayor of Cologne when in 1926 that city planned to build a bridge across the Rhine to the suburb of Mülheim. A committee of experts, five well known architects and four representatives of the city, scrutinized bids submitted by the bridgebuilding industry and selected as the winner the Firm of Krupp which offered a beautifully curved archbridge. But Mayor Adenauer had his heart set on a suspension bridge, because, he felt, only a suspension bridge would not obstruct his beloved view. With the stubbornness, political skill, and unshakable conviction which he was to show later on to an impressed world in matters of wider consequence, Adenauer fought for his pet idea until a year later the city council supported him and Krupp lost the deal. Another corporation spanned the Rhine with a suspension bridge. Thirty years later, when this incident was forgotten even by the Krupps themselves, the firm and Adenauer met again. In the 1950's Adenauer again opposed the efforts of the Krupps to "build a bridge," as they called their projected deals with Soviet Russia.

Krupp struggled along with moderate success for a brief time, until the Great Depression hit the world. In 1929 Germany was hit harder than other countries be-

cause its economy still rested on shifty ground. America
had given it credits mostly on a short-term basis, but the
Germans had invested them for long-term purposes, and
when they were withdrawn the country suddenly and
painfully discovered that it had lived above its means.
While several other great corporations went bankrupt, the
House of Krupp withstood the crisis without great damage. Its debts were relatively small, it had built up new
reserves, and it had ceased paying dividends, which, after
all, consisted only in shifting money from the firm's pockets to those of the family. Under the impact of the crisis,
its old, peculiar structure of a one-man enterprise proved
anew its worth.

Apart from this peculiarity, the House of Krupp would
not have differed basically from many other German
heavy industrial corporations of that time in its growth
and crisis had it not led a secret double life. While Mr.
Krupp-Hyde acted as a manufacturer of steel and steel-based "tools of peace," Dr. Krupp-Jekyll was busy planning and making "tools of war."

With this activity, he violated, of course, the law as it
had been laid down by the Treaty of Versailles, and
Krupp had to operate underground. If the secret double
life seemed somewhat out of character for an organization man, it was less surprising than it seemed. In the first
place, a few members of his government knew of, approved and sometimes even suggested, Krupp's secret return to the arms business. Given their official backing, he
felt he was a loyal citizen obeying the authorities rather
than a lawbreaker on his own. Furthermore, Gustav
Krupp von Bohlen's dominating ambition had grown to
be "a real Kruppian." Like a man who has sworn allegiance to a new country, he was particularly eager to
prove his faith in the heritage of the firm with which
he had come to identify himself. In his eyes the heritage and tradition, if not the existence of the firm, were
closely intertwined with the making of arms, and also
with the power of Germany. Krupp did not differ very
much from many other Germans who considered the
one-sided disarmament of their country an injustice as

well as a danger to peace, since a defenseless Germany could easily have invited aggressions from its armed neighbors. But like Germany itself, he and the firm wavered uneasily between loyalty to the new Germany, which was insecure and shaky in its very foundations, yet based on legality, and loyalty to the past Germany with its power and glory, which was restorable only by recourse to illegality. Little wonder that Gustav Krupp von Bohlen felt his heart drawn to this past Germany, while his reason forbade him to admit these leanings in the open.

The Versailles Treaty did not, and could not, prohibit Germans from blueprinting new weapons or constructing them on a draftboard. Neither could the Treaty and the control commissions forestall the production of, say, trucks; but their production facilities could easily be transformed into those of tanks. These activities occupied Krupp as he infiltrated his peacetime business with possible future military products, gambling on both without violating the law. By an irony of history, the Treaty interdictions of arms manufacture would benefit Germany greatly in the end. With the latest and most efficient weapons in the development stage, their production could begin in earnest, while other nations were still burdened by the old-fashioned and less efficient weapons which they had mass produced and could not scrap overnight.

If Krupp did not stop altogether at the blueprint and development stage, but proceeded to test new weapons as the last stage before production itself, this, too, was legal, provided it was done outside of Germany. Seemingly independent foreign corporations secretly controlled by Krupp took Essen's place. The Versailles Treaty had merely interdicted arms production in Germany, without foreseeing a device which permitted Krupp to take up again its profitable production of new arms for foreign customers.

During the Versailles era, and again after 1945, the Krupps and their mouthpieces denied in deeply hurt innocence that the firm had ever engaged in secret, illegal armament preparations. However, luckily for the historians, though not for mankind, during the years between, those of Hitler's *Third Reich,* they openly boasted that they had given their all to exactly these secret preparations. As Gustav Krupp wrote on March 1, 1942, in his company house organ, the *Krupp-Nachrichten* (Krupp News), his mind had been on nothing but secret rearmament while his firm struggled along in the Weimar Republic.

"Today I may speak about these things, and, for the first time, I am doing this extensively and publicly," he asserted at that time, when he could claim credit for the offenses he had previously denied. "In 1919," he explained, "the machines were destroyed, the tools were smashed, but the men remained, the men in the construction offices and workshops who in happy cooperation had brought the manufacture of guns to its highest perfection. Their skill had to be maintained by any means, also their vast funds of knowledge and experience. I wanted and had to maintain Krupp, in spite of all opposition, as an armament plant, although it could be known as such only in the distant future. I could talk freely only in a very small and intimate circle about the actual reasons which induced me to follow my intention and adapt the plants to a definite type of production. Therefore, I had to expect that many people would not understand me, that I would perhaps even be ridiculed as I soon actually was, but I never felt the inner obligation toward all my deeds more compellingly than in those fateful weeks and months of 1919 and 1920. Then I felt myself drawn into the magic circle of an established working community."

To prove he was a true Kruppian, he himself ridiculed the past peaceful period of Krupp. "Thus to the surprise of many people, Krupp began to manufacture products which really appeared to be very remote from the previous output of the armament plant . . . padlocks, milk cans, cash registers, track-repair machines, trash carts, and similar small junk appeared really above suspicion, and even locomotives and automobiles made an entirely civilian impression."

As Gustav Krupp explained in 1942, the manufacture of these "tools of peace" was only camouflage. "Even the Allied snooping commissions were duped." An official annual report of the firm during the Nazi period elaborated these boasts in detail. In 1938 the German readiness "to manufacture war material in large quantities" under the Nazis was proudly credited to the fact that since 1919, "the firm decided as the trustee of a historical heritage to safeguard its irreplaceable experiences for the armed strength of our nation, and to keep the personnel and shops in readiness for later armament orders, if or when the occasion should arise. With this in mind, we tailored our new production program to a pattern in which our personnel could attain and improve its armament experiences, although the manufacture and sale of some of the products entailed big losses."

Some of these losses, it is true, were covered by secret subsidies given by the government to enable Krupp to proceed on its secret way. As Joseph Wirth, an unsavory politician who was German Reich Chancellor in the worst inflation years of 1921 and 1922 (and who ended as a Communist stooge in the years after World War II), reminded Gustav Krupp in a personal letter, "considerable sums were released to the firm by the Reich to preserve German armament technology . . . to lay new foundations for the technological progress of German weaponry."

What the firm actually achieved in the way of secret armaments was impressive, according to confidential tabulations and memoranda in Krupp's business files. In a lengthy pamphlet, "The Artillery Construction Department of Fried. Krupp A.G. and the Development of Army Artillery from November, 1918, to 1933" (or, from the end of World War I to the inception of the *Third Reich*) the Firm enumerated in painstaking detail its secret achievements in armaments abroad. First of all, Krupp had transferred by secret agreement its blueprints and technicians for the production of weaponry to a Swedish arms manufacturer, the Aktiebolaget Bofors. Safely removed from the Allied Control Commission and sharing the profits, Bofors and its silent partner in Essen

manufactured cannons—some developed by Krupp as
early as 1920, such as the 7.5-cm. mountain gun L/20
— and sold them to all interested countries. Ammunition
for tanks and other war materials were also produced in
Sweden by Krupp. (Only in 1935 did the Swedish government close down Krupp's establishment on its soil, and
"the Krupp officials returned to Essen," as the report
concluded.)

In Essen itself, Krupp continued only rudimentary research and gun tests after the war, until the French Ruhr
invasion interrupted this work and Gustav Krupp had his
secret arms material smuggled to safer places. On July 1,
1925, the firm opened a seemingly harmless and independent machine factory in Berlin, under the name of Koch
and Kienzle. For the next two years KuK E(E for *Entwicklung,* Development), as it was called, was busy designing and developing new field howitzers, naval and
coast guns, anti-aircraft guns, and other weapons. "When
at the end of 1927 these jobs had been completed, KuK
E was dissolved and the gentlemen recalled to Essen
where meanwhile the reconstruction of the artillery design
department had been started," the Krupp report concluded this chapter.

The "summary of a few important developments" in
artillery achieved by Krupp in secret during that period
includes eight new types of cannon, light field guns, and
howitzers, produced under the cover of "heavy tractors."
A new type of howitzer for mountain warfare (ordered
by the Dutch government for use in Indonesia), a self-
propelled gun, a new type of 21-cm. mortar, and a new
type of sprung gun carriage were the main harvest of this
"black" production in the artillery field. The output was
further strengthened by adding weapons for armored warfare when, in 1928, the German Army's Weapons Department invited Krupp to deliver two experimental "light
tractors." This was the code name for light tanks armed
only with machine guns. In 1932 a "medium tractor," a
tank equipped with a gun, followed. All the German guns
used in World War II, as the report found after the war
had begun, "were already fully developed in 1933. The

mortar was then almost completed, and the light field gun 18 was also ready for use. The firm, Krupp concluded, "stood ready to take up mass production upon order."

If Krupp manufactured artillery in Sweden, it did similar secret work for the navy in Holland. At the suggestion, and under the supervision, of two retired lieutenant commanders of the former Imperial German Navy, and with the approval of the chief of the Admiralty, Krupp's agents founded a Dutch company, the *Ingenieurskantoor voor Scheepsbouw,* or Engineering Office for Ship Building. According to a secret memorandum, "Service Publication No. 15, The Fight of the Navy against Versailles, 1919-1935," Krupp succeeded in keeping its submarine-construction staff busy designing and testing new models, after they had been sold to, and built in, Japan, Turkey, and Finland.

In all this secret armament work, the Army General Staff and the Admiralty gave specific orders to Krupp. Mindful of the lessons taught to the military leaders by World War I, the German officers not only realized the importance of industrial production, but took a leading hand in it. In the different secret organizations, officers were assigned to work side by side with Krupp officials. When Krupp produced its cannons in Sweden, officers of the *Reichswehr* were present at the firing ranges to watch the performance. German naval advisers sat in the Dutch Krupp office, and others gained valuable experience in Turkey, Finland, and Japan with Krupp's new underwater craft. In turn, industrial specialists were attached to the staffs of the military districts. Krupp's only original contribution to the new armaments was to weld rather than rivet the caterpillar treads to tanks, an innovation which reduced their weight considerably. Even behind the drawn shades of the secret arms production, the new trend was clearly outlined: the technicians and the military, rather than the arms manufacturers, were taking over the leadership. Krupp received the new ideas from the outside, but his men did the work. In later years—from 1933 to 1945—Krupp and his spokesmen harped on their great financial sacrifices in the cause of secret

German rearmament. After 1945—as though the record were not available—they simply denied that Krupp had taken any part in this secret activity. Both claims were widely off the mark. Foreign sales of the camouflaged foreign auxiliaries must have contributed to, if not covered, the investments and expenses of research and experiment. Alfred Krupp had set this pattern almost a century before when he made his first cannons, although the political conditions had changed.

In a political atmosphere poisoned by the demands of the Versailles Treaty—as well as by the attempts of most German military leaders, several industrial leaders, and a few political leaders to circumvent it—Krupp followed the tradition of the house and gambled on a coming German remilitarization.

In this gamble, Krupp did not take great risks. If earlier the Allies had watched out for secret German rearmament with a particularly keen eye on Krupp, after the early 1920's their role was taken by Germans themselves. Democrats, pacifists, and Left-wingers considered it their duty to track down disarmament violators and to denounce them in public. Although they could not discover every secret deal, they ran considerable risks in trying. Many informers were killed by the *Feme* of the nationalist underground, and the German judiciary tended to sentence the informers as national traitors, rather than the secret armorers. The worst effect of the secret armament was in moral terms. While it led some Germans consciously to violate the Treaty and engage in fraud, public opinion became divided to a point at which national politics became impossible. Germans considered fellow Germans on the other side of the fence as enemies to be silenced by brute force rather than as opponents to be outvoted in open civic discourse.

This division of Germany into two or more enemy camps created what the Germans used to call a *Zwischenreich,* or an Interim State. "There had to be a change" by the victory of one camp until a permanent, peaceful, possibly powerful Germany could again emerge. The democratic order that prevailed and which had been weak from its beginnings was even weaker after fourteen years of existence under the impact of the economic crisis. In this tottering Interim State, Gustav Krupp did not take sides, nor did he proclaim that he would uphold the existing German Republic. He merely accepted the situation as behooved a man as nonpolitical and nonrevolutionary as he. Only in collusion with some of the military did he circumvent the Versailles Treaty. The Firm of Krupp, too, was in an interim state, between adjustments to the peaceful present and preparations for "the big change."

As Gustav Krupp saw it, the re-establishment of the old monarchy, or perhaps the establishment of a military dictatorship led by his friends, the generals, was the most desirable "big change." It would make him again "the German *Reich's* armorer." Beset by economic chaos, desperate mass unemployment, and furious onslaughts by Communist and Nazi civil-war troops since the late 1920's, the lawful government lost its authority, which was a second reason why Krupp hoped for a change. According to the tradition of the firm, a strong government was a prerequisite of the growth of Krupp, whether it produced for peace or war, or, preferably, for both.

First and foremost, Gustav Krupp von Bohlen wanted to preserve the heritage of his adopted family. In his faith to the letter and the spirit of the founder's will, he was to lead his family and his firm to disgrace and disaster.

PART III

Only Yesterday

1933-1953

8

Krupp's *Third Reich*

Adolf Hitler and Gustav Krupp von Bohlen und Halbach had little in common. In fact, the two men were a study in contrasts—contrasting backgrounds, contrasting personalities, contrasting thoughts and hopes. If Krupp was a proper Prussian organization man whose days and mind seemed to run like clockwork, Hitler was an Austrian bohemian driven by demons. Krupp believed in the supreme value of tradition, self-discipline, order, and duty; Hitler lacked all ties to tradition, and he lusted for a "new order" which merely reflected his own, disordered self. Krupp lived behind his mask of cold silence, while Hitler in private and in public raged and shouted savagely. The manners of a gentleman which were Krupp's seemed a doubtful, if not despicable, thing to Hitler. The revolutionary leader proclaimed the primacy of politics and had only contempt for what is called economic reason, while the industrialist regarded politics as an alien, dangerous passion which threatened the regular course of his own, economic world. Krupp worked for profitable production; Hitler dreamed of war and victory. One saw himself as a superman with a mission to change the universe, while the other was a family man devoted to preserving and enlarging his wife's heritage. Every time Germany prospered in the years after World War I, Krupp's firm also prospered, while Hitler's party lost its followers, and vice versa.

Nevertheless, the head of the firm and the head of the party had a few traits and interests in common besides their clipped mustaches. First and foremost both deeply believed in the *Führerprinzip*, the principle by which one man, and only one man, could lead their respective organizations, the firm and the party, as well as the *Reich*. Because of its adherence to this principle the firm had risen from its start with less than a dozen workers, not unlike Hitler who had set out with less than a dozen followers. In their struggle for success both men owed a measure of their rise to the secret support of military leaders out to use them. Even more important than their past common experiences, Hitler as well as Krupp glorified arms and military strength. These common beliefs sufficed for a common platform.

But until Hitler secured, fourteen years after his emergence on the German scene, the nation's leadership, no contact, let alone sympathy, existed between firm and *Führer*. From a distance, Hitler showed more respect for Krupp than for most other German industrialists; he often denounced them for their lack of interest in, and support of, his movement. The platform of his party, written in the early 1920's, demanded socialization of big business, but the official commentary excepted "the really great creators of our heavy industry, the Krupps, etc. . . ." Hitler still held his view shortly before he came to power, when a Nazi subleader of radical Socialist leanings, Otto Strasser, broke away from the movement because it did not meet his revolutionary standards. In his last conversation with Hitler he asked him: "For instance, would you leave everything with Krupp as is?" Hitler's answer was short: "But naturally, yes!" At the same time Hitler's brown-shirted followers were marching through German streets shouting their party anthem: "The comrades killed by Reds and Reaction are marching in our ranks." As they saw him, Krupp belonged to the reactionary enemies.

Fritz Thyssen, one of the few big industrialists who at an early stage openly and wholeheartedly supported the Nazis, noted in his memoirs, *I Paid Hitler*, that "until Hitler's seizure of power, Herr von Krupp was his violent opponent." Krupp did not contribute one pfennig to the funds of the Nazi Party, while a number of other industrialists contributed their share, as they contributed, cautious people that they were, to other, including middle-of-the-road, parties. Alfred Hugenberg, Krupp's old Chairman of the Board, who had led the German Nationalist Party ever since he had left the firm in 1918, had worked since 1931 in a United Front with the Nazis. Together they formed the so-called Harzburg Front, named after a resort town where both groups appeared together for the first time in public. But no Krupp representative, let alone Gustav Krupp, had any contact with either Hugenberg, whom Gustav Krupp now disliked, or the Harzburg Front. In 1932, Hitler addressed the assembled big industrialists of Rhine and Ruhr for the first time at their club in Düsseldorf (which gave him equal time after Cohen-Reuss, a Socialist leader, had delivered a political speech at their previous meeting). Gustav Krupp did not even show up at this first meeting of the industrialists and the Nazi leader.

When in the early 1930's the end of the Weimar Republic was visibly near, it was an open question which form of government would succeed it—communism, a military dictatorship, a monarchy, a semi-medieval "State of the Estates," or the Nazi revolution. With strong forces behind each of these ideas, many Right-wingers suddenly discovered their sympathies were with Hitler. He appeared as the last hope of many unemployed workers, university students and young graduates without job prospects, merchants and craftsmen on the road to bankruptcy, peasants threatened by dispossession, and industrialists facing a work stoppage, in short, the victims of an economic crisis in a sick society. This gave Hitler's party the desirable strong mass basis which, with the exception of the Communists, no other group could claim. In the eyes of many Germans, the Nazis seemed the least of several evils. Others were more optimistic and saw the Nazis as heralds of Germany's recovery. After all, the Nazis promised to end unemployment, the economic crisis, the national frustrations brought about by the Versailles Treaty, and the Communist threat. These were also the hopes of Right-wingers, including many industrialists. They thought they could "use" the Nazis to do the job; after its completion, they would either get rid of the Nazis or tame them until they turned into respectable patriots.

In November, 1932, one of the most influential advocates of such a policy, the former Reich Bank President, Hjalmar Horace Greeley Schacht, who pleaded and schemed at home and abroad in favor of Hitler, drafted a letter to be signed by more than two hundred German business leaders, and addressed to Reich President Hindenburg. The letter implored the President—thoroughly senile and incompetent by that time, yet still entitled by the Constitution to designate the men who would make up the government—to nominate "the best men led by the *Führer* of the largest national group," in other words, a cabinet of non-Nazis with Hitler as a figurehead leader. By this measure "the cinders and faults as they come with every mass movement, would be exterminated." Schacht, as he later described it in his arrogantly apologetic autobiography, hoped "to put brakes on the Nazis and maneuver them onto a moderate course." (When after Hitler's fall fifteen years later, Schacht faced a German court on charges of collaboration with the Naxis, the Public Prosecutor asked him: "Why did you as a little lion enter the big lion's cage?" Schacht answered: "You forget that I did not enter it as a little lion, but as a lion trainer.")

But apparently Gustav Krupp kept aloof. A copy of Schacht's letter, containing Krupp's typewritten signature, was later found in the safe of the I.H. Stein Bank in Cologne, but the original letter disappeared and no copy was discovered in the extremely orderly and comprehensive private or business files of Krupp. Probably Schacht invited Krupp to join and he evaded. Had he really signed the petition, it would have been silly for his fellow industrialists, who knew his aversion to Nazism, to ask him two months later to rush to Berlin and dissuade President von Hindenburg from following the advice given in that letter. Krupp did not see Hindenburg at the time. In sum, before the Nazis came to power, he remained true to his principles as an *unpolitisch* businessman and neither op-

posed nor supported them. In the light of evidence, or
rather lack of evidence, there was no truth to the generally accepted cliché that "Krupp paved financially Hitler's
road to power."

In January, 1933, Hitler was appointed Reich Chancellor. His new cabinet seemed to correspond to the proposals Schacht and his fellow signers had submitted to
Hindenburg. In the new government Hitler was surrounded by conservative Right-wingers who would, as
many observers expected, gradually "use," control, and
soften the Nazi leader.

A month after Hitler became Chancellor, Gustav
Krupp met him for the first time. Herman Göring,
World War I flying ace, Nazi old-timer, morphinist, and
newly appointed chairman of parliament, had invited
more than twenty leading industrialists to his office. The
Nazis wanted them to help finance their campaign in the
coming general election. Hitler came, late as always, and
presented his political views to the assembled moneybags
and managers. Gustav Krupp busily made notes of the
speech and kept them in his personal files (under the
heading "Private Correspondence 1933–1934"). What
the *Führer* said with a sly appeal to the interests and
fears of this special audience, and of Krupp in particular,
was, according to Krupp's notes, that "private enterprise
cannot be maintained in the age of democracy." Rather
than the rule of a majority under which everything "will
irretrievably fall," he pleaded for a rule based on "authority and personality." In short, Hitler threw a sop to
big business and played the role of a sensible advocate of
free enterprise. Göring chirped in to promise political
pacification, economic recovery, and "no experiments"
under the new Nazi rule. Krupp was duly impressed.

Dr. Hjalmar Horace Greeley Schacht (like Krupp von
Bohlen, the offspring of a German family which had emigrated to America and returned home again) was also
present and surprised by the moderation of Hitler's
words. So moderate were they that after the speech Gustav Krupp rose and declared in his brief, dry way his su-
port of Hitler's government. He agreed with Hitler, he

told him, on three points: Time has come to clear up German domestic politics; this must benefit the whole people rather than individual professions or classes; business can develop only in a firm and independent State. Neither Nazis, non-Nazis, nor anti-Nazis could object to these rather vague generalities which ignored Hitler's plans of future conquest by Wagnerian wars and his dreams of mass murder.

After Krupp had spoken, the twenty-five assembled industrialists pledged to raise three million marks, or less than $30,000 per head, for election campaign funds to be pooled among the governmental parties. The Nazis would get a fraction of this fund, which was entrusted to Doctor Schacht. Many other Germans, hopeful or fearful of the Nazis, donated their pfenning or more to the Nazis who at the time walked through saloons and salons to collect contributions in little tin cans.

Gustav Krupp's next letters to Hitler were still signed with the old-fashioned courtesy form of "Very respectfully yours," but he soon changed to "German Greeting," a subtle way of appeasing yet not fully adhering to Nazi rules, until finally he adorned them with the orthodox Nazi salute, "Heil Hitler." He had submitted wholeheartedly to the dictatorship.

The feelings Gustav Krupp held toward the new rulers were clearly revealed by instructions he gave to Karl Stahl, his chauffeur in Berlin, after the *Third Reich* was established. Stahl had to watch him closely on his approach to the car. If he carried his gloves in the right hand, the chauffeur had to greet him with the traditional military salute, but if he shifted his gloves to the other hand, he was to be given the Nazi salute of the raised arm. At first, Krupp carried his gloves on the left only when Nazi leaders were around to watch him, the chauffeur observed.

But Krupp's submissiveness toward the ruling Nazis soon grew with their increasing power. The less respect they showed him, the more willingly he submitted, until in the end he became their devoted and enthusiastic follower. If many conservatives had believed they could "use" and dismiss the Nazis, Hitler demonstrated in his earliest dealings with Krupp that it was precisely the other way round. Gustav Krupp was to learn this by an early and humiliating experience. Since 1931, two years before Hitler, he had served as president of the Reich Association of German Industry (a group roughly resembling America's National Association of Manufacturers), which the Nazi press attacked as a "reactionary, Jew-ridden, liberalistic, plutocratic outfit." In fact, among its leaders and members were, besides a few Nazis, a number of men who were anti-Nazis for different reasons—some were Catholics, others Jews, still others who believed in democracy or in free enterprise. Shortly after Hitler came to power, Krupp, as president of this association, had two lengthy and private conversations with him. After the second interview, in April, 1933, Krupp announced that all Jews had to leave the association and that its executive director, *Geheimrat* Kastel, who was a hard-boiled adherent of economic and political liberty and therefore a "reactionary" in Nazi eyes, was suspended from office. Two Nazi economists would take over leadership in the association in which the *Führerprinzip* was to be established, with Gustav Krupp as its *führer*. The self-administration on which the group had prided itself was abolished. By decreeing this change, Gustav Krupp violated the mandate of his office, the by-laws of the association, and the wish of a majority of its members. Rather than attempt to "soften and influence the Nazis," let alone resist them, Krupp swung the powerful group into the governmental course—*gleichschalten,* or "conform," was the word for it —as soon as Hitler requested him to do so.

If Krupp thought he would emerge from this coup as the *führer* of German industry, he was mistaken. Once the group had submitted to the Nazi command and thereby lost its potential power, Hitler contemptuously finished it off altogether. A new Nazi-directed organization of industrialists was set up to supersede the association and make it superfluous, until it dissolved. In the new Nazi organization, Gustav Krupp was appointed only to head one of its seven sub-groups under the command of the new association *führer*, but he soon resigned from the post.

Yet this experience hardly disappointed Gustav Krupp. He was not power-hungry and did not want to lead the association the way he had led his Essen empire, as its sole master. As the autocrat of his combine, he followed the will of its founder and his family. But outside of it, he followed only the strong will of the government, in keeping with the tradition of the house and his personal inclinations. As an unpolitical businessman, he still followed orders from the "superiorities," as long as they did not interfere with his business.

Several months after the "new order" had been established in Germany he was in full agreement with its program and policies, or, in short, a Nazi. His wife, Bertha, kept her reservations and complained to friends, at least once tearfully, about her husband's sudden political flirtations. But he would admit no doubts. When conversation at the family dinner table turned to the Nazi rulers, he would cut it short, as he had done throughout the pre-Hitler years of the Weimar Republic, with a brief, authoritative *"Hier wird nicht politisiert."* No talk about politics here! When Carl Bosch, head of the I. G. Farben Dyestuffs concern and as powerful in the field of chemistry as Krupp was in steel, made a few snide remarks about corruption among Nazi leaders, Gustav Krupp said, "I cannot tolerate such talk in my presence," and left the room.

Krupp's personal conversion to Nazi doctrine took little longer than the successful conversion of his firm to Nazi goals. The primary goal, of course, was to begin again the full-blast production of arms, though at first still in slightly camouflaged fashion. Hitler had not yet formally renounced the Versailles Treaty which he could safely do only after the other nations were sufficiently impressed by his new armed power. "But as soon as the Hitler government was established, it called on the firm to make war material again, and the call was answered without as much as an hour's delay," Wilhelm Berdrow, the company chronicler, proudly reported in the Nazi war year of 1943. "It could be done because the capacity had been preserved, and the know-how kept alive throughout the dead period, with the whole family fortune at stake." Gustav Krupp himself confirmed this boast when he wrote: "After the assumption of power by Adolf Hitler, I had the satisfaction of being able to report to the *Führer* that Krupp stood ready, after a short warm-up period, to begin the rearmament of the German people." Going into detail, Fritz Gerhard Kraft, Krupp's official industrial historian, stated in 1943 that "since 1933, Krupp's [Germania] Shipyards had built warships of all kinds, submarines, cruisers, escort boats, and destroyers." This was two years before the Allied ban on their construction was lifted. Similar admissions, or, at the time they were made, similar boasts, abound in the company publications.

In strange contrast to these published admissions, after 1945 Krupp's old and new historians went out of their way to point out that Krupp was neither prepared nor willing to respond to Hitler's call and rearm. A noted German writer, Ferdinand Fried, for instance, summarily stated in 1956 in his book, *Krupp: Tradition und Aufgabe* (Tradition and Challenge), that "only in 1936 was armament production begun again at Krupp, as it then was by many other steel works."

A second writer of a recent Krupp-commissioned history of the House of Krupp, Gert von Klass, went even further than that when, in 1954, he commiserated with his hero who, as he wrote, was forced by the Nazis to go into the arms business, against his will. "Since 1934," Herr von Klass wrote, "Hitler attempted to force the Firm of Krupp to build weapons whose production was interdicted by the Versailles Treaty. . . ." But Gustav Krupp, according to this author, "did not want to violate these rules since treaties were inviolable to him, once and for all."

If these claims were true, instead of being a belated whitewash, they would indicate that the Firm of Krupp defrauded the Nazi government. As secret memoranda in the company files show, the firm demanded high monetary compensation from the Nazi Government for having placed its plans, research data, and development results gathered secretly in the fourteen Weimar years at the disposal of other corporations upon the ascent of Hitler, "without a moment's delay," as Gustav Krupp himself asserted in a meeting with high Nazi officials in 1940. In yet another memorandum to support Krupp's compensation claim, Krupp's financial director, Johannes Schroeder, estimated Krupp's sacrifices for this purpose at three hundred million marks—perhaps an exaggerated claim, but the Nazis acknowledged it and Nazi Reich Minister Todt promised payment in full.

After 1933, Krupp again developed speedy mass production of heavy tanks and artillery, including siege guns, tank guns, tank turrets, mortars, and caissons for field guns. Its shipyards constructed submarines—one a month by 1939—a battleship, an aircraft carrier, cruisers, and other vessels for the Navy. The Essen plants armed the new German battleships from the *Bismarck* to the *Deutschland*.

As Krupp's company files show, Hitler and his subleaders occasionally argued heatedly with Krupp's managers on specific armament questions, and at least once threatened that "the *Führer* might lose patience with Krupp unless he obeys." These clashes occurred when Krupp's economic reasoning conflicted with Hitler's power politics. Krupp resisted if and when the *Führer* tried to force him into unprofitable production. While Krupp was eager to fill orders, he was unwilling to invest capital in ventures which would take a long time to pay off, or to speed up production to a degree which upset his calculations or change models and processes in conflict with his business interests. But in contrast to the tradition of the house, which had held its own in similar conflicts with Prussia and the Kaiser's Germany, Hitler won over Krupp. He did not even have to articulate his threats of concentration camp and expropriation which hovered over his commands as a matter of course. Grudgingly, the firm gave in and did what the *Führer* ordered it to do.

To be "as tough as leather, quick as a greyhound, hard as Krupp steel" was the oath of allegiance the boys of the

Hitler Youth swore, holding high the dagger given them as their membership symbol. Whether Krupp himself was as tough as leather and as hard as Krupp steel, apart from other qualities on which he placed greater value than the Hitler boys, remains a debatable question.

But Krupp's profits in the first Nazi years rose steeply, and not only the Nazis kept the old armory busy. As soon as it became known that the Essen firm was back in its traditional trade, weapon orders from abroad abounded. Orders for guns and tanks were placed with Krupp from the governments of Southeast Europe, some South American nations, and Soviet Russia. Krupp supplied them all, after the *Führer* had given his permission. In fact, Krupp supplied better weapons to foreign nations than to his own. This was the paradoxical outcome of the Nazi principle according to which only raw materials available in the homeland could be used for German arms production. The military planners recalled the bitter experience of World War I when the British blockade had succeeded in almost paralyzing German arms production by cutting off its foreign supplies. They wanted to be better prepared in the next war, and they instructed the industry accordingly. Krupp had to use synthetic or second-rate materials for home production, while quality materials went into his production for foreign countries. Turkey, Greece, and the Soviet Union received better Krupp arms than Nazi Germany. Although the Krupp managers tried hard to change the minds of their political leaders on this self-defeating policy, they did not succeed.

To make the firm independent from supplies of the outside world, the firm of Krupp founded a synthetic gasoline plant, and in 1939 completed its first revolutionary invention in the steel field for more than half a century. Krupp designed the so-called *Renn* procedure; this revolutionary procedure freed steel production from its dependence on high-grade iron ore and special coke, which were scarce in Germany but without which formerly no steel could be cast. By an ingenious process Krupp succeeded in casting steel from poor ore without furnaces, using any fuel available instead of only coke, and producing other nonferrous metals from nickel to copper to gold and platinum. Before World War II broke out, the firm had established several such plants in Germany, as well as in Manchukuo, Korea, and Japan, where similar shortages hampered industrialization.

In the years of total war, the difference between the "tools of peace" and the "tools of war," on which the firm had stood as on two legs since the time of Alfred Krupp, faded away. This was one reason why Krupp's new civilian production rose in Hitler's *Third Reich* with the same speed as its military production: Locomotives, motor cars, agricultural machines, and bridges much in need to span the *autobahnen* in an unbroken network formed the mainstay of Krupp's work in the prewar years. But if Krupp had started its first regular program of tank production in 1933 under the cover of an "Agricultural Tractor Project," it foresaw that all its new peacetime production could eventually and speedily be converted into production for wartime needs. Even the *autobahn* network was built with an eye to its use for military deployment.

As it seemed to Gustav Krupp, the *Führer* kept his promise. Employment and prosperity, stability and strength, came back to Germany, and first and foremost to the firm. Its gross profits doubled within the first three Nazi years, from 108 million marks in 1932 to 232 million marks in 1935. The net profits, that is, Bertha and Gustav Krupp's personal income, rose even higher, from 57 million marks in 1935 to 514 million at the beginning of World War II. The old center of the combine, the iron and steel works, alone expanded its labor force from 35,000 in 1932 to 112,000 in 1939, and its output was almost tripled in the same period. The technical research bureau for artillery construction employed twenty designers in 1933; their number soon grew to 2000. If there were also a few "excesses of the mass movement" which pleased Krupp less, he shrugged his shoulders and looked the other way. In 1934 the *Führer* came to Essen for the first time. In the footsteps of Bismarck and the two Kaisers, he visited Krupp's steel factory. Gustav and Bertha

Krupp's daughter, Irmgard von Bohlen, received the guest with a bunch of flowers in the factory lobby, while the leading employees greeted him with the Nazi salute. Trying hard to be on his best behavior, the *Führer* remained friendly and modest. When he was taken on the grand tour through the plants, he asked only questions of a technical nature, and grinned happily at what was shown to him. What was discussed when the head of the firm and the head of the *Reich* retired to the former's private office, we do not know.

After his first visit, Hitler came to see the Krupps in Essen once or twice a year for the rest of his life, and he was followed by a long procession of other German, Italian, and Japanese political and military leaders. While no member of the family or high employee of the firm had joined the Nazi Party before it came to power, three months later the first Krupp directors took out membership cards; the others soon followed suit. Gustav Krupp himself was awarded the Golden Party Badge on his seventieth birthday, by the *Führer*. Other honors from other party leaders came with it. The Minister of Economics presented him with the title of "German Führer of Economics," the Minister of Labor with that of "Pioneer of Labor," the Minister of Armaments with a new order, the War Cross of Merit, and since it came in two versions— the regular and the commander's cross—both were given to the old gentleman at the same time. He was the first German to receive all these titles and honors.

The firm had just finished a large Soviet Russian order for an armed cruiser and duly delivered it, when Hitler unleashed his war. Krupp again employed as many workers as during World War I. In the years to come all Krupp production, as in most other German industries, was converted to total war production. Krupp's assembly lines in his hundred factories turned out guns of all calibers; anti-aircraft artillery, anti-tank cannons, heavy naval guns, and tank armor plates, in addition to tank, submarine, and other ship and airplane parts, and, last but not least, the steel itself to be used by other arms industries. Under Nazi supervision, the Firm of Krupp with its specialized skills also worked on research and construction assignments for other, competing industries to which Krupp's developments had been allocated. While the firm adjusted its cannonry from the requirements of ground warfare to air and motorized warfare, the developments in the technology of new weapons remained outside its range. The army and Nazi coordinators told the firm what and how to produce. On orders, it turned its heavy trucks into the dread Tiger tanks which led German offensives from the Kasserine Pass to the Ardennes.

Krupp's proudest achievement was the Sevastopol cannon, once more "the world's biggest gun." It was a direct descendant of "Big Bertha" and "Big Gustav" of the previous war. Hitler himself ordered its construction as early as 1936 in the hope that it could crash the Maginot Line which France had built as its defense wall against Germany. When Krupp delivered the monster, the 32-inch caliber gun which weighed 1,465 tons and was movable only on a specially constructed twin-track railroad, was able to fire over a distance of 25 miles. But it was used against the Russian fortifications of Sevastopol rather than against the French Maginot Line. Its development involved expenses of five million marks while the actual production cost amounted to seven million marks for one piece. On delivery the army procurement office refused to pay more than the cost of the gun itself. Rather than fight, Krupp announced it would generously donate all its development costs and charge only the actual production price, ten million marks. After the second gun was delivered, the profits surpassed the donation.

As Krupp was to learn, the life of a businessman and industrialist under Nazi rule was more difficult than the early Nazi supporters had anticipated. Hitler did not abolish private property and free enterprise, but he subordinated them to his command and to the command of all his party underlings; an armed, often fanatical bureaucratic giant, this State party organization supervised all phases of economic planning, often decreed what should be produced, and allocated materials and labor according to its own lights. If this often resembled State socialism, it yet retained to a high extent private profits and competition. In the resulting order, the industrialists, as all other citizens, were commanded to do their best of their own will, and enthusiastically, even when they had to submit to commands which seemed uneconomic, if not nonsensical. In the war economy, the master in his mansion was downgraded to a part-time agent of the State, but when he did his job well, the rewards were high in honor and in cash.

Quite literally, Krupp was pushed to the side line when it came to running the factory. Hitler himself, that omniscient man, played, as a secret report of the firm's war-material department in 1942 reported, the role of a weapon-construction expert. At his first meeting with the department's technicians, he "stressed the necessity of simplifying the design" of anti-aircraft equipment. In later conferences, he gave his criticisms and orders with regard to new anti-tank guns and other artillery pieces. Rather than discuss these questions with Gustav Krupp, he disregarded him, and worked directly with the firm's chief technician in charge of gun design, Erich Mueller. He was known—to distinguish him from other men named Mueller—as *der Kanonenmueller*. A convinced Nazi whom Hitler honored with the coveted title of *Herr Professor honoris causa*, he came to outrank in importance the head of the firm, foreshadowing the new times in which the scientist rather than the industrialist played the master role in the field. Behind the political leader who ordered new weapons and the scientist who designed them, the industrialist who merely manufactured them almost disappeared. This was a new and consequential trend.

When "the labor supply" in Hitler's total war ran short, the Nazi authorities took over its distribution. To replenish the source, three groups of human beings were thrown into the labor pool—Allied prisoners of war; foreign workers from occupied countries who were drafted or had volunteered under varying degrees of force, and who were deported to Germany from their native countries; and inmates of concentration camps. Much though the members of these groups differed in nature and in the treatment they received at Nazi hands, they were lumped together in foreign eyes as "slave labor." If the majority of the "foreign workers," many prisoners of war, and all concentration camp inmates were slaves, this term sounds unduly euphemistic compared with the lot of slaves as it prevailed, say, in the United States before abolition.

When Nazi leaders first suggested that the Firm of Krupp employ "foreign workers" to bolster its labor supply, Gustav Krupp was reluctant, though not from moral or political scruples. What he was afraid of, he explained, was that these foreigners might learn the firm's production secrets and reveal them to Krupp's foreign competitors after the war.

In all honesty, the Nazis could assure him that his fears were groundless. Slave laborers were in no position to see and remember Krupp's technological processes, even if they were lucky enough to survive. When Krupp's fears were overcome, the first "foreign workers" arrived in Essen with their armed guards. Over the four war years, the firm employed more than 55,000 foreign workers, 18,000 prisoners of war, and 5,000 concentration-camp inmates. Their total number equaled the native labor force employed by Krupp before the war.

Representatives of the firm—for instance, one Wilhelm Werner Heinrich Lehmann, a manager in charge of labor relations—went on frequent trips to Holland, Belgium, France, Italy, and Poland to recruit "volunteers." When their time of employment was completed and the "volunteers" wanted to leave, they were informed that a Nazi law subjected them to "compulsory extension" of their contract, and they were treated as prisoners. Held in camps behind barbed wire, they were not even permitted to talk with Germans. To those who nevertheless did, or who "rebelled" in other ways, or who "loafed," hard and often cruel punishment was meted out. The Firm of Krupp, according to a statistical table in its business files, "established and used" fifty-seven camps for foreign workers. Several hundred to several thousand prisoners in each camp were guarded by Krupp's uniformed company police.

"In the midst of 1941," Adam Schmidt, a railroad employee of Essen, recalled, "the first workers arrived from Poland, Galicia, and the Polish Ukraine. They came in freight cars jammed full. The Krupp supervisors rushed the workers out of the train, and beat and kicked them. . . . I could see with my own eyes that sick people who could hardly walk were dragged to work."

"Conditions in all camps for foreign workers," remembered Dr. Wilhelm Jaeger, a senior physician in charge of Krupp's camps, "were extremely bad. They were greatly overcrowded. . . . The diet was altogether insufficient. . . . Only inferior meat, such as horsemeat or tuberculin-infected meat which veterinaries had rejected, was distributed in these camps. Clothing was also completely inadequate. They worked and slept in the same clothing in which they had arrived from the East; virtually all had to use their blankets as coats in cold and rainy weather. Many workers had to walk to work barefoot, even in winter."

"Tuberculosis," the doctor continued, "was especially widespread. The TB rate was four times the normal rate. This was caused by bad housing, poor quality and insufficient quantity of food, and overwork. . . ."

But these foreign workers and war prisoners were well off in comparison to the third group of slave workers, the inmates of concentration camps on lease to employers of all kinds, including Krupp. They were owned, as it were, by the SS, Hitler's black-shirted elite guards who, as guardians of the Nazi faith, guarded the concentration camps. This institution, in which hostile civilian elements were held without a court trial and without rights, had been used at the turn of the century by France in its struggle against rebellious natives of its African colonies, adopted by Great Britain in the Boer War, later on set up in style by Soviet Russia, and since 1933 taken over by Nazi Germany. Jews, foreign resistance fighters, anti-Nazi Germans, gypsies, criminals, and "asocial characters" made up their population.

Concentration-camp inmates were a highly sought-after industrial commodity. True, they were *ersatz* labor, like *ersatz* linen or *ersatz* coffee or *ersatz* rubber in wartime Gemany, inferior to the original article, but not much cheaper since the SS demanded its price for this special labor supply. But with the increasing shortage of labor in general, the industry—and Krupp—were happy if they could conclude a contract with the SS to get a trainload of half-starved, tortured human beings delivered to their factory gates, C.O.D.

The industrialists bargained with the SS for prices and amounts of these slaves in a routine business way. When, for instance, the Firm of Krupp leased from *SS Standardenführer* Pfister, commandant of Buchenwald concentration camp, "2,000 Jewish Hungarian prisoners (male)," it contractually agreed to pay the SS four marks (one dollar) a day for every prisoner. It also agreed to provide every prisoner with a blanket, one set of eating utensils, and one drinking cup, as well as to feed him at the cost of 70 pfennig (18 cents) and the guards at the cost of 1.20 marks (30 cents) a day. Krupp also agreed to pay the cost of four guard towers and of the barbed wire with which the new camp was to be equipped. It was a businesslike contract. What happened to the inmates behind their barbed wire was the responsibility of the SS, not Krupp, as long as Krupp's production was helped rather than hindered.

Many SS leaders were not happy about these deals. After all, their supreme leader, Heinrich Himmler, had decreed in the summer of 1941 that all Jews must be exterminated. But later on Hitler upset this order when he persuaded his SS chief that the interests of warfare and war production came first. Therefore, as many Jews as could be found were to be used as laborers rather than killed outright. Dyed-in-the-wool SS men considered this a dangerous decision, since, as one of them put it, "it might help a few Jews to survive." In the end, however, these seemingly conflicting demands for the labor of living Jews and for their mass murder were reconciled. "Untold thousands of inmates used for work died, since practically all minimum conditions of survival were lacking," Rudolf Höss, commandant of Auschwitz concentration camp, reported. Auschwitz prisoners were allocated to two new fuse and light field howitzer plants which Krupp built not far from the camp. Of more than 450 Jewish women from Hungary delivered by the SS to work in Krupp's Essen steel mill, only two, the sisters Roth, survived. They escaped from the camp. A few Krupp workers and other Essen citizens hid and fed them after their escape.

While the SS leaders argued and intrigued with each other on the treatment of Jews, that is, whether to gas or work them to death, they did not see eye to eye with the industrialists, either. Their difference of opinion boiled down to the question whether slave laborers ought to be treated like cattle destined for the knacker's yard or like hard-working animals. Of course, many SS leaders defended the first method, while the industrialists preferred the second; the output of workers decreased when they were weakened by hunger, by a daily one-hour march from and to work, and by the fear of torture. All this was the fate of concentration-camp inmates on lease to Krupp. Outside the factory, the SS remained in charge of these men. They had little patience with the Krupp officials who suggested that the slaves be fed and transported to work. But when slaves collapsed from exhaustion and starvation, Krupp's interest in their welfare ended. The social principles of which the firm was so proud were not applied to these people. They disappeared from the payrolls, the SS payrolls, that is, to be exterminated.

Whether a strong protest by Krupp would have helped much, or whether Krupp could even have voiced one, is an open question which the owner of the firm never asked. Krupp and his fellow industrialists as well as his subordinates submitted to force. But this submission contributed substantially to their production, to their standing in the community, to their profits. Whether or not they liked or approved of the way in which their slaves were mistreated, they dodged all responsibility for it. Nonpolitical as ever, the firm submitted to, and cooperated with, the authorities in the interests of its business.

The commands of "economic reason" and Kruppdom came first. If, as has been claimed later, the firm was raped by the *Führer*, it rather resembled a rape victim encouraging the rapist to proceed "and a bit more quickly and violently, please!"

Gustav Krupp himself hardly knew or understood very well what was going on around him in these days. He was in his early seventies and pathetically senile. His face had turned into a rigid, lifeless mask; like an automaton he appeared at his office every day as punctual as ever, to read files and letters, but without active participation. He seemed to demonstrate the truth of the theory that old age overdevelops the dominant traits of previous life, making stupid men more stupid, wise men wiser, selfish men more selfish, and so on. In his senility, Gustav Krupp gave the Nazi rulers unquestioning obedience.

Early in the war, one of his sons was killed. When his directors and fellow industrialists came to express their sympathies, Gustav Krupp snarled: "My son had the honor to die for *der Führer*." The accent was on the words *honor* and *Führer*. His Golden Party Badge glittered on his lapel.

When it came to the Nazi test, Bertha Krupp proved a "truer Krupp," after all, than her husband. She held her distance from the new rulers of whom she never quite approved. Her reason, and as far as her later public and private statements reveal, her only reason for this posture, was that the Nazis interfered too much with the firm. They were not even scions of the Prussian monarchy or its civil servants, yet they disregarded Krupp's traditional claim to be "master of the mansion." With people of that kind, she would never make her peace, which bought her in marked contrast to her submissive husband who happily served the intruders.

While Gustav Krupp weakened, his directors, executives, and managers formed a collective leadership. As "economic men" they remained skeptical of the program battle cries of their rulers who, after all, were self-admitted "political men," or in Kruppian eyes, fools, notwithstanding the fact that they were "authorities" to be obeyed.

But one director, Ewald Oskar Ludwig Loeser, quietly resigned from the firm in March, 1943. Why he left became known only fifteen months later, although his colleagues, and also the Secret State Police, suspected at a much earlier date that it was for "a political reason" as they called it. If for no other reason, Loeser would have been suspect because he joined the firm in 1937 as a financial expert on the recommendation of Carl Friedrich Goerdeler, who was even then highly suspicious, if not objectionable, in Nazi eyes. In pre-Hitler days, Goerdeler served as Lord Mayor of Leipzig, and Loeser as City Treasurer. As soon as the first waves of Hitler's "national revolution" flooded their country, the two conservative civil servants showed their dislike of the new Nazi ways. When local Nazi toughs marched to the municipal building to hoist the Nazi flag, Goerdeler and Loeser, as the city's ranking officials, simply locked the gates and stayed inside the building until the would-be invaders left with their unhoisted flag. A few weeks later, the two men rushed to the Bruehl neighborhood—a Leipzig quarter in which the predominantly Jewish-controlled fur trade was housed—in full regalia to keep the Nazis from destroying the Jewish stores and beating up their occupants. Loeser resigned from his post a year later, in 1934, rather than cooperate with the new rulers, and joined a Jewish-owned hotel-management corporation in Berlin. Goerdeler was appointed to the rather high post of Price Commissioner in the Nazi government. He fancied it possible to "put the brakes" on its policies and retain a conservative economic course, but after two years he gave up and returned to his Leipzig post. He was widely known for his remarkable ability as a financial planner, and Gustav Krupp von Bohlen sent him a message offering him a job with the firm. When Lord Mayor Goerdeler returned from a vacation to find that local Nazis had removed Leipzig's monument of the German-Jewish composer, Mendelssohn, from its city square, he resigned in protest and wrote Krupp that he was willing to accept the offer.

In the meantime, however, Gustav Krupp had learned of Goerdeler's political reputation and was afraid that his appointment might harm the standing of the firm among Nazi leaders. Somewhat naïvely, he asked for a personal meeting with Hitler "to talk about Herr Goerdeler." Before he hired the man, he wanted to be sure the Nazis would approve. As was to be expected, Hitler did not approve.

Rather than mention his political undesirability, Hitler, as Krupp informed Goerdeler, "disagreed with his economic theories."

Goerdeler then recommended his old friend and colleague Loeser, whose political antecedents and convictions were less well known. Krupp asked his brother-in-law, Thilo von Wilmowsky, who was in charge of the firm's Berlin offices, to sound out this new prospect. "It is highly important," Krupp wrote him, "that his mind be set on cooperation with the [Nazi] Party as honestly and sincerely as is my own attitude toward the *Führer* and the whole movement." Loeser was found satisfactory in this respect and became financial director of the firm. At the same time, Krupp offered to stake Goerdeler's foreign travels if he would send him personal reports on political and economic conditions abroad, and Goerdeler accepted.

What Gustav Krupp did not know was that Goerdeler by that time had become a secret plotter against Hitler and his rule. After his initial attempts to put brakes on his system, he had come to understand that such efforts were in vain. The only way, he felt, to end the rule of terror was to overthrow the government by force. In preparation of a *Putsch,* he gathered an increasing number of other Germans who felt the same way. His Krupp credentials in his travels served as a cover for this undertaking. It had to be carefully hidden from the Secret State Police.

On his travels abroad, Goerdeler warned foreign statesmen and businessmen against Hitler's preparations for war and informed them of his own plan to put an end to Nazi rule. In the two last prewar years, he toured Western Europe and America where he met, among others, foreign policy makers such as Cordell Hull, Sumner Welles, Henry Wallace, Henry Morgenthau, Jr., and Senator Taft. Back home again, he told his friends how shocked he was to find leaders in America, and even more so in England and France, rather placid about Hitler's threats, quite prepared to appease him, and inclined to discount reports of his domestic rule of terror. As to the German uprising against Hitler, they were cool, skeptical, and disinterested. Goerdeler continued his Krupp-financed conspiratorial travels until the war made it impossible and so put an end to his usefulness to the House of Krupp.

But Loeser remained with Krupp for the reasons for which he had joined the firm in the first place. As a director of the combine which was so highly appreciated by the Nazis, he was above suspicion while he helped Goerdeler in his conspiratorial work. In turn, he could act as the latter's look-out in heavy industry, inform him of developments, and provide the conspirators with important information.

A totalitarian system must be either fought or followed. To fight it without discovery and destruction by the secret police, Loeser, like many other secret fighters against the Nazi State, was forced to mask himself as a follower and to cooperate in many actions of which he did not approve. By 1943 he felt unable to pay this price any longer without endangering his integrity.

He resigned from Krupp to give all his strength to the conspiracy, in which by that time Germans of many walks of life took an active part, from priests to army officers, university professors, students, trade-union leaders, civil servants, members of the landed gentry, Protestants, Catholics, Jews, and atheists. For them to resist Hitler was a decision incomparably more difficult than for the resistance fighters of Nazi-occupied foreign countries. After all, the overthrow of the Nazi rule was bound to lead to their own fatherland's defeat and unconditional surrender. The oath to Hitler which the dictator had commanded them to take, and which they were to violate, was a second moral obstacle in the way of many conspirators, among whom were some deeply religious men. Even harder for them was to agree to the plan to kill Hitler as the only way to win freedom; they were reluctant to murder a man, even a tyrant. But in the end, a hard core of conspirators prepared to assassinate Hitler, overthrow his *Reich,* and establish a new, lawful order, and after long deliberations they decided upon a successor government. Goerdeler was to be Chancellor and Loeser Secretary of the Treasury. The uprising, execution of Hitler, and establishment of the new "front of decency," as Goerdeler called it, was scheduled for the twentieth of July, 1944.

At the last moment, their plot miscarried. Hitler's life was saved from the bomb that was to kill him, isolated rebellions were put down, and the leaders arrested. Four thousand nine hundred and eighty German conspirators were sentenced to death and executed, among them Goerdeler. Loeser was jailed, but escaped death; before he could be executed, the Nazi *Reich* collapsed.

Also among the victims arrested by the secret police after the plot of July 20 were Gustav Krupp's brother-in-law, Thilo von Wilmowsky, and his wife, Barbara, who was Bertha Krupp's only sister. They had been on friendly terms with Goerdeler, Loeser, and other conspirators who often visited their estate. Barbara von Wilmowsky was brought to the police jail of the city of Halle where she shared a cell with twelve other women, most of them prostitutes and petty thieves. Her husband was sent to concentration camps, first to Sachsenhausen, then to Schwerin, where he was freed by American troops on their victorious advance. Exactly twenty years before, as we remember, Thilo von Wilmowsky and Bertha Krupp had visited Gustav Krupp in his prison cell. But Thilo and Barbara von Wilmowsky waited in vain for Gustav and Bertha Krupp to visit them in their Nazi prisons. All they did was to order their chauffeur to find out where both were held and bring them food and greetings. Their servant was able to accomplish this mission with the help of chauffeurs of Nazi leaders who were his old friends from earlier days when they too had driven the limousines of leading industrialists. "You know," he explained later on, "the masters come and go, but the chauffeurs remain the same."

While many leading Germans, including one director of the Krupp firm and two members of the Krupp family, risked their lives to save their country from disgrace and crime, Gustav Krupp thought only of one, very different thing. Before he died, he wished to re-establish the firm as a permanent hereditary family monarchy, according to the will of Alfred Krupp. This, he felt, would mark him forever as "a true Kruppian"; the goal preoccupied him more than, say, being a true German, let alone a true gentleman.

But to accomplish his mission, he needed the help of Hitler. No one but the dictator could exempt the firm from the law of the land and abolish in its case the laws of inheritance which decreed that estates be divided among (and inheritance taxes paid by) a number of successors. What Gustav Krupp sought was a special law which would apply only to the Firm of Krupp, stating that it could never be a joint-stock corporation or otherwise owned by more than one person; it was to be passed on from one Krupp to the next, regulated only by its own internal statutes, and preserved forever.

After more than a year's negotiations, Hitler issued the so-called *Lex Krupp,* a law valid only for the firm and the family that inherited Alfred Krupp's empire. In a special decree of November 12, 1943, which became a law with his signature, Hitler proclaimed: "The Firm of Fried. Krupp, a family enterprise for 132 years, deserves the highest recognition for its incomparable performances in boosting the military power of Germany. Therefore, it is my wish that the enterprise be preserved as a family property." The Krupp law that followed saw to it that this wish was fulfilled in legally binding terms. No other German industry or family has been granted a similar privilege.

It was the last action of Gustav Krupp. After this accomplishment, his strength gave out, and the man disappeared altogether behind his mask. In the following year,

he could be seen walking through the gardens of Villa
Hügel with a basket under his arm, collecting stray fragments of shrapnel and shells. The government had encouraged the people to gather all scrap iron and metal
fragments for use in the industrial war effort, and the
head of Europe's biggest steel empire, an erect and silent
ghost, followed the order. This was his last contribution
to German war economy, and to steel production in particular.

With the *Lex Krupp* in force, he could resign his trus-
teeship of the firm and the family, and let another crown
prince mount the throne. He was Gustav and Bertha's oldest son, twenty-nine-year-old Alfried Felix Alwyn von
Bohlen und Halbach. He received title to the name of
Krupp von Bohlen und Halbach along with the heavy
heritage of four generations of reigning Krupps.

His godfather had been Kaiser Wilhelm II in all his rising splendor. Educated by his parents in the severe Kruppian way, he seemed shy and passive, rather than a leader
of men and machines. Never allowed to speak unless addressed, supervised every waking minute, and forced to
account for all his actions throughout childhood, he could
be expected either to remain cowed or to turn into a wild
rebel. Alfried took the first path. His mother often sighed
that Alfried was "the most serious" of her eight children.
He made no friends at Essen's *Realgymnasium*. When in
his later teens his schoolmates persuaded him to join
them for a bottle of wine at the Traube, Essen's most
fashionable bar, he sat silently, never laughing or flirting
with the pretty barmaids as his comrades did. "You
mustn't be always so serious," the motherly proprietress
of the place admonished him and only made him blush.

He remained just as bashful when he attended Munich's Technical University. In those years, the student
body was torn between Nazi and anti-Nazi agitators;
ideological as well as fist fights between both were the
order of the day. The sons of at least two other leading
German industrialists (whose great-grandfathers had been
competitors of Alfred Krupp) attended Munich University at the same time and were leaders in the anti-Nazi

fight. In contrast, Alfried kept aloof from political as well as social life, although he donated ten marks, or two dollars and fifty cents, to a Nazi group. He worked hard at his engineering studies and graduated with honors from Aachen's Technical College.

When he was twenty-two he joined his parents' firm. Every morning he rode to the plant on his motorcycle to punch the time clock like every other Kruppian. When he came late, which happened only twice, his name was posted on the register of delinquents. Thus a modern crown prince is educated.

A year later he surprised his parents with the announcement that he was going to marry. His choice was pretty, gentle-mannered Annelise Bahr, a blond divorcee of good middle-class background. Her father was a well-to-do Hamburg wholesale merchant and as a former cavalry captain, socially acceptable. Her first and childless marriage to another Hamburg wholesale merchant had ended in a quick and quiet divorce. For the first time in five generations of Krupps, if not in Krupp history, an heir married for love. Alfried and Annelise were in love.

But Alfried's parents resented the match and protested strongly. Annelise was a divorcee, and a family as proper as the Krupps would not forgive such a thing. When one of their directors had divorced his wife a few years before, Bertha Krupp insisted that he be fired on the spot, since as she said, "it upsets me to see him." A second reason was her unglamorous, though thoroughly respectable, family origin. In contrast to Alfred Krupp who objected to his son's choice of an aristocratic bride, the parents of Alfried Krupp did not want a commoner as their daughter-in-law. One of their daughters was married to an impoverished aristocrat of a noble family; the second daughter, to a rich Bremen textile industrialist. There was a third reason for parental resentment. A sister of the young woman was the wife of a Jewish lawyer with whom she had emigrated to South America. This made the match most undesirable in the eyes of the authorities, that is, the Nazi Party, the major factor in the eyes of Gustav Krupp.

In the only show of rebellion in his life, Alfried married Annelise. They had a son whom they named Arndt, in memory of the first Krupp of Essen, and, as a Sunday supplement romance would put it quite correctly, they were happy with each other. "These were the only years in which I saw Alfried smile," an old and devoted family factotum remembered later on. "And when he was with Frau Annelise, he smiled almost all the time."

But Gustav and Bertha Krupp advised their son and heir that they would disinherit him unless he ended his marriage. In the same year in which he had wed, the Duke of Windsor married "the woman I love." He also had been warned by powerful people against a marriage with a commoner who was, to make things worse, a divorcee. Yet there was a difference between the heir to the United Kingdom and the heir to the Cannon Kingdom. Alfried Krupp was not a monarch by the grace of God.

Like the former Mrs. Wallis Warfield of Baltimore, the former Mrs. Annelise Bahr of Hamburg was slandered by the peers of her husband, the industrialists of Essen. Alluding to her maiden name of Bahr, a wit called her "the barmaid." The pun was soon accepted as a description of her origin. In German eyes a barmaid is considered on her way to or from a red-light district. The puritanic millionaires of the Ruhr snubbed young Frau Krupp.

Rather than be disinherited, Alfried gave in after four years and divorced the woman he loved. His parents rewarded him with the law which made him the sole heir of the family and the sole *führer* of the firm.

But the new owner did not rule the firm. The collective leadership of managers which headed it in the last years of Gustav Krupp's incapacity continued at the helm, and Alfried Krupp, devoid of aggressiveness, still modest to the point of shyness, little experienced in the ways of men and business, was content as a member of the team. He did what they told him to do, and while he worked hard at it, he achieved nothing which any other sub-manager could not also have achieved. With his managers he negotiated with Nazi officials on the allocation of raw material, on expansion of output, on the type of weapons produced.

Whether it was coincidence or not, the first massive Allied air attack hit the Krupp plants in Essen at the same time the Krupp family was granted its special status by Hitler. Like Hitler, the Allied planes also considered Krupp a "special case" and a specially worthy target. In the next two years the first attack was followed by fifty-four equally or more destructive assaults. The last and most destructive raid, on March 20, 1945, foreshadowed the end of the war. In all, more than 2000 tons of explosive and incendiary bombs were dropped. One air attack alone succeeded in destroying twenty-five acres of sheds, the next, thirty-five. In one night 1000 RAF planes turned the old and strong heart of the Krupp combine, the cast-steel factory, into rubble. Many plants were completely flattened or badly damaged, and although production became increasingly difficult it never stopped altogether. Some plants remained wholly intact. Many had been removed to distant, less exposed parts of Germany. As soon as the sirens announced the end of an attack, the Kruppians hurried to rebuild what had been destroyed only an hour before. As soon as the reconstruction job was completed, the Allies returned for a reconstruction job and completed it, too.

"Under the impact of these air attacks and the war situation," Johannes Schroeder, financial director of the firm, later recalled, "we [the executives] felt that Germany had lost the war, and we said so in strictest confidence among ourselves." It was then that, for the only time in Nazi history, Krupp acted against the law and systematically broke Nazi rules, but only for the business interests of the firm. The Nazi government had commanded that every industrial combine invest all its liquid assets at once in new war production equipment. In view of the coming defeat the managers of Krupp, however, were more interested in "saving at least something for the postwar period; we wanted to lead the firm into the future in a state of financial health that would permit its survival," Schroeder reported. Germany may be destroyed,

but Kruppdom must survive! Rather than invest its assets
in war production and lose them, the firm secretly followed a new policy of "keeping its assets as liquid as possible. It rid itself of all War Bonds, cashed all its claims
for war damages, and collected all outstanding debts
from the *Reich*." Since it was too dangerous openly to
advise the managers of the firm's auxiliaries to follow this
course, Krupp did so in underground ways. "We realized
the risk we were running," Schroeder admitted, but in
this case, it seemed worth while. "We were not traitors,"
he explained, but the firm's interest required this step
against "Hitler's mad policy." No such risks or steps were
taken when interests other than Krupp's were involved,
for instance, when shortly before surrender, with the Allies close by, the SS officers ordered Krupp's 450 Jewish-
Hungarian women slave workers removed for mass exter-
mination. Obediently and efficiently, Krupp's officials followed orders and organized the special train which carried them from Essen to their death.

Faithful to its *"unpolitisch"* principles, the firm had
followed the Nazi course as soon as it had become the
governmental course of authority and power. As Gustav
Krupp and his colleagues could have discerned the aims
and methods of this course more clearly than most of
their fellow citizens, their pose was rather stupid, since
nobody can remain *unpolitisch* under totalitarian rule.
The Krupps refused to face this fact. Whatever the government, they submitted unless or until their economic interests were endangered. While the firm followed the
führer, it was caught in the mesh of the totalitarians,
cooperated with them of its own will, and submitted to
their veiled threats and seductive promises.

In 1945 Hitler's war drew to an end. Allied troops invaded Germany. Only a tiny minority of Nazi die-hards
tried to resist them in a last stand. The majority hurriedly
turned their bedsheets into white flags of surrender,
hoisted them over their houses, and greeted the invaders
as liberators. But the American commander-in-chief,
General Dwight D. Eisenhower, made an announcement;

his men, he declared, had come as "conquerors, not as liberators."

In September, 1858, Abe Lincoln asked his slaveholding Southern fellow citizens: "Are you quite sure that the demon you have roused will not turn and rend you?"

The Krupps had never heard the question which Abe Lincoln asked at Edwardsville, Illinois, and they would not have understood what it had to do with their heritage, their family, their firm, or their fate, if they had.

The demon they had roused would turn and rend them.

9

Outcast in His Ruins

High above Salzburg in the Austrian Alps, with the border of Germany close by, rises Blühnbach Castle. The happy hideaway was built by the unhappy Archduke Franz Ferdinand of Habsburg. Before he could enjoy its beauties, the murder bullets of Sarajevo ended his life and rung in World War I. After that war Gustav Krupp von Bohlen bought Blühnbach as his "little summer place." The eighty-room castle is surrounded by some of the best Alpine hunting grounds; chamois, boar, and fallow deer wait, as it were, for the lord of the manor and his guests to shoot them. Gustav Krupp shot many, as his collection of hundreds of antlers impressively proved.

Toward the end of World War II, while Allied planes pulverized Essen and killed its people, Gustav and Bertha Krupp fled to Blühnbach Castle. When they left their undamaged hilltop palace and the ruins of their factory, the former Cannon King was a ruin himself. Progressive hardening of the arteries had paralyzed his body and his mind. In December, 1944, while being driven to the hospital, he had bumped his head on the car window, and since that time his last powers of movement had left him. He could neither walk nor stand, eat without help, talk or hear. While his wife, servants, nurses, and doctors administered to his needs, the only words he still painfully articulated once in a while were *"Ach, Gott"* and *"Donnerwetter."* The second word is a Prussian curse.

His family was in ruins, too. Of his seven children—an eighth had died in infancy—only Alfried, the oldest son, heir to the family fortune and head of the firm, remained in Essen. Claus, a second son, had been killed in the first months of the war when as a young *Luftwaffe* officer he went down with his plane in a test flight. Ekbert, the youngest son, a first lieutenant, had died in the last months of the war, in the fighting on the Italian front. A third son, Harald, was a prisoner of war in Soviet hands, a fate which seemed, and often was, death on the installment plan. His daughter was a war widow. Only one son, Berthold, was with his parents.

When Allied troops took Salzburg, a jeep drove up from the valley over the winding road that led to Blühnbach Castle. At its gate a scholarly-looking, pipe-smoking lieutenant colonel of the U.S. Army emerged and rang the bell. To the frock-coated butler who appeared, the American officer said that he wanted to see Herr Krupp. "His Excellency is sick in bed," the butler said, but he himself could take care of any business the gentleman might wish. The gentleman told him brusquely that American colonels weren't in the habit of doing business with butlers, and demanded to see a member of the family. Eventually, Berthold von Bohlen was summoned. The American merely wanted to see the place. His commander, General Mark Clark, had asked him to find a shooting lodge where he might entertain his Allied colleagues and Blühnbach Castle was by far the most attractive place in the district. It was available too. Its present owner, as the colonel knew, was to be arrested and tried as a war criminal. By an ironic twist it so happened that the colonel, Charles W. Thayer, was related by marriage to Charles "Chip" Bolen, U. S. Ambassador to Moscow and a member of the American branch of the family of Gustav Krupp von Bohlen und Halbach.

Colonel Thayer found the eighty-room castle too large and sumptuous for General Clark; instead, it was turned into a home for war refugees and Gustav and Bertha were moved to the "Post House," as its servants' annex was called. Since all communications between Austria and Germany were interrupted in those days, the Krupps did not learn the fate of their factory and their place in Essen for many months.

On April 10, 1945, twenty days before Hitler killed himself in his Reich Chancellory, advance troops of the U.S. Ninth Army entered Essen. Among the first to arrive was a jeepload of officers of the Counter Intelligence Corps. With the help of their carefully prepared map, they rushed through streets and plants which Allied bombs had covered with rubble, until they pulled up at the gate of Villa Hügel. Despite its ugliness, the hilltop palace was a pleasant relief from the surrounding ruins; it had completely escaped the assaults, and the greenery in the park was bursting out in fresh bloom. Without so much as a glance at the horticultural, architectural, and other sights, a captain hurried from the jeep to the villa's pompous outside staircase and shouted at Herr Karl Kohrmann, the impeccably dignified butler: "Where's Krupp?" As if the armed visitors were guests expected for formal supper in the villa, the butler at his butlerish best —with that undertone of condescension toward ill-bred people which they themselves would hardly perceive—announced: "Gentlemen, Herr von Bohlen is expecting you. May I ask you to enter?"

Alfried Krupp von Bohlen had been waiting alone since early morning when the first scouts had arrived in Essen. The captain and two soldiers stamped through the giant hall and found him standing in the library. "Are you Krupp?" the captain asked him in purposeful discourtesy. "Yes, I am Krupp von Bohlen," he said in good English, and bowed slightly. When the captain shouted at him, "You are under arrest," Alfried's face did not change. As the shocked butler later observed, a GI grasped the head of the House of Krupp and led him to the jeep in a "brutal police hold."

Alfried Krupp was driven to the temporary command post in Essen City, where the lieutenant who served as his guard started a slightly embarrassed conversation. "Well, sir, what are your ideas about the future?" the American asked Krupp. His answer might have seemed fantastic had he not made it sound commonplace: "I shall rebuild my factories and take up production again, of course. You know, I am a businessman, not a politician." These were his first words in captivity which, he felt, would end "after a few days at most." But it would be "fifty years or more" before the firm was again a going concern, he thought. He was far off the mark in his time estimates of the time of his captivity as well as of the reconstruction of the firm.

On the morning of Alfried Krupp's arrest, the firm was also taken over by American troops. A few weeks before, the Nazi authorities had given orders to evacuate all Essen factories, and Alfried saw to it that this command was followed. "The authorities are still at the helm," he said to his directors, "and we must still obey them." Herr Tubesing, a second-string manager in charge of the firm's real estate, was chosen to hold out in the administration building as caretaker. Well provisioned with wine and food for his stay, he was alone in the deserted building but for Herr Wilhelmshorst and Herr Schuster, a janitor and his helper. The assistant financial director, a rotund, bespectacled man, later also moved in, armed with his umbrella and a rucksack, ready to defend the interests of the firm against all comers. There was ghostly quiet; only a few Stukas circled over the town. The barricades built around the factory for a last stand were scattered with bits of torn uniforms from fleeing German soldiers. "In my thirty years of work for the firm, I had never experienced such stillness," Herr Tubesing recalled later on. Since six o'clock in the morning American vanguard troops had been passing along the street, and at ten their first jeep stopped at the entrance to Krupp's office building where the caretaker received him. An officer pulled his machine gun, held it at the back of the Kruppian, and ordered him in English: "Go!" Together they groped through the rubble-strewn ruins until the officer had made sure that the plant had been evacuated.

An hour later a second jeep pulled up with four Counter Intelligence corpsmen of the U.S. Army. They spoke German, went through the offices, and opened Alfried's locked desk drawers with pistol shots. "My friends outside must think they shot me," thought Herr Tubesing and he rushed to the window to show his consoling lively presence, while the Americans discovered to their disappointment that the desk had been emptied. About noon a group of higher officers arrived and interviewed the Kruppians. Fourteen years later they would still bitterly complain that the American conquerors "stole" a few of Krupp's typewriters, a portrait of Hitler, and a desk model of an old howitzer.

Around the firm's half-destroyed office building stretched miles of once-industrial wasteland. Fond of superlatives in chamber of commerce fashion, the city that had boasted of Europe's hugest industry, richest family, and deadliest armory now called itself Germany's most ruined city, and it was entitled to this boast. At war's end, exactly one half of all its industrial plants and public buildings and 56 per cent of its private housing were totally destroyed; of its 185,000 apartment units, only 6000 stood unharmed.

Also badly damaged were the numerous monuments to numerous Krupps which had filled, though not embellished, the plazas of Essen. While church spires, seemingly miraculously, withstood the bombs, bronze statues of the steelmakers tumbled from their pedestals. The biggest statue of Alfred Krupp had fallen into a bomb crater. And there he stood upright and unharmed, tall, bearded, and forbidding as ever. An incredible omen, as it seemed to the people of Essen.

Kruppians completed the job which the bombs had started and tore down the remainders of all the monuments to all the Krupps. Essen's municipal council solemnly resolved to strike the names of Gustav and Bertha Krupp from the register of honorary freemen of their city. In the postwar months, former German Cannon Kings were without honor in their capital city.

Most of the welfare institutions set up by the firm and family—the housing settlements, the hospital, the department stores, the baker, butcher, and wine shops—were extinguished by the air attacks. Fifty per cent of the 15,503 apartments which the firm had built for Kruppians, and which it still owned, were completely demolished, while 8.7 per cent were badly damaged and 41.3 per cent were damaged to some degree. Not one single house remained unharmed. Dust filled the eyes of the wanderer who tried to make his way through the ruins. On stormy nights, many collapsed and buried those foolish or desperate enough to try to live inside their walls.

Essen was again a dangerous town. More than 10,000 former foreign workers and a few, pitifully few, concentration-camp survivors left their slave-labor camps and roamed through the town in search of their former masters and food. Understandably enough, they were out for revenge, and considered themselves entitled to take whatever they pleased from the firm whose slaves they had been. Managers of Krupp asked the U.S. Army for protection, and the colonel in charge dispatched his men to save Kruppian lives and properties until the freed slaves left for other parts.

Although it was not visible on first glance, Krupp's factories suffered less from the fifty-five Allied air attacks than had the civilian establishments. Thirty-two per cent of Krupp-owned plants were completely destroyed and 29 per cent were heavily damaged. On balance, approximately one-half of the works had ceased to exist, a damage of almost one billion marks.

Before long old Kruppians returned from military service or evacuation and asked their firm for employment. There were few other opportunities for them to make a living in Essen. Since thousands of workable machines remained under the broken steel columns and caved-in walls—the scrap alone worth many millions—the firm hired 3000 men to clear the grounds, to keep ruins from further destruction, and to salvage usable materials. Experts estimated it would take at least five years merely to clear the Krupp plants from their cover of rubble.

The only group of workers which was employed in full force, and even strengthened, was the company police. The people of Essen, including many former Kruppians, scavenged the factory yards for anything salable, from a pailful of nails to a valuable machine part. Right next to the Krupp grounds more than fifty dealers set up shop to buy what the scrap-diggers brought them, and to prosper in the scrap-rush. Thievery, perhaps, according to the law, but many families had no income except from their scavenging. Joseph Cardinal Frings, Bishop of Cologne, said in a sermon that it was no sin to rescue one's family from starvation by that kind of tragic treasure hunt, after which the Essen people felt better about searching out and selling factory remainders. But even if the city police-men had wanted to protect Krupp they could not have done much about it, since they were prohibited by Allied demilitarization orders to carry arms. But the private strong-arm men of the firm defended the works valiantly against the natives.

Two months after the Americans arrived, the British succeeded them in the occupation of Essen. As one of their first measures, they arrested all the directors of the firm. Two months later, British armored troops occupied the central office building. From that day on, their com-mander announced, British Military Government was to run the combine. It appointed a controller as the sole legal head of everything that had belonged to the firm and family of Krupp.

On his first day in office, the controller, Colonel E.L. Douglas Fowles, of the British Army, called Krupp's managers and department chiefs to the general meeting room of the firm. Stiff and erect, flanked only by a uni-formed secretary, he sat behind the long green table. On its other side stood almost twenty Krupp executives. He did not ask them to sit down. Talking in German, "so you can understand me better," in clipped accents he in-formed them of the future of Krupp in Essen, as it had been decided by the victors. He pointed to the window through which could be seen the dim outlines of ruined plants, fallen smokestacks, and broken walls almost dis-appearing in the fog and drizzle of the November day. "Out there, gentlemen," he said with a contemptuous sweep of his hand, coolly and matter-of-factly, "no chim-ney shall ever smoke again. Where once stood the cast-steel factory, there will be greenery and parks and meadows. The British Military Government has decided to put an end to Krupp forever. That's all, gentlemen."

Overwhelmed by the speech, Krupp's gentlemen stood in awed silence. Thirteen years later, everyone then present would still recite the colonel's words on the slightest provocation, *verbatim*. Together with a few dicta of Alfred Krupp they would remain the most popular item in Krupp's Treasury of Familiar Quotations.

After seconds of silence, Assistant Financial Director Johannes Schroeder spoke up. "How shall we pay and collect our debts, Sir?" he asked with the sobriety of a good accountant who is more easily impressed by figures than by dramatic announcements. "By what right do you ask me questions?" the Colonel snapped back. "By the right of a man sentenced to death who is entitled to a last word," Schroeder said mildly. "War criminals," the Colonel told him, "do not collect their debts, nor do they pay debts to other war criminals." The meeting was over.

This was the answer to the question people in the Allied countries had asked and discussed for four wartime years: "What to do with Germany?" The very question assumed that after its defeat the fate of the land was to be in foreign hands, and Germany a passive pawn of the victors. This fate had now come to Germany, and to Krupp too. The master in his mansion was demoted to an outcast in his ruins.

In fact, Krupp, the heirs as well as the heritage, was hit even harder by the war and the victors than Germany as a whole. The plan of converting the firm's real estate into pastures and farmland, as Colonel Fowles had announced it to the distraught second-string managers, only mirrored the pastoral future of all Germany as outlined in 1943 by Eugene Varga, Moscow's leading Soviet economist, in *War and the Working Class*, and subsequently in the Morgenthau Plan, the main author of which is widely considered to be Harry Dexter White, then Assistant Secretary of the Treasury and later identified as a Communist agent. It set out to turn Germany into a defenseless, de-industrialized country, unable either to feed or defend its people; in brief, the kind of country in which communism wins its easiest victories. With this objective attained, Germany was bound to fall under Soviet domination like an overripe apple, and with it, all of Europe.

The so-called Morgenthau Plan for Germany impressed a number of American and British policymakers who were unaware of its origins and consequences. They honestly wished to reform Germany and to free it from Nazi and militarist leanings. In the previous twenty years many among them, or their advisers, had been persuaded by the majority of opinion makers—sometimes led, often influenced, by Marxist and Left-wing theories as they prevailed in Western thought between the two World Wars —that big business was at the root of Nazism and militarism. This theory stemmed from the political bias of Marxian prejudices. After the believers in reform and revolution of America, England, and France had struggled with very limited success to win a victory over big business at home, in defeated Germany they had a heyday.

They set out to break German industry to pieces. In the eyes of the reformers controlling defeated Germany, industrial "bigness," with its horizontal and vertical concentration on ownership at every step from raw material to finished product, seemed not merely an economic development. In the light of Marxist ideologies, they confused economic power with political power. As it seemed to them and as they told the public over and over again, the great combines of heavy industry were the real power behind the thrones, particularly the Nazi throne. And, since the German occupation gave almost limitless powers to the Allies to determine the plans of the military government, their primary aim was a trust-busting job of unprecedented thoroughness and toughness. Every enterprise which was more than modestly middle-sized or which combined more than one branch of production, *esse delenda*. And first and foremost, Essen *delenda;* Krupp, the symbol and Samson's hair of Nazism and of Germany, was to be destroyed.

Krupp was worse hit by the trust-busters than any other German business combine. While Hitler ruled Germany with his theory that the Jewish race was the devil behind democracy, plutocracy, and all the other evils of his world, critics from the Left concentrated their attacks against big business on the big armaments business. In their imagery, it was the devil behind dictatorship, reaction, and all the other evils of their world. Since the early thirties, when the (Socialistic) Union of Democratic Control in England "revealed" and denounced the alleged vested interests in war held by the arms-making *Secret International,* a whole literature had arisen to expose the weapons industry—in books with titles such as *Merchants of Death, The Bloody Traffic, The Hawkers of Death, Cry Havoc!, Iron, Blood, and Profits, War for Profits, The Road to War, The Bloody International, Patriotism Limited;* these and other books warned the people against the power of the arms-makers. Special committees of the late League of Nations, as well as of the United States Congress, where Senator Gerald Prentice Nye and his colleagues investigated, tried to nail down and disarm the armaments industry.

To blame the arms-makers for war was about as fashionable as to blame the bootleggers for the enjoyment of liquor in the days of Prohibition. Of course, both arms-makers and bootleggers merely satisfied demands which were not of their making. If they satisfied these demands, they were entitled to their profits, whether or not one approved of the demands. (But the fashion in devils seems to change rather quickly; by 1950 the world had forgotten all about the weapon industry and its diabolic ways.)

Little wonder that Krupp seemed three times as dangerous and therefore worth destroying as anybody and anything else in Germany. By its size and its products the firm had come to embody the essence of bigness as well as weaponry. But its third feature to provoke accumulated hatred was the fact that it was identified with the reign, war, and victories of the Kaiser as well as those of Hitler. The firm itself had claimed and taken credit for both, and done everything in its power to promote this identification. After it had for years disregarded political responsibilities in favor of its business interests, or as the

Krupps put it, "did not let politics interfere with economic reason," the wheel took a full turn. The victors tended to disregard economic reason for political reasons. Unhappily, the opposite of one mistake quite often turns out to be another mistake.

The most drastic and spectacular blow was aimed at the House of Krupp when Gustav Krupp von Bohlen was included among the major war criminals to be tried by world conscience. As the only representative of German heavy industry, of arms-makers, and of the family empire whose name he bore, he was to be pilloried and sentenced as one as responsible for Nazi crimes as Hermann Göring, Hitler's second-in-command, or Julius Streicher, the mad hog-caller to the mass murder of Jews.

At the time, the world did not yet know the strange story that had brought about this trial. As early as 1941, in the second year of World War II, the French, Belgian, Greek, Dutch, Yugoslav, Polish, Luxembourg, Norwegian, and Czechoslovak governments-in-exile had resolved to try and sentence the Germans responsible for the aggressions and horrors of the war, according to the Hague Covenants and Treaties which were international law. But only the governments of the Nazi-occupied nations supported this proposal. At the Yalta Conference, Stalin drank his toast to the firing squad which would summarily execute the first 50,000 captured German war criminals without trial, by a bullet in the neck. Winston Churchill did not join in the toast. He rose in fury and shouted that the British people would never stand for such mass murder; the idea, he said, was wholly contrary to the British sense of justice. As Elliot Roosevelt reported later, President Roosevelt joined the dispute with a wisecrack in support of Stalin's stand. "Let's agree on a compromise and settle on a smaller number. Let's shoot at first only 49,500 Germans," the president of the United States said.

The question came up again at the Teheran Conference of the three wartime leaders, when Churchill—manifestly in opposition to the Soviet plan and to uphold Anglo-Saxon ideas of justice—submitted the idea of an international trial of war criminals. Such a trial would forestall lynch justice by mobs, drumhead courts, and Soviet firing squads and try the defendants by the standards of the civilized world. The idea found strong American support when Harry S. Truman followed Roosevelt in the presidency. In the meantime, the British Foreign Office had cooled toward the proposal, which the French had disliked from the beginning. But Washington insisted on an international trial against war criminals. Supreme Court Justice Robert Houghwout Jackson rushed to Europe to lay the groundwork. Judge Samuel Rosenman, aided by Herbert Wechsler, assistant to Secretary of Justice Francis Biddle, worked out the juridical framework. To avoid the stigma of a victors' court, neutral nations were to be appointed as judges, but the idea was dropped when it seemed apparent that there were not enough neutrals left. By no means was the jurisdiction to be left to German courts, which once before had tried only six defendants out of almost 100 war criminals whose trial was requested in the Versailles Treaty, and they had acquitted them. Among those who in 1919 had gone scot free, the victors recalled, was a flyer named Hermann Göring and an industrialist named Gustav Krupp von Bohlen. As a better solution and an alternative to having any trials at all, the British Foreign Office supported Anthony Eden's "St. Helena proposal." It suggested that all defendants be banished to a lonely island the way Napoleon had been exiled to St. Helena. But American spokesmen insisted on holding the tribunal and they got their way.

Two months after the German surrender, the delegates of the four powers agreed on an international tribunal composed of American, British, French, and Soviet Russian judges to try the war criminals. This being settled, the four powers disagreed thoroughly on what constituted a war crime, and how to try it. The Soviet delegate objected to every proposal of his Western colleagues and suggested that there was no need to define crimes at all. In the end diplomatic rather than legal agreements were reached. Nuremberg—where Hitler had held his great Reich Party conventions and where a court building of

the required size had survived the war—was chosen as
the scene of the trials. The indictment was completed on
the sixth of October, 1945, five months after the German
surrender. In the bill of particulars, Mr. Justice Jackson,
American chief counsel for the prosecution, denounced
the firm and the family of Krupp as the "focus, the symbol, and the beneficiary of the most sinister forces engaged in menacing the peace of Europe."

Seventy-six-year-old Gustav Krupp von Bohlen was
presented with his indictment in his sickbed at Blühnbach
Castle. As two American army surgeons found, he was
unable to understand the charges, let alone travel to Nuremberg and take his place in the defendant's dock.
Theodor Klefisch, his German defense counsel, moved to
defer his trial, but the American prosecutor, supported by
the British prosecutor, objected. The Soviet prosecutor
abstained, while the French prosecutor supported the
German motion. The court decided to send a delegation
of six medical experts to Blühnbach Castle. Its members,
three Soviet Russian physicians and one each from America, Britain, and France, agreed that the defendant was
physically and mentally unable to stand trial.

On this report, the American and British prosecutors
presented a new motion. Gustav Krupp, they submitted,
was to be tried *in absentia*. When the British Lord Judge
asked them whether they thought it corresponded to British and American ideas of justice to try a man unable to
defend himself, they could not answer in the affirmative
and their motion was quashed. A second suggestion came
from the French prosecutor. Gustav Krupp should be replaced by his son and heir and Alfried Krupp named as
an alternate defendant. Robert Jackson seconded this
proposal. "Public interests," he stated, "which transcend
all private considerations, require that Krupp von Bohlen
shall not be dismissed unless some other representative of
the Krupp armament and munitions interests be substi-
tuted." He realized, as he added, that he might be criticized for taking this position; but he was reconciled to
criticism of this kind, if a member of the Krupp family
was to be tried. "The United States respectfully submits,"

he asserted, "that no greater disservice to the future peace of the world could be done than to excuse the entire Krupp family." The Russians adopted this formula. The French Judge, Donnedieu de Vabres, spoke up: "Do you really believe," he questioned, "that you can ask the court simply to substitute one defendant's name for another?" When he received only an embarrassed reply, Lord Judge Lawrence said: "Thank you," and this settled the case. Krupp's seat in the dock remained empty.

"At this stage it is too late to substitute another industrialist in his place," reported Victor Heine Bernstein, an American writer who covered the trial for the New York daily newspaper *PM*. He correctly indicated that Krupp had been arbitrarily singled out among industrialists for his family name rather than for his personal guilt. Gustav Krupp had escaped a war crimes trial for the second and last time in his life, and Alfried, his son, was not to take his place, or so it seemed. Rather than a victory of the Krupps, this was a victory of Western principles. According to two German authors, after that day the prosecution knew that "the court was a court of justice."

For a brief moment it also seemed as though the Firm of Krupp would escape the trial by which the victors planned to sentence it to death. The surface appearance of "total destruction" to the contrary, only some 20 per cent of German industry had been destroyed by bombing and fighting, while four-fifths of its equipment remained intact under the debris that covered it, as a survey conducted by the Foreign Economic Administration of the United States found. Krupp had been more severely punished as the favorite target of Allied bombs. Thirty per cent of its industrial plants were destroyed. Yet with almost two-thirds preserved, and with manpower not only available but still in relatively good physical condition in the first postwar year, Krupp's reconstruction did not seem an impossible challenge, once the shock of defeat with its contemporary chaos was overcome.

But instead of reconstruction, there followed final collapse. The greater part of the Krupp works that had remained intact during the war years was destroyed in the

first five postwar years, more in fact, than was destroyed
in the war itself. The war bombings had annihilated 30
per cent of Krupp's producing capacity, but an additional
40 per cent was destroyed in the postwar period by what
was called "dismantling." Like the war crimes trials, this
punishment was suggested by the Western powers as a
compromise to particularly intolerable Soviet demands.
At the Yalta meeting, the Soviets had demanded that a
defeated Germany pay Russia reparations of ten billion
dollars. But the Americans recalled the lessons of the
Versailles Treaty, when German reparation payments had
upset the whole European economy, and their country in
the end had to give to Germany what other countries had
taken from her. They wished no repetition of that error
and at the Potsdam Conference they reluctantly agreed
that many German industries be torn down, or "dismantled," and given to the Russians and other victims of German aggression as reparations for German damages in
their countries. The United States did not wish to share in
the operation, and dismantling in the American occupation zone was ended at an early date. But Essen, with the
bulk of the Firm of Krupp, was in the British zone.

The Borbeck Foundry, one of Krupp's two central steel
mills and Germany's most modern one, was the first target of the dismantling crews. It took them over a year to
complete the job. The whole plant, from the giant furnaces to the last nails and pencils, was sent to Soviet Russia—75,000 tons of machinery, blueprints covering approximately 1000 square miles, and all the formulas for
production. Among the output of the Borbeck Foundry
had been the dread Tiger Tanks; the capacity to mass-
manufacture them on the assembly line was, perhaps, the
most valuable, and dangerous, present given to the Soviets by the British Labour Government which controlled
Krupp's dismantlement.

While construction costs of the Borbeck works had
amounted to 120 million marks, the cost of dismantling
them amounted to 27 million, but Russia's credit to Germany's reparations account was 7.5 million marks. A dismantled 15,000-ton forge was sent to Yugoslavia where

its parts and pieces were nicely stored away. A few years later, they were corroded and had to be scrapped. But then, scrap iron was badly needed by most countries after the war, and the war-ravaged works in Essen yielded a great amount, which was shipped to victor nations. In addition to scrap, 2000 dismantled tool machines and 180,000 tons of other dismantled machinery were removed from the Krupp grounds. Frequently more Kruppians were working on dismantling than on reconstruction jobs.

According to Krupp's British controller, even the plants which had begun again to produce agricultural machines, locomotives, and high-quality steel, were to be dismantled, and many machines were destroyed accordingly. In the end, dismantlement turned out to be self-defeating. It deprived Germany of its means to recover, and, by consequent economic necessity, retarded also the recovery of all of Western Europe. Once again the United States was forced to subsidize the victims threatened by starvation and chaos. If it then seemed a worthwhile goal to destroy the German capacity to make "tools of war," and Krupp's capacity in particular, a less desirable by-product was the destruction of the capacity of the German people to make the "tools of peace" so desperately needed to feed them and to restore their economic life. With the results of dismantling added to those of the bombings, more than two-thirds of Krupp's total prewar production was demolished.

But dismantling was not the last blow to fall on Krupp. A third blow was dealt in the form of Allied Law 27, a brainchild of American trust-busters, which was issued to carry out "the elimination of excessive concentrations of economic power" in the defeated country. True, this law was not a *Lex Krupp*, but while it was aimed at all the eleven steel combines which before the surrender had controlled 90 per cent of German steel and 55 per cent of Ruhr coal, it hit Krupp particularly hard. What this law set out to do was to put an end to "bigness," to decombine the combines, to slice and carve them into a lot of small, independent units.

If an earthworm is cut in half, both parts will automatically turn into new, independent earthworms that go on living, a process which can be multiplied. But it is another thing to divide economic combinations which have grown into one unit for compelling economic and technological reasons, particularly in the steel industry. "You can't unscramble eggs," J.P. Morgan had cracked when similar suggestions were made with regard to American concerns. If the Allies set out to prove Morgan mistaken, at least in Germany, they ignored the fact that many steel combines in the U.S. dwarfed in size and extent the Essen empire, and they overlooked similar combines in Soviet Russia, for instance, the Ordshonikidse Trust in the Don Basin which combines an impressive number of mines, furnaces, rolling mills, and armor construction plants. In fact, the Soviets started building bigger trusts and combines in their East German occupation zone at the same time the Allies were smashing the trusts and combines in their zones. When the Soviets expropriated all the Krupp holdings and auxiliaries in East Germany, they continued running them for their own profit. Most important among these new Soviet industries of Krupp vintage were the Gruson Works in the East German town of Magdeburg which specialized in the construction of heavy machines for war and peace. Even Krupp's name was exploited by the Communists who proudly called it, rather than Max-Engels Mill or Stalin Works as was their custom, the Krupp-Gruson Works. With these Gruson Works went secret tungsten steel formulas which, in the opinion of experts, enabled the Soviets to design their MIG jet fighter plane.

Was this, perhaps, one of the reasons why at the Potsdam Conference, as in 1959, State Department papers would reveal, "Stalin especially wished to make certain that German industrialists—he specifically named Krupp —were included."?

In accordance with the Allied Law, the House of Krupp had to divest itself of all its raw-material producing facilities—its coal and iron ore mines and its huge Rheinhausen steel mill, as well as other, minor installations.

They were handed over to Allied trustees with the assignment to sell them. At least one half of that third of Krupp's former producing capacity that had survived the war and postwar destruction was cut off by deconcentration. After five post-war years, more than nine-tenths of the firm's holdings, including the cast-iron factory which had been its heart, were gone.

The end of the House of Krupp seemed close by. Its material as well as its spiritual heritage seemed lost in defeat and disgrace. Worse yet, the heir himself was still under arrest. But the deepest fall of the Krupps was still to come.

None of this had been foreseen by Alfred Krupp when he laid down the laws which would preserve his legacy through all emergencies and generations to come—"for eternity."

10

Heritage on Trial

When the International Military Tribunal in Nuremberg on October 1, 1945, pronounced its sentence against twenty-two "major war criminals," the twenty-third defendant, Gustav Krupp, was absent. Whether he would have been acquitted like three of his fellow defendants, or sentenced to death like eleven others, or have been punished by prison terms like the rest, we do not know. But the International Trial against Major War Criminals was held merely as the first in a long series of international trials against other war criminals, and the men who were after "Krupp" did not give up in their attempt to get their man, or rather, their symbol. Hardly had the court refused to substitute the son for the father in the opening trial, when a new, independent trial against Alfried Krupp was put into operation.

However, after the conclusion of the first trial, the wartime alliance of the four powers had broken up. The British, French, and Russians refused, though for different reasons, jointly to hold any new international trials. With the Allied Law still on the books, the Americans decided to go it alone, and to continue "international" trials all by themselves.

Still on the American prosecution agenda were the cases of 1762 Germans indicted for individual crimes, such as the murder of concentration camp inmates, captured American airmen, and American unarmed soldiers. In addition to these cases to be tried in the so-called Dachau trials, many others were still pending in Nuremberg, among them those of German diplomats and business-men. When large sectors of American public opinion voiced strong protests against these victor courts, the United States Department of the Army suggested that the Nuremberg Trials be brought to an early end. But influential spokesmen of the American Military Government in Germany were dead-set on continuing them. In the end, a compromise was reached; of the many Nuremberg Trials planned and prepared, only three more were to be held. One of these trials was the "Krupp Case," or, formally, "The Case of the United States *v.* Alfried Felix Alwyn Krupp von Bohlen und Halbach, et al."

Two other groups of leaders of two huge German combines were also still to be tried in Nuremberg—Friedrich Flick and his fellow managers of a heavy-industry trust in the Ruhr and the directors of the giant chemical trust of I. G. Farben. These men were the most spectacular German industrialists, and Alfried Krupp was the most spectacular of them all. If he was tried as a name and an heir, he was not tried—in a legal sense—in the place of his father, although this legend has since come to be almost generally asserted and believed.

The Krupp Case was tried in the sprawling dirty-gray sandstone Nuremberg courthouse, called the Palace of Justice, where the other major war-crimes trials had been held. On November 17, 1947, a marshal in the uniform of the United States Army solemnly called out: "The Honorable, the Judges of Military Tribunal III A. Military Tribunal III A is now in session. God save the United States of America and this Honorable Tribunal."

High above the large courtroom, under the barely visible Stars and Stripes, sat the three judges: middle-aged men without experience in foreign law or affairs. Since U. S. Supreme Court Justice Fred Vinson had decided that no federal judges could be granted leave of absence for this purpose, these men had been drafted from the United States state courts. The Presiding Judge of the Krupp Case, fifty-seven-year-old Hu C. Anderson of the Court of Appeals of the State of Tennessee, was flanked by fifty-five-year-old Judge Edward James Daly of the Superior

Court of the State of Connecticut, and fifty-year-old
Judge William J. Wilkins of the Superior Court in Seattle,
Washington. The three black-robed men held in their
hands the fate of what had been Europe's largest industry
for almost a century.

The prosecution was led by Colonel (later Brigadier
General) Telford Taylor, at the time United States Chief
Counsel for War Crimes. The forty-one-year-old lawyer
had served in various agencies of the New Deal, starting
in the AAA with Henry Wallace, until he was drafted
into the army, where he assisted Mr. Justice Jackson in
the prosecution of war criminals. After the "major" trial,
he succeeded him on the job.

Guarded by steel-helmeted GI's, the twelve defendants
sat side by side on their bench. They were managers and
sub-managers of the House of Krupp; on their right, as
chief defendant, sat the heir and head of the house. Alfried Krupp looked more haggard and serious than ever.
Since his arrest at the hilltop palace a year and a half
ago, he had been held in detention camps and prison cells
unaware of the fact that a trial against him was in the
planning. Only a few months before it opened did he
learn the nature of the charges leveled against him and
the facts that his frequent interrogations had attempted to
establish. These interrogations were conducted by a specially organized "Krupp Trial Team." A battery of German lawyers—with their assistants numbering more than
thirty—was present to defend Krupp and his directors,
while hundreds of interpreters, researchers, technicians,
newsmen, and visiting dignitaries from back home
crowded the courtroom. Everybody but the military
guards was equipped with earphones which transmitted
simultaneous translations from German into English and
vice versa. In both atmosphere and appearance, the
courtroom recalled a big and businesslike international
conference.

The Krupp Case went on for approximately eleven
months. Over 200 witnesses were heard and the tran-
script of its proceedings ran to 13,454 mimeographed

pages, with more than 4200 written exhibits. In outward appearance it was a thoroughgoing trial.

It was also a unique trial. Conducted under the American flag by an American court according to new, international rules of law valid in neither America nor Germany, it tried German defendants for alleged crimes committed when and where German law had been applicable. The American prosecuting staff and the German counsel for the defense struggled like a team of boxers with a team of wrestlers, each bound by its own rules and techniques, which were based on the different legal and cultural conceptions of two different peoples. Because German lawyers could be expected to be at a disadvantage in a contest with the victors on the basis of laws they hardly knew, Alfried Krupp tried to strengthen his defense battery by adding Earl J. Carrol, an American lawyer from California, who specialized in foreign occupation cases. But the court refused to admit him. In protest, Alfried Krupp declared that he would prefer no lawyer at all, and his chief counsel resigned, until the court appointed him as defense counsel and forced him to serve.

The court and the defense counsel clashed again when the latter objected to witnesses being heard by commissioners in camera rather than in court, which excluded cross-examination. The German attorneys asked for a recess to consult on this question, but the court refused to grant it. When they left the room under protest, the court had them brought back by force and arrested six of them for contempt of court. Neither German law nor international law—on the basis of both of which the Germans were being tried—incorporated the concept of "contempt of court" for which these lawyers were punished. Throughout the trial, the defense was at a conspicuous disadvantage while the prosecution was favored to a degree which would hardly be tolerated in American courtrooms.

As the prosecutor read the charges on which Alfried Krupp and his fellow defendants were indicted, their crimes seemed grave. According to the prosecution, they had committed "crimes against peace," since they "participated in the initiation of invasion of other countries and

wars of aggression in violation of international laws and
treaties"; as was explained, they had planned, prepared,
and waged World War II. Next they were charged with
"war crimes and crimes against humanity," which consisted of their "participation in the plunder, exploitation,
spoliation, devastation, and other offenses against property and the civilian economies" of Nazi-occupied countries. Furthermore, Krupp and his directors "participated
in atrocities and offenses including murder, extermina-
tion, enslavement, deportation, imprisonment, torture,
abuse, and other inhumane acts against civilians; and also
in their persecutions on political, racial, and religious
grounds." The fourth and last count charged all the defendants with "a common plan and conspiracy" to com-
mit these crimes against peace and humanity.

The lengthy and passionate charges made it appear as
if "Krupp," rather than Hitler and his henchmen, bore
the main guilt for the crimes of the totalitarian regime in
peace and in war. Nazism, the prosecutor submitted,
"was, after all, only the temporary political manifestation
of certain ideas and attitudes which long antedated Nazism and which will not perish nearly as easily. In this
case," he explained the Krupp Case, "we are at grips with
something much older than Nazism, something which
fused with Nazi ideas to produce the *Third Reich* but
which has its own independent and pernicious vitality." If
this sounded vague, it also sounded ominous. The steel
combine seemed surrounded with mysteriously sinister secret powers.

But after studying the indictment, the court dismissed
the counts of preparation for war and conspiracy against
all twelve representatives of Krupp. A mountain of implications had been built against them to prove their guilt.
But it proved merely what was well known, denied by nobody, and in accordance with the law, that is, that the
firm for a century had produced weapons at high profits.
If, as the prosecution claimed, the Firm of Krupp had
been preparing for an aggressive war since the end of
World War I in 1918, Alfried Krupp was at that time still
a school boy and none of his fellow defendants had then

been with the firm. In fact, among all the defendants only Alfried Krupp and Ewald Loeser—who, as we remember, joined the firm in 1937 as a cover for his anti-Nazi and antiwar activities—had been directors before the war which they were alleged to have prepared. Instead of evidence, only glimmering generalities were submitted to prove that the defendants participated in, or even knew of, Hitler's conspiracy to unleash his aggressions.

Over the next three months, the court heard testimony on Krupp's guilt of wartime thievery and inhumanity. The Nazi times—which had hardly passed, but had already paled in the minds of many—were revived in all their fear and fury while the witnesses, some themselves victims of the evil-doers, told their stories.

A few of these testimonies seemed surprising. For instance, an elderly art historian reported that on a Saturday afternoon of 1940 he had visited the director of a huge soap concern to sell him a painting. This happened to be the afternoon on which Germany invaded Holland, and by chance four fellow industrialists, Alfried Krupp among them, were guests of his customer. When they heard the news over the radio, the witness told the court, they jumped up, rushed to a map, and pointing to it, distributed among themselves the Dutch industries. "They resembled vultures gathered around their booty, and you may believe that a man like I, an art historian, who has dedicated his life to the preservation of culture, was bound to be very much shaken by this," the witness said. That Europe's hugest industrialist should stake his claims to foreign holdings under these circumstances, and in such a way, would seem more likely in one of the less realistic comic strips than in Ruhr reality. What seemed even more surprising was that the judges accepted this testimony at face value, and based their judgment on it.

But other testimony was heard from witnesses who knew quite well what they said, and whose reliability could not be doubted. Among them were a few owners and managers of industries in Nazi-occupied countries whose plants had been taken over by the Krupp combine. They were followed by Kruppians who denounced the sadistic treatment which a number of Krupp's foremen had meted out to slave workers. There appeared also before the court a Catholic priest, a government official, a newspaperwoman from Belgium, and a young Jewish woman from Hungary, former slave laborers who had suffered greatly while working for Krupp. Other witnesses included Nazis in and out of the firm who described their past misdeeds with the same "sense of duty" with which they had committed them; highranking officials who explained the working of the slave labor organization with the technical accuracy of specialists; Germans who had helped the foreign victims and other Germans who had seen it all and had done nothing about it.

The cruelty, cowardice, and misery brought about by the Nazi rule were presented to the court with impressive examples, and they proved that the House of Krupp had been deeply enmeshed in the evil. Following the tradition of the firm, Krupp and his fellow managers had tried to remain *unpolitisch* to the point of self-deceit. This point was reached when the totalitarian system forced and tempted its armorer to be its accomplice. If the totalitarian system led the House of Krupp and its heir into this trap, Krupp's very heritage set the direction. It was its legacy which commanded that the firm be profitably preserved.

It was this heritage of five generations of Krupps that was on trial. For his heritage, the youngest heir was charged with crimes of whose commission he could not have been personally aware. While he headed the firm for a year and a half, he was at best only the titular head of a collective leadership and not able to oversee all that went on in the seventy auxiliaries of his combine, which employed close to a quarter of a million people. But then, "the tradition" which he had inherited and upheld made him the sole leader of, and solely responsible for, his whole empire. While he inherited the claim to responsibilities which he could not fulfill, he was also accused of crimes for which he was not responsible. Where did his responsibility begin?—where did it end? Was irresponsibility—which surely is a grave sin—a crime according to law? Were the moral myopia, cowardice, and callousness of the "economic man" crimes? Can the actions of men under totalitarian rule be judged by the standards of a society which safeguards freedom of conscience and action for every citizen? These moral questions transcended by far the legal questions.

Alfried Krupp did not attempt to answer the questions put to him. He sat through his trial as quietly and passively as he had sat through his meetings with his directors, with authorities—Nazi and others—with his workers, a perfect gentleman who listened and tried to understand. Throughout the court proceedings he remained silent. His lawyers had advised him to let them do the talking. Slim, serious, elegant even in the defendant's dock, Alfried resembled Alfred Krupp only in outward appearance. He kept his temper, if he had any, under complete control. In his posture he appeared to be watching a stage drama of no concern and little interest to himself, and his mind seemed often to wander off altogether. His twelve managers in the dock did not speak up, either. When they were asked a question, they answered as matter-of-factly as if a business deal were under discussion.

Before judgment was pronounced, Alfried Krupp and Ewald Loeser made the final statement in their own as well as their fellow defendants' names. Loeser spoke first to outline the political background of the Nazi years. "Once liberty is lost, it is too late," he quoted U. S. Secretary of State Edward Stettinius, and went on to explain that when the Germans had lost their liberty in a moment of crisis it was too late for them to recover it. While he denounced Hitler's abuse of power, his contempt for the dignity of man, and his destruction of individual responsibility, he admitted: "The evil which emanated from the head of State asserted itself throughout the country with all-embracing power until the foundations of law and order were shaken." This was the first and only time that the moral dilemma of citizens under totalitarian rule was articulated in the trial. And although he did not elaborate on it, Loeser himself was a living example of this dilemma in its extreme. In order to plot Hitler's fall and to

prepare a reign of decency, he had been led to mask, and
sometimes act, as one of his followers. If he was guilty,
his guilt was only cloak and consequence of his innocence.

Different, and less lucid, was the final statement of Alfried Krupp who spoke, as he emphasized, "as a member
of the fifth generation [of Krupps] which produced steel,
and the fourth generation which forged weapons." He
considered himself an innocent victim of old slanders
against his family and his trade, a victim of misconcep-
tions on the nature of economics and of his own role.
Much as he regretted the mistreatment of foreign workers, he asserted that he had not known of it, and that he
had acquired foreign properties only under Nazi pressure.
"In the final analysis," he said, "we are charged with
cooperation, while we did only our duty during the war,
as did millions of Germans at home and at the front." As
he saw it, his first duty was toward the tradition and the
survival of the House of Krupp. The Commandments,
which put other duties first, did not seem to have left a
deep mark on his mind. He felt the same love for his firm
which others felt for their fatherland and their faith.
Though his words were manifestly honest, they disclosed
that he lacked the moral and intellectual perspicacity to
understand what he had done, and what was done to him.
He did not perceive the demon which had turned and
rended.

The three judges of the Nuremberg tribunal found all
the defendants in the dock guilty on both counts. In the
court's opinion, Krupp and his managers had violated international law as individuals when their firm took over
—in one case, leased—six French and Dutch industrial
properties; while the prosecution had charged them with
the same offense in five additional occupied countries
under German military rule, the judgment did not mention these charges, nor did it acquit the defendants of
these charges. Second, they were held guilty as heads of
an organization in which foreign workers, concentration-
camp inmates, and prisoners of war were employed, exploited, and mistreated.

The sentence recognized no mitigating circumstances, much to the discomfort of the presiding judge. Alfried Krupp was sentenced to twelve years in prison. Ewald Loeser, who had escaped the Nazi hangman three years before, was sentenced to seven years. Their colleagues received prison terms up to twelve years.

In addition to his prison term, the head of the House of Krupp was sentenced to forfeiture of all his property, both personal and real. With his freedom, he lost also his firm and his fortune, a fall from which it seemed there could be no rise.

In the words of an American trial interpreter, Alfried reacted to the pronouncement "as if the whole theater didn't concern him." A few German spectators came to press his hand, but rather than accept their sympathies he shrugged his shoulders and wished them well. When Dr. Stefan Graf von Schlippenbach, a German engineering expert involved in business negotiations with the firm, wanted to console him, Krupp reassured his well-wisher instead: "Don't you worry, your case will be straightened out to your complete satisfaction." The penniless convict was still a *grand seigneur* in every word and gesture.

That the personal properties of convicted war criminals be expropriated as a special punishment had been proposed by the Soviet representative when the four Allied Powers prepared the statutes of the tribunals. The representative of the United States, Justice Jackson, however, had objected. "It would be somewhat obsolete as a penalty . . . like drawing and quartering," he sarcastically remarked. (In its Report 3080, the United States State Department published this remark shortly before sentence in the Krupp Case was pronounced.) While such a penalty was in line with Soviet totalitarian thinking, it violated the standards of justice which free nations uphold. According to these standards, property can be confiscated only if and when there is a causal connection between the criminal act for which the defendant is tried and the acquisition of his property. In less legal terms, it can be taken away from him only if he has been sentenced for having stolen it. But the trial neither submitted nor showed that Krupp's fortune had been acquired by theft or in other illegal ways. Therefore, Presiding Judge Anderson did formally "dissent from the order confiscating his [Alfried Krupp's] property," which he considered illegal. Of the almost two hundred German culprits before the Nuremberg tribunal, none but Alfried Krupp had his property expropriated. The tribunal did not explain why it seemed to ignore the American principle of equality before the law in the case of Krupp.

Who, then, was to take over Krupp? According to the sentence, the new heir was the Allied Control Council in which the United States and its two Western allies, as well as the Soviet Union, were represented. In practical terms, these four powers would settle in the Ruhr and run Krupp. This disposition, which had been suggested before in the Morgenthau Plan, had been the goal of the Soviet leaders throughout the war and postwar years. If they held their hands on this industrial heart of West Germany as owner of its iron and coal, its steelmaking and manufacturing power, they shared in the control—economic and political—of Western Europe. With partial control of the Ruhr, Soviet industrial potential would be on a par with that of America. In the course of their postwar expansion into Europe, where they annexed, subdued, exploited, and colonialized captive nations from Czechoslovakia, Hungary, Poland, and the Baltic countries to East Germany, the control of Krupp was the last stepping stone to total control. When the American tribunal in Nuremberg decided to invite the Soviets to Essen and to let them share in the Krupp combine, the Soviets had begun their blockade of West Berlin which the United States defended by its great airlift. Surprisingly, America offered control of the Krupp combine to its enemy in the cold war.

Seven months later General Lucius D. Clay, Military Governor and Commander-in-Chief of the European Command of the U. S. Army, confirmed the sentence against "Alfried Krupp, et al." "On the whole, though," he reported, "those of us who were responsible for the trials feel that the full evidence will provide history with an unparalleled record of how greed and avarice attract unscrupulous hands to bring misery and destruction to the world. Certainly in reviewing the cases which came before me, I felt no hesitancy in approving the sentences."

But on one point, he did revise the judgment. He annulled the provision that Krupp's forfeited and confiscated properties be handed over to the Allied Control Council with its Soviet partner. In the first place, this Council had ceased to function, since the Soviet partners consistently had violated their agreements with the Western powers. And General Clay knew full well what would happen if the Ruhr gates were opened to the Russians, a catastrophe he wished to avoid. In a brilliant move he decreed that Krupp's properties were "subject to confiscation by the Allied commanders of the occupation zones in which they were situated." Essen and the Ruhr were in the British occupation zone; Krupp's Bertha Works at Markstaedt went to Silesia, which had been occupied by the Polish Communists; only the huge Krupp machine works in Magdeburg lay in the Soviet zone. The Soviet commanders alone took advantage of the American-granted privilege and operated the former Krupp works in their zone as part and parcel of the new Soviet arms production. The United States did not claim for itself a share in the loot.

Alfried Krupp and his fellow convicts, Ewald Loeser, the anti-Hitler resistance fighter, among them, were sent to the fortress of Landsberg-am-Lech, a medieval stronghold converted into a prison. In this fortress, in 1924, Hitler had served his term and written his *Mein Kampf*, after his beer-hall *Putsch* had failed and he was convicted of treason. Alfried Krupp shared the prison with more than one hundred and fifty other war criminals. The motley mass of men included killers, diplomats, and generals.

While Alfried was spending his first year in prison, Gustav Krupp died. A week later, Bertha claimed the family fortune which she and her lawyers estimated at well over 500 million dollars. The *Lex Krupp*, she suddenly submitted to the Allied authorities, which estab-

lished her son Alfried as the sole heir and owner, was unlawful since it was issued by the *Führer* in violation of the
law of the land. She asked the Allied High Commissioners to disinherit her jailed son and to allow her and her
other children to share the inheritance. Alfried's brothers
and sisters supported the petition. Apparently they hoped
to restore the legacy to the Krupp family. But the Allied
High Commissioners did not comply.

Alfried Krupp was assigned to the prison smithy-team.
In his spare time, he welded cast-iron candlesticks for a
neighborhood church and read novels from the prison library. According to his fellow prisoners and the GI's who
guarded him, he was a model prisoner. He spoke little,
and almost only with former Krupp managers, but he
shared his cigarettes and his food packages with anybody
who seemed in need. Although his prison routine was severe, he never complained. He received and wrote few
letters, mainly concerning business and family affairs. The
only exception was his warm, uplifting correspondence
with Annelise, the woman he loved, and whom he had
deserted to preserve his inheritance.

While he wore the red-and-white-striped Landsberg
prison uniform, he made it a point, as he often said, not
to think of the past, and he refused to discuss it with his
jailmates, let alone with his jailers. Like his father at the
dinner table of Villa Hügel, Alfried cut off all questions
with a *"Hier wird nicht politisiert."* No politics here!

A young and friendly German-born GI guard in
Landsberg once asked Alfried how he preferred to be addressed: *Herr* Krupp, or *Herr* von Bohlen, or possibly by
his full, legal name, *Herr* Krupp von Bohlen und Halbach? "Call me Krupp," the prisoner told him. "It's on
account of that name that I am here." And, in an attempt
to joke, he added: "This cell is my share in the great
Krupp legacy." He did not smile, however, while he made
this remark, which seemed quite serious indeed.

PART IV

Krupp in Our Time

1953-1959

11

The New Look

Alfried Krupp had begun his sixth year in prison—and his third in Landsberg Fortress—when John J. McCloy, the recently appointed American High Commissioner for Germany, studied his case anew. McCloy's succession to General Lucius D. Clay marked a new era of the United States in Germany. While the General had ruled as Military Governor, McCloy, a distinguished banker with a good record in public service, served as High Commissioner. This change in titles signaled the transition from the military occupation of a defeated enemy to the civilian supervision of a friendly nation on its way to sovereignty and freedom. The hurricane that devastated Germany had run its course. Gentler winds had begun to blow, and the economy, the democratic spirit, and the peaceful community were recovering. Visibly this new Germany stood on the side of the West which in turn was waging its cold war with the totalitarians of the Soviet world.

After two years in Germany, McCloy had made great progress toward the proclaimed goal of binding Germany more firmly to the West, and the West more firmly to Germany. A partnership between the two nations was evolving in defense against the common Soviet enemy.

By the end of 1950, with the Korean War going full blast, McCloy recommended that the Clemency Board for War Crime Trials—a body under his supervision—revise the punishment meted out to Alfried Krupp and his fellow Kruppians. On January 31, 1951, two and a half

years after sentence was pronounced, McCloy granted an
amnesty to all the convicts of the Krupp Case. He ended
their prison terms and set aside the confiscation order of
Krupp's fortune which, as he declared, was "generally re-
pugnant to American concepts of justice."

This decision was reached only after intensive study.
As McCloy explained it, Alfried Krupp had had little active influence on the leadership of his firm. The other
Ruhr industrialists, all of whom had employed slave
labor, had received much lighter sentences or none at all.
And the confiscation of Krupp's fortune did not correspond to civilized standards of equality before the law.

Hardly had McCloy announced his decision when a
storm of protest broke loose, particularly in England. As
he explained in a private letter, he could not understand
it. The British themselves had originally protested the in-
clusion of German industrialists among the war criminals,
and had called it an unwarranted act of revenge on the
part of the Americans. Now that the decision had been
reversed, they attacked America for showing mercy to
Krupp. But in matters like this, McCloy felt one cannot
follow the public temper, but only one's own conscience.
He acted accordingly. Early in the morning of April 9,
1951, crowds of weary-looking women, prosperous-look-
ing men, photographers, and reporters arrived at Landsberg Fortress. In a tensely cheerful, expectant mood, they
assembled before the gate at which they stared fixedly. At
nine o'clock sharp, the bored GI guards came to attention, the prison commander opened the heavy door, and
twenty-nine prisoners were on their way to freedom.
Among them, and towering over them, was Alfried
Krupp.

While some of his colleagues hastened to the prison
cemetery to bid farewell to dead comrades, he shook
hands over and over with his personal reception committee—his brother, who greeted him with a bouquet of tulips, his managers, his lawyers. After six years in jail he
appeared hardly changed. As ever he was chain-smoking,
well dressed, haggard, and serious. When the newsmen
cornered him for an interview he answered their ques-

tions politely but shortly. He refused to describe, let alone complain about, his prison experiences. One must never see the world through the eyes of a prisoner, he said, who sees things only in distortion. Neither did he answer a reporter's question about what he thought of Nazism. "We would have to rehash the whole trial record," he said, nervously shrugging his shoulders. "Please spare me all that." Would he produce cannons again in his new freedom? another reporter wanted to know. "I have no personal desire or intention to do so," the son and heir of the Cannon Kings answered, "but I think the problem will be solved by the German government, not by my private inclinations." Other reporters took up the question. "I hope it'll never again be necessary for Krupp to go into the arms business," Alfried Krupp elaborated, "but what a factory produces depends, after all, not only on the will of its owner but on the politics of its government." And in an aside, making humility sound haughty, he added: "My life has always been shaped by the course of history rather than by myself."

In the manner of a well-bred guest who has long enjoyed the hospitality of a friend, he found kindly words of thanks for his host. The American colonel commanding the prison, he said, was "a real gentleman." His lawyers took him to a champagne breakfast in the local inn before he left for Blühnbach Castle where his mother awaited him. But Alfried could not go home again.

Villa Hügel was still occupied by the British and the firm still subject to a British Controller. Since 1950, when the leaders and public opinion of the United States had begun to realize that it weakened the free world, dismantling had been discontinued. But the industrial giant of Essen stirred only sluggishly when its collective leadership of six devoted and able managers tried to put it back on its feet. With the authorization of the Controller, the Widia tungsten-carbide works was the first Krupp factory to start producing again. Its output was badly needed for hard-cutting parts of coal-mining and industrial tools. Next the locomotive section began repair work on locomotives and rolling stock of the German railway. The third step was the opening of the heavy engineering section at Rheinhausen. Besides producing boilers and electrical machines, it also contributed to the vast postwar bridge-building program for the broken-down West German road and rail systems. Twelve thousand seven hundred men worked again at Krupp, about one-twentieth of the labor force employed before its heir was arrested.

But all this was merely a miscellany of more or less healthy independent factories rather than a strong combine. Missing was the firm's old and steady heart, the cast-steel factory, much of which had been shipped to victor countries, mainly in Eastern Europe, and the rest destroyed. The firm had also lost other one-time vital and procreative organs, particularly the iron and coal mines and mills that had supplied its raw materials. The financial worth of these lost subsidiaries amounted to more than half of the Krupp fortune. The Firm of Krupp had always been primarily a steel plant on which its subsidiaries depended, whether they supplied raw materials or manufactured finished products. They had grown like branches from an old and strong tree. But since the Allied Law had "deconcentrated German heavy industry," Alfried held in his hands only a dozen branches, with some deadwood among them. The trunk was gone.

Whether he was to head his firm again remained as doubtful as his actual property rights and his present position as its heir. The occupation law still banished him from his office in the firm. The exiled ruler of a detruncated empire moved to a modest furnished apartment in the Essen suburb of Bredeney which lies nearer to Villa Hügel than to the factory grounds. "I thought it might take fifty years, or more perhaps, until we were on our feet again," he admitted later, "but I never doubted that the day of our new rise would come."

Alfried Krupp felt despoiled, but not despondent. In his new freedom, he wanted to start a new life, and not merely as far as the firm was concerned. He wanted also a new, happier life for himself. He was forty-five years old, healthy, lonely, and on the rebound.

About a year after his release from jail, on a visit to

Hamburg where he attended business meetings by day and opera performances in the evening, he chanced upon an old acquaintance whom his first wife had introduced to him as Vera Hossenfeld. At present her name had grown to Vera Hossenfeld von Langer Wisbar Knauer. She was in Hamburg on a visit from the United States where she made her home. In her thirties, groomed by America's best beauty experts, aggressively gay and worldly, she bore little resemblance to the provincial Essen *hausfrau* and to the pompous mistresses of the Ruhr manors whom Alfried was accustomed to meeting, and she also seemed quite different from his soft-spoken, retreating first wife.

The daughter of a German insurance agent, Vera had been married three times. After a Baron von Langer, she wed Frank Wisbar, a promising German drama producer with whom she emigrated to Hollywood. When America accepted the newcomers with less generously open arms than they had expected, she worked as a clerk in a Los Angeles department store, then as a receptionist for a refugee doctor. After a Las Vegas divorce from her still hapless husband, she married the doctor, was naturalized as a United States citizen, divorced her third husband, too, and went on a trip to her native land, where she ran into the heir of the House of Krupp.

A few months after their brief encounter, Alfried married Vera. Their secret wedding was performed at Berchtesgaden, a beautiful Bavarian resort village hidden away in the Alps, where Hitler had once had his mountaintop retreat. The couple drove to the registrar in the battered car of their innkeeper who with his wife served as a witness to the ceremony. They were the only guests at the wedding dinner in the inn's dining room, whose sole decoration consisted of empty chianti bottles. The groom presented the bride with an expensive Porsche sports car and fifteen tulips. After a brief honeymoon, Frau Vera—as the successor to Frau Bertha, Frau Marga, and all the other *frauen* of Krupp tradition—was received in Essen with full honors due to the new queen.

Alfried Krupp searched for new faces and new avenues

in his days of new freedom. It was in this mood that he met Berthold Beitz, a thirty-nine-year-old businessman, and, by German standards, a very young and very successful one. Their chance encounter was to ring in the comeback of the Firm of Krupp under a new leadership and with a new look, or, perhaps, a new spirit.

Beitz had come to Essen to see Jean Sprenger, an equally young and successful sculptor devoted to that slick linear style much in demand by postwar German businessmen. They liked to decorate the stripped façades of their barracklike new office buildings with "a little art" —nudes, or dolphins and buffaloes, or slightly blasphemous saints and madonnas. Berthold Beitz wished to commission a nude statue for the new office building of the Germania-Iduna Life Insurance Co., which he headed and for which he had built its glass-walled administration building. After the artist and his Maecenas came to terms, they went to a dinner given by Sprenger's friend, Berthold von Bohlen und Halbach. Casually the host asked Beitz whether he had met his brother, Alfried Krupp. No, the visitor said, he had never met him and he should be delighted if a meeting could be arranged. "After all," Herr Beitz later on explained with a smile, "I was a young man and Krupp's name sounded sort of magic to me."

Three days later Alfried Krupp and Berthold Beitz were introduced to each other. In their backgrounds and personalities they could hardly have been more different. Beitz stemmed from Pomerania, a North German country still untouched by modern industry and little touched by modern ways. On the expansive "knights' estates" of which it largely consisted, the *junkers* grew their wheat and upheld their feudal past as if serfdom still were the order of the day. Beitz's ancestors had been estate managers, a position far below the noble owners but high above the semi-serfs who did the menial work. Young Berthold Beitz left these surroundings as a boy when his father, a former sergeant in the Pomeranian Lancers' regiment, became a state bank teller in a neighboring small town. After graduation from the *Gymnasium* young Berthold learned banking as an apprentice in the local bank, but seeing only poor prospects of advancement there, he found a new and better job with the Hamburg office of the British-Dutch Shell Oil trust. Although these were the Hitler years, he never joined a Nazi organization. "I can't stand them," he confided to his best friends. Soon his business abilities were noticed by his superiors at Shell and he was promoted.

During the war, he was appointed administrator of the Borislaw oil fields in occupied Poland. Polish resistance fighters and Jews later testified that he had courageously helped them while they were hunted by the Nazis. Toward the end of the war he was imprisoned by the Russians but succeeded in escaping and made his way to West Germany. For a while he lived in a suburban garden-tool shed with his wife, his two daughters, and his refugee parents. Impressed by his good political record, his promising business background, and particularly by his former work for the Shell concern, the British occupation authorities appointed him a director of the Hamburg Private Insurance Control Authority. As he told this writer, he did not know a thing about insurance at the time, and it bored him. He invited the oldtimers of his and other firms—all of whom had been involved one way or another with the Nazis, and were therefore sentenced to clean streets and do other chores for the occupation rulers—to come up to his office and teach him the elementals of his new craft. He quickly mastered it. Three years later, when the Currency Reform of 1949 laid the groundwork for German economic recovery, Berthold Beitz resigned from his post to go into private business as director-general of the Germania-Iduna Life Insurance Co. This company was then sixteenth in size among German insurance companies, and Beitz pushed it by aggressive sales campaigns and mergers to third place. To be an imposing director-general in accordance with the image of his own dreams, he took up puffing cigars, although they made him sick.

Beitz's meeting with Alfried Krupp was pleasant. They chatted about cars and planes, music and sailing, the

Essen and Hamburg climates. No talk about business, although this would seem to have been the main subject of mutual interest. Strangely the tired heir and the young man "hit it off with each other swimmingly," as Beitz, a devotee of American slang, put it after their first meeting. While Alfried Krupp looked older than his forty-five years, Beitz looked much younger than his thirty-nine. In contrast to Alfried's shy and taciturn manner, Beitz was bubbling with jokes, ideas, and laughter; Krupp was serious about the most unimportant questions, while Beitz seemed cynical even about the most important ones. In psychological terms, one was as complete an introvert as the other was an extrovert. But there were still other and deeper contrasts. Alfried Krupp spoke of his mother in the ways of an hagiographer, while Berthold Beitz reverently described his mother, in the American slang which he loved, as a "tough baby." Alfried was burdened by the family tradition of four previous generations. Beitz lacked a sense of tradition, but the war and postwar years had taught him that to survive it was every man for himself.

After a month, Alfried and Vera Krupp came to Hamburg where they met Beitz and his wife for dinner at the *Hotel Vier Jahreszeiten.* A week later, the Krupps invited the Beitzes a second time. After dinner they had a few drinks at the hotel bar, with the ladies doing most of the talking. Toward midnight, when the bar began to empty and the waiters demonstrated discreetly that they wanted to close up, Alfried Krupp asked in a stuttering embarrassment whether he might ask Beitz a question. "Frankly," Beitz said later, "I expected him to ask me for a loan." But Krupp asked him for a favor of a different kind. "I think we could work together very well," he said. "Will you come to Essen and help me rebuild my firm?" Without a moment's thought and without showing his surprise, with his best smile of boyish innocence, Beitz said: "Yes, I will, if my board of directors will let me go." It was a year before the board agreed to release Beitz.

As he told it later, he never regretted his decision, and neither did Alfried Krupp. Tired and burdened by his heritage of five generations, he felt that fresh blood, and fresh elbows as well, were needed to keep the House of Krupp alive. Shrewdly he looked for a manager who, in contrast to all the other able men in the firm, was an outsider without ties to the steel and other heavy industries, and free from past traditions. Beitz knew nothing whatever about steel, had no experience in the iron and coal industries, but had proved his worth as an aggressive modern businessman of the postwar school. Krupp could hardly have found a better man for his new firm.

The part assigned to the young outsider initiated a managerial revolution in the House of Krupp. If up to now the owner had ruled the firm, he would content himself in the future with reigning over it and letting Beitz do the managing. The manner in which Beitz appeared on the scene at Essen demonstrated the New Look that went with the managerial revolution. The workers and other Kruppians called him "the American" because he was informal and brash, two qualities which the good people of Essen associate with America. He showed his cheerful, almost cruel, contempt for the stuffy, overly dignified ways in which the older Kruppians gloried. Rather than be addressed by his resounding title of *Herr Generaldirekto*r, he told everybody, "Just call me Beitz." And added, "If I like the job you do, I'll call you by your first name." He dressed in the latest Madison Avenue style, let it be known that he was an addict of hot jazz, and liked to spice his speech with generous helpings of "O.K." as well as "k.o.," applying the latter expression to everybody in his way. He would have cut a very strange figure in America, but Essen accepted him as "the American." Such pseudo-Americans, copying what they think is native, although it does not conform at all with reality, have become familiar characters on the foreign postwar scene. Beitz personified and shaped Krupp's New Look; in the years to come, he would lead it to victory.

On his very first morning in the firm, he ordered the old-fashioned *"paternosters,"* an antique kind of elevators still operating in Krupp's office building, to be overhauled and made to run more quickly; employees were wasting too much time moving from one floor to the next,

he said. After he had been on his job for a while, one of
his directors objected to a rule given by Beitz. The
general manager fired him on the spot. When this writer
asked Beitz whether it was true that he had told the director to pack up and leave the building within five minutes, Beitz smiled his toothiest smile. "That shows how
people make up stories," he said. "There isn't a true word
in it; in fact, I gave him fifteen minutes to leave."

The innovation most surprising to a first incredulous,
then skeptical, world was the repeated assertion that the
new Krupp wanted to desist from the production of arms
both now and in the future. This reflected the outlook of
many younger Germans of Beitz's generation. They had
come to hate militarism and all things military. *Ohne
mich*—without me—which was their slogan in response
to the call for a new German defense army became,
under Beitz, Krupp's new public-relations as well as production principle. Alfried's own unhappy experience laid
the groundwork. Beitz expanded it into the business policy of the firm. But then, this was less of a break with
Krupp tradition than it seemed. In the first place, rockets,
missiles, and atomic weaponry had taken over the spot-
light of arms production; cannons, armor plate, and the
like which had made Krupp famous, began to look old-
fashioned. In the second place, Krupp, as we have seen,
had produced arms because, or when, they brought or
promised profits. *Unpolitisch* from the very beginning, the
Krupps had satisfied the demands of other countries and
their own country as businessmen. The Nuremberg trial,
and the fall that preceded and followed it, left them with
a trauma. While they still remained as *unpolitisch* as before, they mistook cause for effect, and decided to give up
the arms business rather than the irresponsible business-
only, nonpolitical principle. In terms of profits and prospects, it seemed more advantageous for the firm to concentrate on making articles other than arms—anything
but arms. "After the next war," Beitz told us with a
smile, "it will be the electronics manufacturers and the
missile makers who will stand before a war crime tribunal, not us."

A third and decisive reason for Krupp's radical break with its most traditional, most glorified, and most denounced business was the new industrial structure that had been imposed on it by the victors. In its whole previous history, the Firm of Krupp had been a steelmaking concern which had expanded to include everything from raw materials to finished goods. Since the Allied dismantling and deconcentration measures had excised the core, there remained for Krupp only its former secondary production in engineering and related fields. This was to be the new mainstay of the firm and to determine its New Look.

The old firm with the New Look won freedom of action in the beginning of 1953, when the American High Commission in Germany jointly with the two other Western former occupation powers arrived at an agreement with Alfried Krupp; as it were, a state treaty concluded by three soverign powers with a fourth. The treaty reinstated Alfried as the head of his firm and settled the new frontiers of his property. Negotiations between his lawyers and American, British, and French government lawyers and economists had begun almost immediately after his release from Landsberg Fortress, when his firm was still threatened by Allied seizure. Allied Law 27 forced him—along with all the other great German heavy-industry combines—to "deconcentrate" his holdings, that is, to sell the heavy industrial (mining and steelmaking) sections of his empire.

But could he be restrained from acquiring new steel-mills after he sold his old plants? The new West German government was doubtful whether it could lawfully enforce the deconcentration policy. On the other hand, the Allies planned to let Alfried Krupp return to his firm only if they received from his special, ironclad, personal guarantees that he would live up to their intent and not build up again the traditional family empire in horizontal and vertical concentration. Reluctantly supported by their American colleagues, the French and British spokesmen insisted that Krupp's holdings could be returned to their owner only if his power was broken forever by a special settlement. Not only was the former heart of his empire —all the iron, coal, and steelmaking facilities—to be wrested from him, but safeguards had to be set up to prevent him from acquiring new ones. For more than eighteen months, negotiations for a peace treaty between Krupp and the Allies continued. It was as hard a struggle as any at an international conference table between big powers with conflicting interests The spokesman of the German government who came to participate uneasily shifted between Allied and Krupp viewpoints.

At the very first meeting, three Americans clashed— Mr. Carrol and Mr. Robinson, representing the House of Krupp, and Mr. Willner, representing the United States. Mr. Willner brought a statement which Alfried Krupp was to sign, with his pledge: "I have no intention of going back into the basic coal and steel industries in Germany, and I undertake not to use any of the funds received from the sale of any of the properties or securities under this plan for the purchase of an interest in the basic steel or basic coal-producing industries in Germany." But Alfried Krupp and his lawyers refused to sign. Such a statement, they submitted, violated the Basic Law, as the new democratic constitution of Germany was called. It guaranteed equal rights to all citizens. The statement, Krupp claimed, would discriminate against him and deprive him of his civil rights, as it would make it unlawful for him to engage in a business in which everybody else could freely engage. In short this would be a new, special *Lex Krupp*, applying only to him and his house, though this time taking his civil rights away rather than granting him personal privilege. It was only the latter kind of special law which Krupps found acceptable.

Krupp submitted a counterdraft with the validity of his pledge limited to the next ten years. By then everything would be forgiven and forgotten. The American government representative agreed. After all, he said, it was merely a political statement to throw a sop to "certain elements" of public opinion in the countries of wartime Allies (as Krupp's lawyer informed his colleagues in a letter). But the French and the British refused to go along. The treaty was to be valid for Alfried's lifetime.

Negotiations almost broke up again when Krupp insisted that the term "steel or iron-producing industry" was too vague. For instance, the Widia tungsten-carbide works might be included in the ban, although they did not produce steel in the technological sense and he planned to keep running them. After much wrangling, a "letter of definition" was worked out to be annexed to the treaty. It explained that Alfried Krupp was to be barred from "the making of alloy steel by any method except in small quantities incidental to the enterprises which will remain in the possession of Alfried Krupp." The same was set down for "the hot rolling of steel." But, it was added, "the production of Widia is not regarded as part of the steel-producing industry." Krupp won his point, since the definition left him free to produce the steel "incidental" to new orders if he bought the raw-steel ingots and did not make them himself.

Struggles over other formulations continued over many meetings, one being exclusively concerned with two commas in the draft, another with subtleties of a translation from the English original to the German language.

After eighteen months, Alfried Krupp signed the declaration affirming that by his own free volition he renounced what was considered the basic tradition and trade of his house. The reasoning that led him to sign this treaty, as it was described in confidential files of the firm, in the private arguments of his lawyers, and in his own personal statements, revealed the vigor with which the old tradition survived under the New Look.

His signature, the Allies said, would bind him in a legal as well as in a moral way. It was a treaty, and as the British representative insisted, a gentleman's agreement. Alfried seemed to agree with them, but felt not at all bound by a pledge which, he privately said, had been "extorted" from him by a "form of blackmail." "If we hadn't signed," his chief lawyer explained later on, "they would not have given anything back to Krupp; they would have taken away everything." Literally, the same words had been used before to explain Krupp's compliance with

Nazi orders. Krupps never say no when it would endanger their control of the firm

His lawyers informed him that he had little to fear from signing this treaty since it could not bind him legally. In the first place, they claimed, a signature given under duress—that is, under the threat of losing his fortune—violates the moral code and is therefore illegal. Second, the promise never again to engage in steelmaking violated the equality of citizens before the law, and was therefore unconstitutional and illegal.

Under these circumstances Krupp felt he could sign "the scrap of paper," as the legal head of the firm called the treaty. He explained that "we attribute to it only a declamatory meaning, for instance for publicity in American newspapers." In less legal terms, the pledge was given to deceive foreign public opinion. True, the moral, political, and economic grounds on which Krupp was forced out of the steelmaking industry seemed shaky, and he had a right to attack them. Nevertheless, one wonders about the cavalier manner in which he solemnly pledged to renounce control of part of his empire in order to be granted full control of the rest, with the secret intention of never renouncing anything at all and of violating his given word.

The treaty which Alfried Krupp finally signed at Mehlem, seat of the American High Commission which pleasantly overlooked the Rhine River, committed Krupp to sell the huge Rheinhausen steelworks, formerly known as the Friedrich Alfred Forge, through German trustees over the next five years at prices acceptable to him. The three Krupp coal mines were to be sold and incorporated with this steel mill. Three other coal mines, and an iron mine, in which he owned a 51 per cent interest, were to be sold independently. Two small manufacturing firms were to be transferred in equal shares to his surviving brothers and sisters, or their heirs, who had been disinherited by the *Lex Krupp,* and in addition he was to pay each of them three million dollars.

The old cast-steel factory with its affiliated locomotive factory, truck factory, machine-tool plant, tungsten-carbide works, and all the retail, printing, and building auxiliaries of the empire in Essen were his again, as well as his shipyards at Bremen, the Germania Shipyards in Kiel, and the large bridge-building and steel engineering plant of Stahlbau Rheinhausen. Nobody could say how much all this was worth, except that it surpassed hundreds of millions of dollars. Against all this, he was to pay twelve million dollars to his family and twenty-four million to the firm's pensioners.

When this agreement was published, a wave of protest followed. In legal terminology, the agreement dealt with the "compensation" Krupp was to receive for the holdings he was forced to sell. This was misunderstood by politicians and the public to imply that Krupp—like, say, the victims of Nazism—was being compensated for his damages. The misunderstanding was difficult to clear up. "The uproar caused by the McCloy decision [to release Krupp from prison in 1951] was remarkably violent, especially in the British press. But it was nothing compared to the furor which arose when the Allied High Commission were forced to reveal . . . the terms of their plan to 'liquidate' the Krupp empire," Alistair Horne of the London *Daily Telegraph* reported at the time. Members of Parliament bombarded Foreign Secretary Anthony Eden with inquiries and complaints. There was a similar public uproar in France, which was to continue for some time.

What the public saw was only that the convicted "war criminal" of yesterday, heir to one of Germany's feared and hated names, symbol of German military power, was back on his throne and again Europe's richest millionnaire. The fears and hatreds of the past stirred again, and old wounds were opened. With this reminder, and seeming revival, of the past, "again" was the key word. It was understandable, particularly in the light of past experiences with the House of Krupp, if foreign opinion distrusted, if not disbelieved, the New Look. They did not want "to be fooled twice."

It was up to Alfried Krupp and his firm to prove whether the firm was as new as its look, or whether this

was merely a new camouflage. It was up to him, too, to
show whether he was merely the recipient of his forefathers' industry or "a real Krupp" who would multiply his
inheritance.

His fellow workers, with bouquets of flowers in their
hands and happy grins on their soot-blackened faces,
lined the streets when, as a monarch returning from exile,
Alfried Krupp, his new wife by his side, drove for the
first time again to his firm in March, 1953. The streets of
Essen through which they rode and the factory which was
their goal were still mostly ruins. The picture of destruction and decay still was seen almost everywhere. But here
and there the debris had been cleared and occasionally
there were even signs of new construction. Krupp was in
the race again, with a New Look and a very old heritage.

12

Miracle in the Ruhr

In 1953 the Firm of Krupp began to rise again and it has continued on its ascent ever since. If the seven postwar years brought fall, disgrace, and destruction—in the eyes of many, the end—the next seven years led to a complete comeback.

Some of the hardest blows of the postwar period turned out to be blessings in disguise. With almost half the equipment of the firm dismantled and carried away, it was forced—and free—to install new equipment and build new plants. This put the firm at an advantage in its competition with other European producers, who were burdened with old equipment. Among these foreign competitors some were even stuck with Krupp's old equipment which they had received as reparations. With its more modern machinery, Krupp was often able to out-produce and outsell its competitors.

The first new investments were financed with money which the planners of destruction themselves made available to Krupp. The sale of a few properties under Allied deconcentration rules supplied Krupp with almost three million dollars in cash, and he borrowed nearly twenty million dollars from West German banks to finance reconstruction projects. In contrast to corporations obliged by law to publicize their assets, profits, and sales, the one-man business of Krupp was under no such obligation. Although, perhaps because, no outsider knew its financial status, the banks granted credits on the strength of the Krupp name. "Had we been forced to publish our balance sheet," Krupp's financial manager, who shared in the collective leadership of the postwar years, admitted later on, "we could not have lasted. Our situation was much worse than anybody would have guessed." A fourth financial shot in the arm came from the German government, which allowed Krupp substantial tax write-offs. In all he spent some forty million dollars for initial reconstruction. This was a modest expense compared to the profits which began to show after 1955, two years after Alfried Krupp came back and Berthold Beitz came in. These profits, which Krupp plowed back as capital investments, financed the continuing growth of the firm.

The main reason that the firm was able to come back was the great change in its industrial character. Rather than steel and arms, which had been its main production items, the firm now made and sold practically everything, with the exception of steel and arms. Even in the well-stocked toy department of its Essen department store, a customer would not have found one single tin soldier or toy tank.

To enumerate all the goods and services offered by the House of Krupp since the mid-1950's would fill a book. In fact it did; the firm's catalogue which listed all a customer could buy or lease from Krupp was a complete and rather impressive book. Nicely bound in fluid-resistant patent leather—presumably for customers and salesmen to carry under water—it listed in its 150 pages, in alphabetical order, the names of almost 4000 products and services offered by Krupp, with the addresses of the auxiliaries that sold them. By an accident of the alphabet which seemed symbolic, the long and lavish list began with *Abbauhämmer*, or wrecking hammers. On the next pages, a customer could find and order almost anything else he desired. If, say, he wanted to take up, or was engaged in, mining, all he had to do was to look up mining apparatus. If he produced condensed milk, or beer, iron, coal or oil, chemicals, textiles, soap or movies, Krupp offered him the machinery required. If he was interested in buying a bridge for pedestrians, Krupp had it ready for sale, and for that matter, bridges of every other kind, too—railroad bridges, canal bridges, pontoon bridges, and a dozen more esoteric types. To order palm-fuit presses or palm-kernel cutters from the Krupp catalogue was just as easy as to order, perhaps, a whaling ship, a research boat, or an ocean-going passenger liner.

In this giant hardware store serving industries rather than consumers, steel, the oldest staple of the firm, was missing. But Krupp offered instead to supply its customers with steel foundries. "Total planning and production of complete installations, for iron, steel, and metal productions, including entire construction of attached housing projects, transportation systems, and power plants," as Krupp succinctly advertised. Krupp would supply also packaged steel mills, from a team to survey the local ore reserves to the finished forges. While the firm itself was unable to make steel, it helped others to make it, not unlike, say, the Swiss who, after their medieval era of martial glory, became thoroughly devoted to peace but still supplied their more martial young men as soldiers to foreign powers. While Switzerland remained a peaceful country, its sons remained a great supply of hired hands for other nation's wars; so with Krupp's steel.

Steel itself had found new, peaceful uses. New cities came to rest on, be sheathed in, or have skeletons of steel as a basic structural material. According to its catalogue, the firm was ready to deliver steel structures for private housing and factories, railroad stations and movie theaters, trade-fair halls and airport hangars. While Krupp expanded and excelled in the engineering and manufacturing fields in the postwar years, it developed only one new type of material, titanium. This new metal, about 80 per cent lighter than steel and with practically the same strength, was highly resistant to cavitation and erosion. It was extracted from semiprocessed ore and began to be used industrially in 1955. But the innovations which Krupp had developed after Work War I in the fields of locomotives, heavy trucks, Diesel motors, and railroad cars, in the production of non-corrosive steel, and in the development of the Widia hard metal, were still important and profitable in its post-World War II program.

The demand from Krupp surpassed by far the supplies. In 1956 its backlog of orders would have kept the firm busy at full capacity for two years even without new ones coming in. But new ones did come in at a rate that increased with every year. About four-fifths of Krupp's total production was bought by German industry. If Krupp's growing strength reflected and led West German recovery after the postwar crisis, the firm profited from it in the first place. The sudden, surprising, steep economic comeback of Germany coincided with the return of Alfried Krupp to his firm. As Germany bounced back, the firm bounced with it, adjusting and changing its character until it showed little resemblance to its past.

While Germany recovered at a speed and with a vigor which took the world and the Germans themselves by surprise, the Germans began to speak of their *Wirtschaftswunder,* or their economic miracle. The phrase had been coined in the 1920's when Julius Hirsch, a Berlin professor of economics, described in a book the prosperity he had seen on a trip to America. Twenty years later it was in turn an American—the philosopher-reporter Max Eastman—who, after a trip to the new Germany, used the term to describe what he had observed there. Since then, in German usage this name has designated the whole era of the 1950's with its prosperity, its sudden satiety, and its emphasis on material rather than spiritual values. In this era of the *Wirtschaftswunder,* the businessmen, industrialists, and economists were once again central and triumphant figures who towered above "the poets and thinkers," but the element that was new and revolutionary was that they towered also above the government officials and the generals.

When Germans call their country the *Wirtschaftswunderland,* or the Economic Wonderland, they point to the Ruhr district as the core of the miracle. This 2000 square-mile district—overly rich in resources and energy, but pitifully underdeveloped in beauty and culture— which occupies only 2 per cent of the area of West Germany, contains Europe's tightest industrial concentration. Almost a third of the industrial equipment of West Germany, and a tenth of its labor force, are found in the Ruhr around Essen. Nearly all the steel and coal of West Germany are produced in this patch of land that was the powerhouse of German recovery.

Some of the Ruhr ghost towns of 1949 had tripled in size by 1959, when the postwar ghosts had been replaced by traffic jams and labor shortages. By 1959 Germany led Europe again in the size of steel output, ranked only behind the United States in the world's shipbuilding, and truck and auto production, and exported more manufactured goods than any nation except America—a total of seven and a half billion dollars in 1958. Once again Germany won the old race against the British competitor on the world market, and the steel market in particular, with the House of Krupp far out in the lead.

To some degree, this was again caused by the disguised blessings which the postwar planners of destruction had enforced on Krupp. "The restraints imposed by the Allies forced the Firm of Friedrich Krupp to take an increasingly active part in the world market," an authoritative German economic survey reported in 1955 ". . . It is a paradox that, through the policy of the Allies, especially of the English, the Firm of Krupp is forced to compete successfully against the British in their very oldest markets, such as India and Pakistan. This is a result of the deconcentration policy unforseen by its originators." A rather understandable undercurrent of *Schadenfrende*—a German expression without English equivalent, describing joy over somebody else's misfortune—can be perceived in this analysis.

With one-fifth of its total production being exported, hardly a spot remained on the map which did not buy some products or services from Krupp. The conquest of customers abroad became Krupp's most spectacular postwar victory, due mainly to new tactics which Krupp developed in search of markets. But this was not another case in which, as tradition had it, "the trade followed the flag." On the contrary, where Hitler's conquerors had failed, Krupp's salesmen succeeded.

The industrialization of "underdeveloped countries"

offered a great opportunity to the firm, which latched on
to their demands with the ingenuous energy with which in
the past it had latched on to the militarization demands of
underarmed countries. Rather than merely sell them its
products, it sold a package consisting of Krupp materials,
Krupp know-how, and Krupp men. If, for instance, a
country wanted to exploit its mineral sources, Krupp
would send a "team of explorers" from the Essen home
base. In its full strength it included one geophysicist, two
geologists, five mining engineers, one surveyor, one chem-
ist, two general engineers, and six drilling specialists.
This team was rented out at a flat fee of from $250,000
to $1,000,000. In one single recent year, Krupp's teams
worked on assignments in Pakistan, Yemen, Iran, and
Greece, and in the following year, Ethiopia, Turkey, and
Labrador. On the return of the team to Essen, a second
team took over to draw the blueprints, work out the calculations, and outline the industry to be built on the basis
of the explorers' findings. When the country accepted the
final bid, crews of Krupp workers and supervisors rushed
to the scene with Krupp material to turn the drafts into
reality.

In this way Krupp received and filled orders in the past
few years to set up, in Greece for instance, a $10,000,000
hydro-electric project, a second $20,000,000 project to
exploit lignite deposits near Ptolemais, an iron-ore smelting plant at Larynma, and a twenty-three-million-dollar
oil refinery near Athens. At the same time, Krupp was just
as busy in other lands. For instance, it built a bridge
across the Bosporus and an 800,000-ton steel plant in
Turkey, six bridges in Portugal, an industrial plant in
Afghanistan, freight quays in Holland, a vast ore-dredg-
ing installation in Australia, a low-grade iron-ore processing plant in Spain, a steel plant in Iran, and so on in
Bolivia, South Africa, Indonesia, and Thailand, where
Krupp took charge of the erection of a new $20,000,000
harbor in Bangkok.

While Kruppians in Pakistan were constructing a steel-
mill and iron-ore mines at a price of $75,000, India, the
hostile neighbor across the border, invited Krupp to build

its steelworks too. In the neighborhood of Rourkela—a name on the map and little else, in one of the most "underdeveloped" parts of an "underdeveloped" country, two hundred miles from the nearest city—Krupp's surveying teams found rich iron reserves and valuable coal fields. This was all that was needed to build a new Essen in the wilderness. But if it took several centuries to break ground for Essen's industrial growth, Asia's new "Essen" was to be built by Krupp in ten years, according to the contract signed in 1955. The project cost $178,000,000 of which the Indian government paid half and the World Bank one fourth. The remaining 25 percent was financed by a German syndicate of thirty corporations associated with, and led by, Krupp. Ironically, among them there was the *Gutehoffnungshütte,* or Forge of Good Hope, that first and failing industrial venture of the Krupp family a hundred and fifty years before. It supplied three 1000-ton blast furnaces to Rourkela.

In February, 1959, the President of the Union of India inaugurated Krupp's Rourkela steel plant and assisted the first blast-furnace tapping. The men from the Ruhr beat their Rourkela deadline. In addition to the huge steelworks themselves, they had to conjure up a whole new city to house the 100,000 members of its labor force and their families. Before the arrival of Krupp only a few native peasants dwelt in the valley and worked in the rice paddies. Five of Krupp's own city planners drafted charts in Essen. "It had been agreed," as Konrad Steiler, their chief, reported, "that no consideration was to be shown for the existing primitive buildings." In a rush, they blueprinted a modern city of one-family houses, connected by a circular highway and embellished with all the greenery dear to the hearts of city planners. Drinking water supplies and sewage systems were laid out with efficiency, and there were high schools, theaters, hospitals, and club houses, to satisfy "cultural needs." Even the future traffic problem was anticipated, with a shrewd system of separate paths for pedestrians and roads for cars and trucks. As in Essen the main shopping streets were closed to all motor traffic, and also as in Essen each house was de-

signed with two rooms, plus a kitchen and bath, differing
only in that Indian courtyards were surrounded by walls
to protect the workers from roaming tigers. There was
nothing, though, to protect the Indian workers from their
wage scale of one and a half rupees a day, or four cents
an hour. (At the same time, the average West German
steel wage was 68 cents an hour, average United States
steel wage $3.03. By 1957 U.S. steel wage costs including
fringe benefits had risen to $3.22, and German steel
wages, excluding fringe benefits, to $1.01, while a Japa-
nese steel worker received 46 cents an hour, and a
French worker, 96 cents.) Soon after their arrival,
Krupp's technicians and engineers reported happily that
everything was going according to plan. In a few years
the neo-Kruppians in Rourkela would forge steel for their
country as efficiently as the old Kruppians in the Ruhr.

In contrast to gigantic jobs of this kind, Krupp was not
averse to accepting minor, seemingly profitless jobs.

In the spring of 1959 Krupp built the hollow steel
globe inside which the Swiss scholar, Jacques Piccard,
and the U.S. Marine Lieutenant, Don Walsh, in the bathy-
scaph, *Trieste,* established a new depth diving record in
the ocean near Guam. This intricate, glamorous feat paid
better in publicity for the firm than in dollars and cents.
Similarly, Krupp accepted the challenge of the Obelisk of
Heliopolis which had slowly sunk into the mud of the
Nile over the 4000 years since Pharaoh Sesostris I had
erected it in honor of himself. When Nasser wanted to
re-erect it on one of Cairo's public squares, Krupp agreed
to elevate the obelisk with hydraulic presses, to clean it
from the filth of four millennia, and to set it down on a
cement pedestal, all for a measly $10,000. But the value
in public relations was incomparably higher, as was soon
demonstrated when Krupp was awarded new contracts by
Nasser to build a shipyard, a paper factory, and two huge
bridges over the Nile.

The real aim of Krupp in Egypt was the multimillion
dollar Aswân Dam. As the House of Krupp proposed,
one stage of this revolutionary project was to be given to
Soviet Russia, a second to England, and a third to West

Germany, represented by Krupp. If the United States financed Krupp's part, a great work of peaceful co-existence could be achieved. Neither Egypt nor its presumable contractors in Moscow and Washington agreed with Krupp on this project.

Krupp pursued the same idea on a world-wide level. Beitz, general manager of the firm and father of the idea, called it the Point Four-and-a-Half Program. It was to follow, and improve on, the United States Point Four Program, designed to give economic and technological help to underdeveloped countries on a self-supporting basis offering longterm investments rather than gifts. Yet many recipients, and sectors of world opinion, often misled by Soviet propaganda, suspected that secret political strings were attached to these American offerings. This was where Krupp planned to come in.

As Beitz saw it, if the firm—well-known for its absolute lack of political interests—gave this aid and helped the underdeveloped countries to build up their industry, nobody would suspect it of ulterior motives or political strings. But since neither the firm nor West Germany was potent enough to finance such ventures, the United States was to finance them for Krupp. The underdeveloped countries would receive their stringless development, Krupp would receive his orders, and America would attain its aim of helping other nations without running the risk that its gifts would be rejected or, as happened more frequently, accepted and sneered at. American generosity seemed to Beitz as suspicious as the American determination to defend world-wide freedom, which was a "political" and therefore objectionable aim in his eyes. Since he himself was as *unpolitisch* as Krupp tradition, he proposed to substitute Krupp's business interest for American generosity, or, to be more exact, to finance Krupp's business interest with American generosity. The idea would have been very smart if everybody had felt the way businessmen, and Essen industrialists in particular, felt. Since this was not so, the naïveté in Krupp's Point Four-and-a-Half Program by far exceeded its shrewdness.

This new pet project of Krupp was presented by Berthold Beitz to Robert Murphy, the State Department's brilliant trouble-shooter, and Douglas C. Dillon, then Assistant Secretary of State for Economic Affairs. They listened to the Essen visitor's proposals with polite detachment, and so did the American business leaders for whose cooperation Beitz eloquently and persuasively called. And that was about as far as he got.

In the meantime, Krupp continued with what might be called its more traditional program, with private profits as its Point One. Older than the governmental programs and more feasible too, this program relied on superior salesmanship, higher quality, and cheaper prices. It was promoted by a powerful organization with excellent public relations. The firm of Krupp had always excelled in these techniques, but in the postwar world, industry in general was shifting from its previous emphasis on production to emphasis on distribution. New advances in production were often arrived at almost routinely by rather bureaucratic research departments, a movement in which Krupp had been a pioneer, but now the competitive struggle centered around new methods of organizing and pushing distribution, and in this Krupp also preceded its competitors.

In its drive to do business abroad and to build up the industry of the world, the firm was deeply attracted by the Soviet economies behind the Iron and Bamboo curtains. From Russia, and its captive nations, to China, Krupp saw a growing, tempting demand for its products and services.

The thought that by trading with the Reds the firm would be helping to build up and strengthen an enemy out to dominate and destroy it, together with the whole free world—not unlike the Nazis, though with even more brutal determination—did not distract Krupp. In the first place, this was, to Beitz and Alfried Krupp, "a political objection" and should have no effect on the mind of an *unpolitisch* businessman. In the second place, the Soviets would build up their industries anyhow, Beitz and Krupp argued, and as they saw it, here was an opportunity for the firm to come in on the ground floor. Of course, Russia had been a favorite customer since way back, before and after the revolution, and as we remember, profitable trade relations between the Russian Communists and Krupp took place between the two world wars.

Krupp's Red trade began in earnest again in 1957 when the Soviets ordered a synthetic-fiber plant worth three million dollars and chemical works worth close to nine million. The Soviets agreed to pay cash for this vast enterprise in which—with the help of 285 machines, 93 pumps, 1515 electro-motors—three separate factories were to produce fibers from xylole, a by-product of Soviet oil distillation. With its huge capacity, the operation produced enough material to make half a million suits a month for Soviet men. Krupp manufactured the machinery in Essen and built the plants in Russia.

This contract re-established a close relationship between the firm and the Soviets, and both Krupp and the Kremlin continued wooing each other on a broader and more lasting basis. When Anastas I. Mikoyan, the leading Soviet trade official, visited West Germany in 1958, he had long and friendly talks with Beitz. He quoted Khrushchev's announcement to the effect that Soviet Russia would outproduce America, and added: "But this drive can succeed only with Western technological assistance." Meaningfully, he added: "The products of Krupp have an excellent reputation among our people." The Soviet representative held out additional inducements. "A smart businessman," the very smart Mr. Mikoyan told Krupp's general manager, "always cultivates alternative markets." He recommended that Krupp, much as it depended on the markets of the Western world, follow his advice and select the Soviet sphere as an alternative market. It would come in handy in the event of American recessions or Western depressions. Russia, he said, was ready to offer many contracts for the construction of factories, power plants, pipelines, refineries, bridges, and roads. It was also ready to buy German railroad rolling stock and trucks. In short, it was shopping for almost everything Krupp had for sale. The supreme Soviet salesman asked the supreme Kruppian salesman to come to Russia and see for himself. He could be sure of receiving red carpet treatment. A few weeks later, Khrushchev mentioned in a speech before the Central Committee of the Communist Party that "the Soviet Union has entertained good trade relations with the Krupp firm in Essen in the past."

In May, 1958, Beitz went to Moscow for a one-week visit. Accompanied by his engineering manager, Beitz was received by all the trade officials of the country from Mikoyan down. Before he left, he bought Tchaikovsky records as presents for his two daughters. If he brought no new Soviet orders, it was only because he could not agree with the Russians on the terms of payment. But he returned with the conviction that the Communist customer was worth being cultivated. He was deeply impressed by the country's industrial potential and the promises it held for the firm. He also noted with favor that Soviet managers resembled Essen managers in that they were not the rabid "political" rabblerousers he had expected to find. "These men," he reported with a look of surprise, "have fingernails as clean as we have!"

Among the Germans who criticized Krupp for this Red trade was, first and foremost, Chancellor Konrad Adenauer. While he successfully resisted the Communist threat and led Germany in the Western community, he denounced Krupp's mission to Moscow in a bitter public speech. When he met Beitz at a reception he asked caustically: "Why don't you wear a red carnation in your buttonhole, Herr Beitz?" Beitz and the Firm of Krupp felt once again that they were innocent victims of misunderstanding and prejudice. "Our business interests in the Eastern block have been judged by political standards," Alfried Krupp complained in 1959 in a speech to his workers. "Such a point of view misjudges our purely economic tasks. We sell to the Eastern countries in order to increase employment, and not for political reasons." In this, he echoed the tradition of his house, and Beitz renewed the tradition when he answered Adenauer: "I can't understand my critics; what could be more logical than to shake hands with a customer who buys fifty million marks worth of goods from you?" Then and on many later occasions he explained: "I am a businessman, do not understand politics, and want to steer clear of politics. . . . Let Adenauer have his politics, and let us do our business." After his trip, he repeated: "Private industry works without political considerations, while governments change. . . ."

It seemed that Beitz had indeed become, as he proudly assured visitors, "a real Kruppian." Once again, the firm seemed to follow merely "the economic reason" of profitable sales (in line with other businessmen in West Germany as well as England and other free countries), and to disregard its responsibilities to the community. The House of Krupp had still not learned its lesson.

After his Moscow trip in early 1958, Beitz, and other Kruppians, often traveled to Poland, Rumania, and other satellite countries, and their salesmen were active in the Red capitals. Sales contracts were concluded with Red China and with most Soviet-captive nations of Eastern Europe. Krupp's spokesmen called these deals "building bridges between East and West." Krupp's public-relations agents, however, worked hard to suppress news of these trips and sales, in view of the bad impression they created in the Western world. When, nevertheless, they became known, the same public-relations agents got busy publicizing deals and contracts of the firm with Western countries, including America, as a counterpoint. But most negotiations and contracts between Krupp and its Red customers were kept secret. In 1958 they amounted to somewhat less than $30,000,000, or about 4 per cent of Krupp's total sales.

At the East German Leipzig Trade Fairs, where the Soviet world meets its Western customers and suppliers, Krupp stood out among the Western companies with its impressive offerings. On the streets, Communist posters shouted their denunciations of the "Western warmongers —Wall Street, the House of Rockefeller, and the House of Krupp," and Communist propagandists chirped in hysterically. But the management of Krupp complained to the Communist leaders, and promptly the posters disappeared and the denunciations quieted down. In a press

conference, Heinrich Rau, Vice-Minister-President of
East Germany, commended the firm for its "contributions
to peace." Karl Edward von Schnitzler, chief East German state-radio commentator, welcomed Krupp to "the
camp of peace." Minor Communist officials who by a slip
of the tongue still added to the name of Krupp their ha-
bitual prefix of "war criminal" and "monopoly capitalist"
were severely reprimanded.

To put the final and inerasable seal of Communist approval on the House of Krupp, Khrushchev himself went
out of his way to show his friendly feelings. On his visit
to the Leipzig Fair in March, 1959, at a moment when
the Soviets threatened once again the freedom of West
Berlin and the peace of the world, the Soviet leader visited the Krupp exhibit. Previously informed of this visit,
Beitz rushed from Essen to meet him, but was dissuaded
in the last minute by Fritz Berg, chairman of the Association of German Industries, and sent instead an elderly,
semi-retired manager to receive the Soviet leader.
Khrushchev studied the firm's offerings and "regretted
that he could not meet Herr Alfried Krupp himself."
When Khrushchev and Kruppians clicked glasses—to be
precise, tumblers made from Krupp's stainless steel, decorated with the three rings, the trade-mark of the House of
Krupp, and filled with French cognac—Khrushchev
toasted "the continued health and prosperity of the firm."
When he left, he expressed his "warmest personal wishes
to Herr Krupp." As a souvenir, he was presented with
one of the Krupp arms-emblazoned tumblers, which he
pocketed with a grin. On the well-worn path to Krupp,
Khrushchev followed the Kaiser and Hitler.

Alfried Krupp, who approved of the Red trade of his
firm without understanding its consequences, worked as
his own foremost traveling salesman, surveyor, and nego-
tiator, and he worked very hard. For two or three months
of every year he went abroad, preferably in one of his
two private planes which he liked to pilot himself. In
1957, for instance, he traveled to Turkey, South America,
Southeast Asia, the Middle East, and Canada, where he
received, and was received by, the governmental and

business leaders of each country. In their ceremonious trappings, these business trips resembled state visits. A flood of announcements, often soon denied, would tell of the contracts which Krupp had concluded or was negotiating, as though he brought a cornucopia overflowing with gifts and a magic wand by which to turn "underdeveloped" countries into lands of plenty. The expectations that accompanied his visits indicated the new Krupp myth; it seemed quite different from the old myth of the Cannon King. True, echoes of the past resounded from the streets as demonstrators picketed the hotels in which Alfried Krupp stayed, and shouted their protests against "the war criminal" and "Nazi," but they had little bearing on the present, and Alfried preferred to ignore them. Nobody protested against the help he gave the Soviets. This demon had not yet come to turn and rend. As happens often, people tend to cling to the stereotypes of the past and under their impact overlook the realities of the present.

How eager the new Krupp was to stamp out the image created by the past was shown in 1954, when, by accident, the firm was linked to an unreconstructed Nazi of the more spectacular kind. When the firm concluded contracts to build in Argentina an iron forge ready for production by 1961 to exploit the iron reserves in the Rio Grande Valley, and to construct an Argentine cement factory, the Krupp manager in charge of foreign sales came to the country. Newspapers duly and reverently reported his visit, and also published a routine picture showing him among other "Krupp representatives" at an audience granted by Juan Perón, who then ruled Argentina. The picture would have been filed away among thousands of similar ones had not the highly respected *Neue Zürcher Zeitung* in Switzerland discovered that one of the "Krupp representatives" depicted was none other than the notorious SS Colonel Otto Skorzenyi, one of Hitler's roughest riders; he had led the commandos which liberated Mussolini from his captors on Monte Sasso, had attempted to liberate Hitler's friend Rudolf Hess from British captivity, and had disappeared after the war. As it developed, he was one of the go-betweens between President Perón and the House of Krupp. But the Essen directors promptly, and probably truthfully, announced that they had no knowledge of his cooperation. The old Nazi soldier and new businessman, they said, acted as the representative of a Spanish company which had some dealings with the Krupp firm, as well as with Perón. Krupp continued to do business with Perón, but Skorzenyi was dismissed and Krupp's public-relations image cleaned of Nazi spots.

Merely to mention the arms-producing past of the firm was considered quite ill-mannered by its head and executives. If one ill-manneredly alluded to it nevertheless, they would shrug it off. Armaments had never played a primary role in the firm's production, they would say, and there had been and were other big arms manufacturers in the world besides Krupp. Also, no stigma was attached to making arms as such, they added. If these claims even approached the truth, they were somewhat contradicted by Krupp's defensive attitude, not unlike a lady of easy virtue who has embraced respectability and is being reminded of her past.

But the mark of "the Reich's armorer" stuck to Krupp almost fifteen years after the last cannon and the last shell had left the plant. Thorough as his conversion to peace-at-any-price production was, public opinion, particularly abroad, continued to identify Krupp almost automatically as "the former arms-maker." The firm's own previous publicity and the terror impact of its former products kept the past alive. "My argument is," Thomas Hardy said, "that war makes rattling good history; but peace is poor reading." For the same reason, people tended to remember the armorer of war rather than the plumber of peace. To offset the old image, and to be accepted, if not liked, throughout the world in the new image, the new Krupp applied the new American public-relations techniques and ordered its public-relations department to see to it that the first rather than the second word be underlined in the phrase "*former* armaments maker," until it could be omitted altogether.

As a plumber and a salesman to the world, Krupp was on the lookout for new raw-material reserves. Its old Swedish supplies neared exhaustion. Germany itself could satisfy only a third of the demand. In its years of rebirth, the firm participated in new companies to explore the Sahara desert for iron ore and copper and established a foothold in northern Canada, near Ungava Bay, where a prospector had discovered ore reserves estimated at close to two billion tons. The Cleveland financier and steel manufacturer Cyrus Eaton, Jr., who owned the rights to operate in the area, invited a West German syndicate headed by the Krupp firm to share with him in the venture. Alfried Krupp and Cyrus Eaton, Jr., circled the district—1000 miles north of Montreal, 500 miles south of the Arctic Circle—in a helicopter, and the contract was concluded. Where only a few Eskimos had wandered, a little Essen-in-the-Arctic was planned for 1500 workers and their families. Since the ore was of low grade, a special processing plant had to be built to convert it into pellets, and new harbor and transportation systems had to be created in the Arctic wastes to ship the iron via the Rhine River to Essen or via the St. Lawrence Seaway to the Great Lakes area. A $200,000,000 project, its first output in 1961 was scheduled to be half a million tons, and by 1965 an output of five million tons was anticipated. These iron-ore discoveries were considered as important as the earlier uranium discoveries in the Blind River district and the oil and natural gas boom in the prairies of Canada. Cyrus Eaton of Cleveland, Ohio, and Alfried Krupp of Essen, Ruhr, seemed fitting partners. What they had in common was an interest in the Soviet Union. Both had been personally invited to Moscow by Mr. Mikoyan, and happily accepted the invitation. But while the Soviets seemed customers like anybody else in the eyes of Krupp, to Eaton they appeared as favorite customers, as the champions of peace and freedom. Since the Canadian-born, self-made utilities and steel millionnaire had lost his corporation battles in the Great Depression, he had developed into a maverick of American industry, denounced the American system of government, law enforcement, and economy, and praised the Soviet way. He was host to Mikoyan when the Soviet leader visited the United States in January, 1959.

But in 1959 the partnership between Krupp and Eaton seemed to come to a dead end. Krupp's spokesmen suddenly denied any future plans of coöperation with the Canadian-American industrialist. Krupp and Eaton, it appeared, were not made for each other—at least, for the time being.

Krupp shifted his eyes from the Arctic to the Republic of the Philippines: Toward the end of 1959 it planned to erect a steel works on the island of Luzon which would produce 150,000 tons of steel by 1963. Krupp's participation in the venture was shared by the Associated Management Company.

In a race for raw materials to keep its foundries going, Krupp searched out sources of power previously unknown, to be developed, of course, by Krupp. In March, 1958, in conjunction with the West German machine factory of Brown, Boveri & Co., Krupp ordered an atomic reactor with a capacity of 15,000 kilowatts to be completed by 1961. In Australia Krupp's team prospected for uranium reserves. At about the same time Krupp acquired a share in a small Munich plant to process hydrogen.

At the same time the new House of Krupp was conquering world markets as a contractor and salesman, it was again expanding its production empire. The Mehlem Treaty was still in force. By this treaty the head of the house was pledged to sell his steelmaking plants, mainly the Rheinhausen Foundry which had again become one of Europe's most modern establishments. Although the management of these plants was independent of Krupp, until they were sold, their profits accrued to him. But Alfried Krupp did not sell them; he could find no buyers, he asserted, who were willing or able to purchase the plants.

Nobody could prove the opposite, but the claim appeared highly doubtful in view of the fact that since 1958 the shares of the *Preussag* mining and oil combine had been sold to almost 1,000,000 individual Germans. The

seller was the West German government, which had inherited the holdings from the Nazi government and felt
that in its free economy industries should be owned by individual citizens rather than the State. Therefore, they
were offered to the public in small "peoples' shares," and
proved a quick sellout. But Krupp would not, of course,
consider transferring his holdings to public corporations
and selling shares to the people as other big Ruhr corporations, such as the DEMAG engineering firm, were
doing.

In September, 1957, Beitz had had himself elected to
the board of the Rheinhausen corporation which Alfried
Krupp had pledged to sell. Everybody understood that
this gesture symbolized the return of Alfried Krupp to
this part of his empire from which he was still banished
by the treaty. Yet legally there could be no objection to
the presence of Beitz. A shrewd division of labor between
owner and manager had emerged. While Gentleman Alfried seemingly lived up to his pledge and remained on
the outside of the Rheinhausen companies, his major-
domo plenipotentiary—bound by neither personal pledge
nor gentlemanly honor—shouted, schemed, and clamored
for reunification of the old Krupp empire and voidance of
the Mehlem Treaty. It had become a personal battle to
Beitz.

After 1958 the claim that Alfried Krupp was waiting
for buyers was merely a transparent pretense to help the
Allies keep face while Krupp reneged on his pledge. His
company statisticians began to list the plants with their
profits and production as though they still belonged to the
Krupp combine, or, more accurately, as though they
again belonged to it. When the five years had passed in
which Alfried Krupp had committed himself to sell them,
he asked for an extension of one year, which was granted
but without much doubt anywhere that this extension was
only a step to annulment of the pledge and eventual complete reunification. In 1960 another extension of a year
was granted again.

It seemed only a matter of time before Krupp would
achieve this goal. In anticipation the firm announced in

January, 1959, that it had purchased the *Bochumer Verein für Gusstahlfabrikation A.G.*, a mill producing specialized steel products, and a competitor of the firm from way back. Three years before this purchase, an option on a controlling interest in the Bochum concern had been obtained by Axel Wenner-Gren, a Swedish mystery man of international finance and a close friend of Alfried Krupp. Rumors that he had acquired the option on behalf of Krupp, though, had been violently denied at the time. The purchase in 1959 justified the suspicion that Krupp was behind the Swedish transaction. The merger of the new steel plant with Krupp's still-separated Rheinhausen steel mill added a crude-steel capacity of 1,600,000 tons a year to the latter's 2,400,000 tons. With a four-million-ton capacity, Krupp was able to make more steel than the Potsdam Agreement of 1945 had conceded to all of Germany. By 1960 a new Renn-process plant able to work poor German ore, which had been under construction since 1957, would be ready to produce an additional half million tons. Once again Krupp was Europe's biggest steelmaker.

From an economic point of view, it was healthy progress. Modern steelmaking depends on its concentration, and for technological and business reasons has a built-in need to expand. "If we allow our big, integrated industries to be made smaller and disintegrated, we may be sure that other nations will not. They will use the very principles of high-volume, low-cost output that we invented to drive us out of world markets. . . ." This message was published almost simultaneously with Krupp's new expansion move. But it referred to American corporations, appealed to Americans, and was published in *Look* magazine, an American publication noted for its liberal rather than "reactionary" tendencies. Its defense of American heavy industry under attack for its "bigness" could well have referred to Krupp, too.

The tendency to merge and expand was stimulated in postwar Germany by the fact that the country, rather than legislate against trusts in the American way, legislated instead against cartels, voluntary associations of individual corporations formed for the purpose of establishing prices, markets, or details of production. Since this was unlawful, German firms went one step further and merged altogether.

"There is a great future danger," Chancellor Adenauer commented in 1958, "that a handful of economic structures will control the German economy to such a degree that the government will be forced to take drastic steps against them." What worried him, as well as many other Germans, was the economic power wielded by these new giants, among whom the new Krupp was the most gigantic. Of considerably less danger was the political—domestic and international—power in their hands, for the reason that they did not want any political power. Their idea of freedom was to be let alone by the government when it came to business, and let the government take care of politics. From Alfried Krupp and Berthold Beitz down, the allegedly powerful leaders of Krupp privately talked of the policies of their government—*die Obrigkeiten,* or the superiorities, as they still called it—with the same slightly resentful and deeply fatalistic submission as the man in the street. As long as the government did not interfere with its growing business and created favorable conditions for its further growth, Krupp would go along.

The new German army, which evolved at the same time as the new Krupp, was built up without the help of Krupp. The firm's contribution to the new defense forces of its country was negligible. In 1958 it sold a 43 per cent interest in an aircraft assembly plant at Bremen— one of the less important units in its empire—to United Aircraft, which assembled American jet aircraft shipped to the West German republic for the West German NATO air force. And a Krupp subsidiary, Flugzeugbau Weser, was commissioned in January, 1959, by the West German Defense Ministry to design and develop a medium-range military transport aircraft. These were all the weapons under development in the Krupp empire.

"Military production is not profitable," Alfried Krupp said in 1958. "Civilian production is more continuous in peacetime, and there is always the risk of losing a war."

In short, it pays not to make cannons, or so the new House of Krupp had come to believe. The firm again stood securely on its Essen grounds without producing any arms at all.

But the line between defense production and civilian production became increasingly blurred. Krupp's Widia tungsten carbide, for instance, the hardest metal known to man, could be used on the tips of heavy-duty industrial drills or in knives. (These knives were the first knives in 2000 years with a cutting edge from a material other, and better than, steel.) But tungsten carbide hard metal was also required for nozzles of jet engines and for vital parts of space satellites. In the latter area the individual "arms manufacturer" was succeded by a team of dozens, sometimes hundreds, of manufacturers producing the thousands, and sometimes tens of thousands, of parts required for one single product. In this teamwork the individual arms manufacturer lost the glamour or the notoriety once associated with his name and became almost anonymous. If Krupp's Widia auxiliary supplied materials for jets, for instance, it was involved in military production. It had no other choice, unless it wanted to be the Don Quixote of big industry. Its disclaimers to the contrary were not, and could not be, altogether accurate.

Since 1953 Krupp—then literally and financially in ruins—had won again its old place, or perhaps a new place, if not a combination of both, among the world's industrial leaders. By 1959 its working force had grown from less than 2000 after the war to 89,000. Its plants, which had seemed mere rubble heaps, were again stretching over many miles, equipped with modern machinery, and busy on a twenty-four-hour shift. Its turnover in 1958 amounted to 3.45 billion marks—or almost a billion dollars—with 2.30 billion marks' worth of sales by the Firm of Fried. Krupp proper, and 1.14 billion marks by the separated, yet Krupp-owned, Rheinhausen steel mill. Five hundred eighty-two million marks' worth of goods and services were sold abroad, with the firm itself taking the lion's share of 495 million marks. In 1959 slightly more than 100 companies belonged to the combine still mock-modestly called the "Firm of Fried. Krupp," although it had all the characteristics of a world-wide industrial, engineering, and trade empire.

Ten years after he was sentenced to a twelve-year prison term and stripped of all his properties, Alfried Krupp reigned again over the empire which he had inherited, transformed, and owned. Its exact value and his personal income are a secret which he and his managers discuss with no one. According to the most conservative estimates, his present fortune surpasses the one billion dollar mark. ("If you are in my bracket," J. Paul Getty, one of America's richest billionaires, said, "you don't know exactly what you own, a few hundred million dollars more or less." But then, his fortune seems to be slightly smaller than Alfried Krupp's.)

Yet it was apparent that the Krupp leaders felt a new sense of limitation. "We're only little fish," Beitz remarked to the writer, the humility of his words overshadowed by the complacency of his voice. "We are small compared with our foreign competitors," Alfried Krupp in his more dignified way assured us. Compared with America or Soviet Russia, Krupp, like West Germany as a whole, was a second-rate force, Krupp said. If this point of view implied a wish to be free of the responsibilities of leadership, it also implied that its holders had no ambitions of hegemony. The new European iron and coal community binds Krupp, and West Germany as a whole, closer to the West of which it has become an integrated part.

The changing mentality as it expressed itself in the industrial character of the new Krupp seems almost more miraculous than the "economic miracle" of Germany. If the Krupp firm seems the very personification of this economic miracle, Alfried Krupp himself does not think so. "In what is unhappily called the 'economic miracle,'" he told this reporter, "there is nothing that is miraculous." What, then, led to the German—and Krupp's—comeback, in Alfried Krupp's opinion? "First," he explained, "the Germans learned after World War I that they could recover from defeat. This lesson inspired us all the time until we really recovered again. The main factor was hard work. This time we had to start from scratch, and we had to work even harder. A shot in the arm was given us by the Marshall Plan and other American aid. Another push in the upward direction was political; we could grow again when the wartime alliance broke up and the common effort to hold down Germany was abandoned." He added, "But there was still another factor to lead us over the mountain; we had good luck . . . don't underestimate our good luck. Take all this together," he summed up, "and it spells recovery . . . but not a miracle."

Other businessmen would have added other reasons to explain their recovery, in particular the economic policies of the Bonn government. Its Economics Minister, Ludwig Erhardt, stuck to his ideas of free enterprise and free competition when he was called to office. He established the new German economy along these lines, while he encouraged exports by government-backed credits and helped the struggling industries by liberal tax concessions. Given this framework and American shots in the arm, the Germans, led by Krupp, could re-assert their energy in a drive for security.

Whether to call the outcome a miracle is largely a question of semantics, if not theology.

13

The Managerial Monarchy

The 220-room hilltop palace, Villa Hügel, as much a symbol of Kruppdom as sprawling plants and mushrooming production, had a new look in the years of the Economic Miracle.

When it was returned to the heir after he signed the Mehlem Treaty, plans were under way to donate the palace with its parks and gardens to the State of Rhineland-Westphalia to which Essen belongs. The donation would not only save taxes and the high costs of upkeep, but also demonstrate in a nice gesture that the Krupps had taken to new ways. But the State was not particularly eager to accept the white elephant which, on closer inspection, turned out to be a gray and somewhat moth-eaten mammoth. While negotiations between Krupp and State officials dragged on, his firm and fortunes rose again. With new wealth coming his way, Alfried Krupp decided that there was no more need for him to be generous. He could afford again not to give away his possessions and to keep them all for himself.

But in the new era, the heir used the familial residence only on great occasions. In the block-wide halls of the villa, he received the potentates who came to visit. As crowned peers and customers of Krupp, King Paul and Queen Frederica Louise of Greece, Emperor Haile Selassie of Ethiopa, President Soekarno of Indonesia, Prime Minister Adnan Menderes of Turkey were among those who drove up to Villa Hügel. On such occasions, a bugle corps of trumpeters lined the driveway, the firm's band, attired in Krupp's black-and-gold livery, would strike up the national anthem, and a choir of Kruppians enter-

tained the guests, while the flag of the House of Krupp—
the three intertwined black rings on a white background
—waved over the palace.

On less festive days Villa Hügel was—in a democratic
effort, perhaps—open to the public. The residence was
turned into a part-time museum, where occasional art exhibitions and concerts were held. This note of beauty
served to announce that Kruppdom's New Look took culture as well as the commonweal into account, not to mention tax benefits.

At other times, when neither a State reception nor a
cultural event lent a festive air to Villa Hügel, sightseers
were invited. The old servants doubled as guides, although they showed little love for the job. The more than
six hundred paintings collected by the owners since the
death of the art-hating founder had been taken off the
walls and stored behind locked doors, and the equally numerous antlers collected by Krupp's gun-loving guests
were packed away too. There remained only a few tapestries, the most beautiful one bearing a legend which proclaimed: *"Ars deprimit bellum,"* which, as the guide explained, meant "War suppresses the arts but the arts aid
war." The translation might well have startled visitors familiar with Latin and/or the history of Kruppdom. Yet
few visitors paid much attention to the Gobelins and their
legends. They were interested in the paintings, statues,
and in the snapshots of the Krupps with which the house
abounded. From Alfred to Alfried, none was missing.

"Shave off his beard, and you think it's Herr Alfried,"
the family factotum of Villa Hügel would say to visitors,
pointing to the paintings and sculptures of Alfred Krupp,
the founder of the dynasty. In fact, although no Kruppian
guide would dare mention it, the resemblance between the
ancestor and his equally tall, tautly erect, bony-faced
great-grandson did not stop at appearance. They also
closely resembled each other in their bitter, lonely lives.
Exactly like his great-grandfather, Alfried Krupp had led
the firm to amazing triumphs after his father's pitiful
death. But exactly like his great-grandfather, too, he
failed pitifully in his search for human happiness.

After she had become Alfried's wife, Frau Vera was rarely seen in Essen. A woman accustomed to the sun and the high-life of California, the Esseners sadly admitted, could find little to attract her in their ugly, provincial, cheerless city. While her husband restored the old splendor of the firm with the New Look, Frau Vera enjoyed the fashionable resorts of Europe and America.

In 1956, four years after his wedding to Vera, Alfried Krupp found in his morning mail a letter from her lawyers. She sued him for divorce. A settlement of $5,000,000 and a yearly lifetime income of $250,000 was her price for freedom in silence, and it was hinted that she could disclose quite a few secret foreign accounts and even more secret political schemes of her husband. The matter was settled *in camera,* a move which violated the law of the land. German divorce laws rule that forthcoming trials as well as their outcome must be announced to the public; this was not done in the case of *Krupp* v. *Krupp.* A surprised German public learned of it only by chance some time after the decree became final.

"The divorced wife of the German ammunitions tycoon," as American gossip columnists called her, more colorfully than accurately, left the smokestack society of Essen for the café society of New York and Nevada. For a while chroniclers busily reported her adventures, as she was seen with George Sanders and other night-life celebrities. In June, 1957, Dorothy Kilgallen of the Hearst papers told her readers that "Nevada officials are expected to subpoena Vera Krupp, divorced wife of the German munitions tycoon, to question her about certain shady figures she knew when she owned part of a Nevada hotel." According to other reports, Frau Vera invested $185,000—Krupp dollars, certainly—in the New Frontier Hotel and gambling casino in Las Vegas shortly before it went bankrupt for tax liabilities. Only after Frau Vera Krupp settled on a 400,000-acre ranch near Las Vegas did she disappear from the public eye. As she explained it, Alfried worked too hard and his mother, Bertha, ruled the household with a hand too iron for the daughter-in-law's pleasure.

After the fifth heir of the House of Krupp lost a wife for the second time, he retreated more than ever into his work and into himself. He moved to the fifteen-room "bungalow," which he had built on the grounds of Villa Hügel. Hidden behind old trees, accessible only by a private road, and guarded as cautiously as an atomic-bomb stockpile, it seemed as impersonal as a cigar box. Every morning at nine o'clock sharp, Alfried drove in one of his two custom-built Porsche sports cars to the factory. He used his other two larger cars on travels out of town. On trips to more distant places he piloted his small private airplane or flew in his second plane, which held a full-sized office and meeting-room. Outside the firm, his main interest was amateur photography, and on his return from far-flung business trips the company magazine would publish his tourist snapshots—of the Acropolis in Greece, say, or of a Siamese temple—with a devotion otherwise reserved only for economic and technological reports. Flying and sailing were his other hobbies. He never visited a church and rarely read a book or attended a concert. "In a life like mine," he explained matter-of-factly, "one has very little time left.'"

"Alfried is the loneliest man we know," his associates sighed in their rare references to the private life of their ruler. "Herr von Bohlen is a most unhappy gentleman," his servants and the waiters in the North Sea resort where he spent his sailing vacations sympathized. Even one of Essen's Communist chieftains told us: "I feel so sorry for Krupp . . . and that has nothing to do with politics . . . it's just because he is such a poor fellow."

Those who knew him were more deeply impressed by his personal misfortune than by the fortune which made him one of the richest men in the world. With King Saud of Saudi Arabia, the Sheik of Kuwait, the Sheik of Quatar, the Nizam of Hyderabad, and a quiet American oilman by the name of J. Paul Getty, Alfried Krupp is among those who belong to the rather exclusive club whose members own more than a billion dollars each. If the heir to the House of Krupp outranks in riches the heirs of, say, the houses of Rockefeller or Morgan, Ford, Mellon, or DuPont, whose ancestors amassed fortunes greater than Krupp's, the reason is that Krupp's inheritance was not split up among a growing number of heirs as were the legacies of the American multimillionnaires. Alfried Krupp leads the world's wealthiest men because his family ruled and inherited its industrial empire according to his great-grandfather's monarchic will.

"I believe that I have to follow my great-grandfather's last will, even if it is now a hundred years old," Alfried often declared. In the year of his fiftieth birthday, Alfried brought up to date the monarchic constitution which Alfred Krupp had willed. On January 1, 1958, he signed and published the new "Plan and Principles of Organization of the Firm of Fried. Krupp." Although in order to demonstrate the New Look of the firm, Professor Carl Hundthausen, then his chief public-relations counsel, had suggested that no reference be made in this document to the old "General Regulative" of 1872, in the next edition Alfried inserted the reference to this past constitution by his own hand.

"The Organization Manual," his preamble proclaimed, "continues the tradition of the General Regulative of the Firm of Fried. Krupp, which was released in 1872 by my great-grandfather and the purpose of which was to detail the rights and duties of office and officer in both factories and administration, to delineate their areas of responsibility, and thereby, in so far as possible to guarantee stability, order, and harmonic cooperation for the present and the future, and to provide for the commonweal of the firm and the welfare of its individuals."

As it emerged, however, the new constitution seemed more devoted to the commonweal of the firm than to the welfare of its individuals. Or, perhaps more accurately, the authors and signers of that constitution took it for granted that the second depended on the first.

"The owner, or his general plenipotentiary, shall lead the whole firm," the first article of the new constitution proclaimed. The monarch and his "general-plenipotentiary" manager had full control over the empire. The manager was Berthold Beitz, who by that time had succeeded in breaking down the distrust and resistance of the old Kruppian bureaucracy against him as an outsider and newcomer, and Beitz saw to it that his role was invested with almost unlimited powers. "I consider myself as a lion trainer," he explained to us with his boyish smile. "I make the lions, that is, the personnel of the firm, perform well, keep them from eating one another, and think up new tricks to teach them." But he did much more than this; he pleased the audience. As a master at public relations he drummed, barked, and cajoled; as an unorthodox, hard-working salesman he filled the tent with customers; and, using his lion trainer's whip with the brutality of a Pomeranian drillmaster, he made the Kruppians perform. Prime Minister Beitz ruled while King Alfried reigned. After this managerial revolution, the Krupp empire became a managerial monarchy.

Due to the bigness and the geographic dispersion of the one-hundred-company combine, the dangers of bureaucracy were inherent, and the constitution set out to overcome them by turning the firm into a federation of firms —as it were, a United Companies of Kruppdom. Its individual and semi-sovereign units were granted the equivalent of states' rights. According to the new constitution, the empire—still named the Firm of Fried. Krupp—was divided into twenty-one so-called "chief companies," from, say, Fried. Krupp Raw Materials to the Forge, the Shipyards, and the Coal Dealers of Fried. Krupp. To each "chief company," a number of auxiliary "companies" were attached, ninety-four altogether, ten among them located abroad. Each company was given "as much freedom as possible and only as many commands as necessary, while it fulfills its task in independence." In the combine that had grown too big for the traditional centralized leadership, "the initiative and ability of the individual is given wide leeway, subordinated only to the common good." While the individual companies were run as separate units, competed in the open market for the business of their sister companies, and planned their own courses, the pattern recalled the "socialist competition" which the Soviet planners—not very successfully—tried to establish in their dictatorial economy.

Like a federal government, the supreme leadership of the combine ruled over its semi-foreign companies from the old Administration Building on the Essen factory grounds. The government of the United Companies of Kruppdom consisted of a cabinet of directors who were, respectively, in charge of sales, technology, finances, and administration, set the general policy of their departments, and supervised the coordination and application of their policies. Each director was assisted by from three to six sub-directors in charge of specialized sub-departments. The director of technology, for instance, had assistant directors of research, development, production, and patents. Beneath these cabinet posts "staff departments" —federal authorities, as it were—planned and directed the firm's accounting, law, public media, and liaison. "They are my boys," Beitz used to boast.

In addition to the form of Kruppdom's government, the new constitution delineated also the rights and duties of Kruppdom's people, more precisely of the workers of the firm. This part of the constitution was embellished by axioms that seemed excerpted from a Rich Richard's Almanac. "He who works conscientiously must never fear his superiors, but regard them as necessary to help him in his own activities," the Constitution proclaimed. "The individual must merge all his efforts with those of his fellow employees into a total effort of cooperation. In addition to performing his own task, each employee must consider also the interests of the other companies." Behind these commonplaces was the attempt to combine individual initiative with unquestioning subordination. "Everybody has a right to present his own ideas," one director explained to us, "until the directors have made their decision. Then he has to do what we tell him to do, whether we are right or wrong." In confidential talks we found the workers, as well as the office personnel, rather pleased with his mixture of freedom and dictatorship, while more intellectually oriented employees, such as the researchers and scientists and some sub-managers, disliked and resented it.

In marked contrast to the old constitution which Alfred Krupp had decreed in the nineteenth century, relatively few orders were laid down to the labor force. The reason was that the rights and duties of all workers were to an increasing degree settled by the government of the new Germany itself. If the old firm had lorded it over, and taken care of, its Kruppians, by 1955 neither was possible. The State saw to it that the rights of employers were limited, and the State itself took care of the employees. With the new Germany turning into a welfare state, there was little room left for a welfare firm. The workers and leaders of the new Kruppdom agreed that the "race of Kruppians" which Alfred Krupp had tried to breed was becoming a vanishing race.

True to tradition the firm still faithfully paid pensions to old Kruppians, which took a big bite out of the firm's income. "To heal the wounds suffered during World War II," Krupp announced in December, 1959, that the firm would pay $1,190 to every Jewish person who could prove that he or she had been a slave laborer for Krupp. Most were dead and could not claim their dues. To the non-Jewish laborers Krupp offered no compensation at all. The firm continued to subsidize the hospital and nursing home for its workers and again erected housing units for the Kruppians, but much of the latter was State subsidized, with rents slightly below standard.

Many of the old welfare tasks of the firm had now become profitable outlets of its free enterprise. If the firm supplied the world's industries with its products, it did the same for the consumers of the Ruhr district, who could buy at "Krupp" furniture to outfit a whole housing settlement or a pound of cheese. Krupp's old "consumers' cooperative" was now the center of a Krupp-owned chain of department stores, supermarkets, and self-service shops, with its own bread factory, slaughterhouse, and soda-water plant attached. Krupp even operated an elaborate wine and liquor store, where a customer could order from its lengthy and inspiring price list more than three hundred different kinds of wine. Several cheap inns, some elegant hotels in and around Essen, even the greenhouses and vegetable gardens of Villa Hügel, served the public and brought profits to the owner.

Somewhat more generous than his ancestor, Alfried Krupp donated here and there a million or so—on his fiftieth birthday, for instance—to causes not entirely alien to his economic interests. He granted scholarships to foreign youths to study engineering or business administration in the Krupp firm and also to sons of Kruppians in search of a scientific education. Every year Krupp's ten apprentices with the best performance record were sent at his expense to a summer sailing school.

If in the past the firm had cashed in on rewards for its paternalistic care, the old policy still bore dividends in the postwar years when Kruppians backed "their" factory and its owner against public hostility. They had a commanding self-interest in the preservation of the firm. Their pension claims, and perhaps their jobs, would be lost if Krupp disappeared. Whether they could find employment elsewhere in Germany was highly doubtful. Therefore, they protested the dismantling and all other measures of discrimination and destruction directed against Krupp. Although many had hoped that the concern would be socialized, they greeted Alfried Krupp with sincere joy on his return to the firm. When he asked the assembled workers whether they agreed with his decision to reconstruct the firm and whether they would support him in this effort, an old Socialist named Hermann Waldeck, who served as the elected spokesman of the factory crew, answered with conviction: "Sure, we're all still Kruppians." Hence the legend that "the old Krupp spirit" among the workers contributed much to the comeback. But the fact is that workers in all other German industries worked just as hard and well as their comrades at Krupp.

The Kruppians, like all workers throughout West Germany, received "fringe benefits" from their government, which in 1959 channeled almost one-half of its budget revenues into social uses. It provided every German worker and his family with government subsidized medical care and with high old-age pensions, the two benefits which had characterized Krupp's early contributions to its

working force. But in a measure which the Krupps would
never have undertaken on their own, the German government brought about worker participation in the firm's industrial relations. By law, the elected representatives of labor were paid wages by the firm while they devoted their full
time to the interests of their fellow workers. With almost
every worker in Germany to share it, the old special Kruppian sense of security and belongingness lost its meaning.

Furthermore, Kruppians, again like other German
workers, lost their physical tie to their employer in the recovery years when they bought their motor vehicles—
from scooters to Volkswagens—and gained a new feeling
of mobility and independence. Any day they could leave
Krupp to drive toward the green fields which abounded
throughout the land under the sun of the economic miracle. The workers of Krupp, as well as those of West Germany in general, lost their status as the proletarian class
as, in turn, the members of the upper classes lost theirs.
In income, style of living, and leisure-time activities, they
began to resemble their one-time betters. They saw the
same motion pictures and television programs, and the
difference between the bar in Essen where a young
worker celebrated a night on the town and the bar in
Dusseldorf where a director entertained customers on an
expense account was visible only in minor details of de-
corum and prices. Even the people of Kruppdom felt almost the peers of their rulers and no longer took off their
caps when the bosses passed through the factories.

The thirty-five members of Krupp's Workers' Council
got along extremely well with the management. Seven
among them were secret members or sympathizers of the
Communist movement now outlawed in West Germany.
They had been elected on the strength of their record as
active and able advocates of their fellow workers rather
than for their political opinions. When the Communists
tried to agitate for political ends in the Krupp firm, they
failed. "If the firm would produce arms again the workers
would protest, but not strike," they admitted. After the
Hungarian uprising, one worker defended the Soviet in-
tervention and his fellow workers threatened to strike un-

less he was fired. The Workers' Council and the management persuaded him to retract and apologize for his statement. But then, "politics" as such remained an undesirable, if not improper, activity to engage in, or to discuss on Krupp grounds. The Workers' Council and the management bargained only on routine matters. In a typical one-month period of 1958, their only issue was the extra payment a number of workers on an outlying project would receive for their daily transportation. A second question was settled in a quick and peaceable way, not entirely in the Krupp tradition. An old storekeeper in the winery was caught stealing a bottle of liquor. According to the rules he was to be fired on the spot, but because he had served Krupp for forty years without a fault and was to be pensioned in a few weeks, the Workers' Council representative pleaded for forgiveness and management agreed.

Alfried Krupp believes that the monarchic principle, by which one personal owner rather than an anonymous mass of stockholders personifies the organization, has succeeded in tying the workers closer to management and has strengthened their personal identification and job continuity with the firm. "They know that I am responsible for their lasting employment, as Krupps have been since my great-grandfather," he asserted.

According to Alfried Krupp and his managers, there were other and more important advantages to the unique principle of personal one-man control by the family heir. In their eyes the most important advantage was the fact that they remained free of interference by, and obligations toward, stockholders. They could re-invest their profits rather than distribute dividends. Second, the firm was not obligated by law, as were stockholders' corporations, to report figures or information on its capital, profits, and debts, or to publish its financial statements. According to Krupp, this state of secrecy permitted a more purposeful system of doing business. Third, the personal one-man leadership made it possible for the leader to make decisions more quickly than could corporation executives bound to satisfy the members of their board, their shareholders, the stock exchange, and government

authorities. Fourth, the system protected Krupp's management to some degree from its workers (the only advantage which was not pointed out by Krupp himself, but
by his workers). They would have a better position in
their labor negotiations if they were more familiar with
the financial status of their firm.

In short, we asked Alfried Krupp, you do believe that
the monarchic principle in modern corporations is superior to the democratic principle? He answered that his
was an enlightened monarchy, and whether it was good
for others or not, it had proved its worth to Krupp. His
managers agreed with him.

More critical observers in and out of the firm were
more doubtful. In times of crisis, they said, it had been a
collective group of leaders rather than the heir who had
steered and saved the firm. They wondered whether the
present enlightened and managerial type of monarchic
rule would withstand the next crisis, if and when it
comes, or whether, perhaps, some leaders and sub-leaders
of semi-sovereign companies might try to strengthen their
independence and gradually break away until in the end
the empire would cease to exist. They wondered, too,
whether public scrutiny, criticism, and control as applied to
other corporations of comparable size would not benefit the
firm in the end. It could help to forestall or correct grave
mistakes, which are bound to happen under one-man rule.

The answer of the Kruppian monarchists was that the
same doubts and objections had been voiced a century
ago when Alfred Krupp set out on his experiment of industrial monarchy and that, despite much intermittent un-
pleasantness, it was going stronger than ever. Theirs is an almost mystical belief, "There will always be a Kruppdom."
They take for granted what to others might seem incredible.

In 1957 the family assembled to lay Bertha Krupp to
rest. The foreign press published the news of the death of
the seventy-one-year-old woman with reminiscences of
the "Big Bertha" gun to which she had given her name
and which in many minds still stood for the firm. But no
Kruppians in Essen seemed to recall this episode of the
past. What they did recall was the continuity of Krupp-

dom that shaped her life. Bertha Krupp von Bohlen had been named after her grandmother whom she had never seen, since the elder Bertha Krupp had fled from Villa Hügel before her birth. But her grandfather, Alfred Krupp, had still glared at her when she was an infant. And when she was in her teens, her father died, or as rumor had it, committed suicide, and left her as his heiress. The Kaiser had addressed her on her wedding day, and Hitler had kissed her hand. Later she and her invalid husband had to flee to what had been their servants' quarters. The firm was in ruins and had been taken away from the family. But in her last years, she saw the firm again on its way to acquiring its old strength under the rule of her son Alfried, its heir, owner, and ruler.

Alfried Krupp led the funeral procession. Next to him walked Arndt Krupp, his only son. The good-looking, seventeen-year-old boy stayed with his divorced mother in Munich on his vacations from a cosmopolitan Swiss boarding school. He was named after Arndt Krupp, the first Krupp who came to Essen almost four centuries before and he was the heir-apparent of the Firm of Fried. Krupp, whose previous four generations of owners had been haunted by their heritage.

Ten years later, when Alfried Krupp died in 1967, he left his industrial empire to a new foundation for the benefit of the arts, sciences and social progress of Germany. His son Arndt renounced all his claims to the billion-dollar heritage. A few years before, the Krupp concern had overextended its foreign credits so badly that the Bonn government had to help out. Krupp was saved under the condition that it become a regular corporation with its stock available to everybody. Arndt was to receive merely royalties from two companies which had been previously separated from the Krupp combine. They assured him of a life-time income of more than half a million dollars a year— enough to keep him happy in his three palaces, his luxury yacht, and his oversized sailboat. An active addict of the *dolce vita*, he announced that he never wished to live in Essen again. The empire has come to an end.

14

As Germany Goes . . .

Time present and time past
Are both perhaps present in time future,
And time future contained in time past.

T. S. ELIOT, *Four Quartets*

How new, then, was "the new Krupp" as it had evolved
by the end of 1959? Had the house mended its old ways
or merely undergone a spurious change?

Many observers in and out of Germany doubted that
there was anything new in this new Krupp. They feared
that it was merely the old Krupp all over again, with the
newness added as window-dressing to attract contemporaries, and to fool them. In the light of the past, their
fears were understandable enough. Since they had come
to see Krupp as the symbol of "everything that was bad
about Germany," as a British critic put it, they wondered
whether the return of Krupp also signaled the return of
past dangers and terrors. The leopard, they said, never
changes its spots; yet, the House of Krupp did not happen to be a leopard, nor any other species of animal—
some of which, incidentally, do change their spots when
the season comes, and therefore the analogy was of little
help in answering the question. What kind of future was
contained in Krupp's past and present?

Looking at the history of the House of Krupp, as we
have in this narrative, the history of Germany itself ap-
pears in clear outline. As in a piece of a shattered mirror,

the profile of Germany is reflected in the image of Krupp. As Germany changed over the years, so did Krupp.

To be sure, no one family can wholly personify its country; least of all the Krupps, whose individual members over five generations were lonely eccentrics and therefore something less than "typical Germans." But the way of this family and its industrial empire mirrors—sometimes in a focus so sharp as to present an overexposed, distorted picture—the changing currents which have dominated the political nature of their country and the national aspirations of their society.

The Krupps always wanted to be *unpolitisch,* to bear no part in the shaping of their community but to take the authority of their rulers and their order for granted, to preserve family principal rather than strive for general principles, to be left alone to work and prosper. Exactly because of their *unpolitisch* character did they follow the course of their country without ever falling out of step. As Germany went, so went Krupp.

From the very beginning, the lifelines of Germany and of Krupp seem to run in parallel directions. Both entered the world scene from a starting point of insignificance. Germany was a nation that wasn't, and Krupp did not qualify as an industrialist. Both deeply sensed their insecurity. Combined with the Protestant ethic of work and success, their sense of insecurity led them to develop overwhelming energy. According to a dictum of a German nineteenth-century historian, Leopold von Ranke, which became quite popular in his country, Prussia showed its greatness because it stood firm "against everybody else." Thus Alfred Krupp could have described his own endeavor. In its fear of losing its independence to neighbor nations, blessed by rich reserves of raw materials and forging its manpower into a military machine, Prussia struggled out of its insignificance. It aimed at hegemony over the other German States and attained it at the same time it defeated the French neighbor nation. Substitute foreign competitors for neighbor nations and labor force for military machine and Prussia's struggle becomes Krupp's struggle. Krupp followed, sometimes led, this

German march toward industrial and military hegemony over the European Continent.

After Prussia attained supremacy on the Continent by the unification of Germany and the defeat of France the next step was supremacy over the world, in what German historians have called *hubris*, or demonic pride. While Germany tried to win a cold war, or a "dry war" as it was then known, Krupp marched along. Both Germany and Krupp outreached themselves and brought about their fall. Their nemesis was in their past triumphs.

When after this fall new German leaders tried to build a new, peaceful, democratic country, many Germans supported them, while others fought the attempt and hankered for a return to the old ways of military power and nationalism. ("What is nationalism? The urge of the German people to spread its influence over all the globe," proclaimed Friedrich Naumann in 1897.) Divided within itself, until one side should win, Krupp again reflected exactly this "Interim State" of the Weimar Republic. The House of Krupp adjusted itself to, and accepted, the official peaceful new order, but at the same time, on the side and in secret, it also prepared for a return to the old. Up to the very last moment of indecision Krupp followed both lines. Only when the attempt at German innovation failed under the onslaught of domestic and foreign enemies, did Krupp join the winner.

Krupp followed Hitler, the winner, on Germany's road while he unleashed his war—first a cold and then a hot war—for German supremacy. Like many Germans, Krupp joined the leader, to some degree under the force of threats, yet in the main under the impact of seductive promises, willingly and sometimes enthusiastically, notwithstanding a few infrequent reservations. Since a totalitarian order of the Nazi kind turns its *unpolitisch* people into accomplices unless they choose to resist, Krupp became an accomplice.

Yet a minority of Germans chose to resist the ruling terror at the risk of their lives. They were even represented inside the House of Krupp by one leading manager and two family members. A small minority among the

Kruppians, as among Germans at large, they could not change the dominating order in which Krupp went along with his rulers, as a glove does with a hand—both glove and hand being manufactured of first-quality steel and spotted by the blood of the victims. When Germany was defeated, disgraced, desperate, in ruins, Krupp was too, only more so. When Germany became the prisoner of the victors, so did Krupp, literally. The plan of the victors to turn industrial Germany into a pastureland was bound to cripple the country. With the announcement that Krupp's industries were to be razed until grass grew on the factory grounds, they sentenced the House of Krupp to death. As Germany went to lower depths, so went Krupp, but Krupp's fall was deeper.

Then came the great turning-point, for Krupp as well as for Germany, and for Krupp a little later than for Germany. The end marked a beginning; the fall initiated a new rise. How Germans felt was expressed by Ludwig Dehio, a leading contemporary German historian, who stated in 1953 that the task of the historian "is no longer to demonstrate the continuity of history, but rather to show the break that has taken place . . . and to knock down what must fall." In German minds, the spell and validity of the ideas, hopes, and aims of their past was broken. This fall of old idols led to the turn in their destiny.

Germans abandoned their century-old goal to attain supremacy over the other peoples of Europe. They ceased to build up the power that was to lead them to this goal and turned their backs on armaments as the tool of that power. There were two reasons for this. The first was psychological: since their previous belief in these goals had plunged them into misfortunes which left a trauma, they never wanted to repeat the experience again. Their second reason was rational: they began to understand that in the world as it was they could not escape their new status as a second-rate power under two new power giants, the United States and the Soviet Union. If in their minds they no longer had a desire for power, they were also well aware of the political fact that they no longer

could attain it. They could survive only in the wake of
one of the two world powers, and in joint action with
their neighbor nations. Taught and led by Konrad Adenauer, the first great German statesman since Bismarck
and the first German statesman to convert Germany into
a Western nation, Germans chose partnership with the
United States, friendship with France, integration with
Western Europe. Only reluctantly, under threat of Soviet
expansion, did the German people agree to the formation
of a new German military establishment as part of the
Western defense community. And they agreed to this only
after they were convinced that it could not be used by
German nationalists as a tool of expansion by force. If in
the past Germany had striven for security by the power of
its arms, it was still striving for security, but without
armed power.

Germany's—and Krupp's—seemingly boundless energy and willingness to work, industrial know-how, ability
to serve the economy and to satisfy the customers, a special sense of duty and discipline, in brief, the old source
of success, survived the fall and soon reasserted itself
again. But rather than toward national power, it was directed toward economic growth, a term which, significantly, has come to replace the older term of economic
progress. If progress seems boundless with the sky as the
limit, growth, in accordance with organic laws, is limited.
No tree reaches the sky, nor can it be forced to outgrow,
or feed upon, its neighbor trees.

This new order of Germany found a willing follower in
the House of Krupp. Paradoxical though it might seem,
the turn was, in fact, less revolutionary on Krupp's road
than it was on the German road. As ever before, pos-
sessed by energy and equipped with industrial, commercial, and engineering know-how acquired over almost a
century and a half, Krupp continued to produce and sell
its products and services. It also continued to prosper.
And it stuck to its old principle of being *unpolitisch*,
looking only to its business interests, following only the
principle of its principal. The new order of Germany sup-

plied Krupp with a perfect opportunity to remain true to its old self.

More paradoxical still, Krupp's new reluctance, if not refusal, to make arms showed that Krupp in our time has changed less than has Germany as a whole. In fact, Krupp's new insistence on making "tools of peace" exclusively, and no "tools of war" at all, was in accordance with its traditional *unpolitisch* and, therefore, irresponsible posture. After Krupp was punished for supplying arms to help Hitler's aggression in World War II, Krupp resolved to produce no arms of its own will to help deter Soviet aggression and to prevent a World War III. With the growing market for Krupp's "tools of peace" this resolution was a source of profit rather than sacrifice. The basic values of the greater community to which the House of Krupp belonged still were of less concern to the Krupps than their short-term business interests and their personal resentments and fears.

In the same vein, the old traces of Kruppdom were revived when the firm continued, and fervently pursued, its Red trade. In this, too, Krupp remained faithful to the heritage of the house. In 1869 Alfred Krupp had refused to let the German Emperor halt his sales to Napoleon III and other enemies of his nation ready to attack it. In 1959 Alfried Krupp refused to let the German Chancellor halt his sales to Khrushchev and other enemies of freedom ready to attack it. The *unpolitisch* businessman tends to be rather short-sighted and somewhat irresponsible when he comes face to face with politics, that is, with those responsibilities toward his community that conflict with his personal interests and internal business affairs. In this Krupp seems also to reflect the posture of many Germans today, but once again, in sharper focus.

Yet we see many signs and portents in present-day Germany that the youngest generation differs from its forefathers. Less burdened by debatable and unhappy traditions of the past, unhurt by triumphs and nemeses of yesterday, growing up in the new era of a peaceful, free Germany, the majority of young Germans seem awake to their responsibilities as citizens and as members of the Western community.

A minority of other young Germans—reflecting minorities of the young all over the world—try to reject all traditions, the good together with the bad. It was in their style that the former heir-apparent of the house of Krupp retired at the age of 29, foreswearing work, living on profits from former family enterprises, supplying the scandal sheets of Germany with frequent stories of his latest amusements. They were his own private affair, without impact on Krupp business. But the house which his ancestors built still stands. It is no longer the biggest of the German corporations, nor is it intrinsically different from other large corporations, nor is it still owned or controlled by the family whose name it bears. Part and parcel of the general German economy, the Krupp concern has lost its old, unique, half-glamorous, half-sinister and often incredible personality.

As Germany went, so went Krupp. And it has become apparent in 1969 that Germany has taken the road of free and peaceful growth which is also ours.

Appendix

Genealogical Line

- I   Arndt Krupp 1624
- II   Georg Krupp 1590-1623
  (Anton, Katharina, Margarete Krupp)
- III   Mathias Krupp 1621-1673
- IV   Arnold Krupp 1662-1734
  (Georg Dietrich Krupp 1657-1742)
- V   Friedrich Jodocus Krupp 1706-1757
- VI   Peter Friedrich Wilhelm Krupp 1753-1795

- VII Friedrich Krupp (Founder of Firm) 1787-1826
- VIII Alfred Krupp 1812-1887
- IX   Friedrich Alfred "Fritz" Krupp 1854-1902
- X   Bertha Krupp 1886-1957
  m. 1906 Gustav von Bohlen und Halbach 1870-1951
- XI   Alfried Felix Alwyn Krupp von Bohlen und Halbach 1907-1967 (Claus (+), Irmgard, Berthold, Harald, Waldtraut, Ekbert (+) von Bohlen und Halbach)
- XII Arndt von Bohlen und Halbach 1938-

Bibliography

NOTE: *Official or authorized Krupp firm or family publications are marked* K.

Aldington, Richard, *Pinorman; Personal Recollections of Norman Douglas, Pino Orioli, and Charles Prentice.* London, 1954.

Anon. *Die Familie von Bohlen und Halbach.* Essen, 1921 K.

Anon. *Der Prozess Krupp vor dem Kriegsgericht, nach dem einzigen vorhandenen Stenogramm.* Muenchen, 1923. (French Courtmartial).

Anon. *Der Fall Krupp.* Muenchen, 1903. (Capri Affair)

Baedecker, Diedrich. *Alfred Krupp und die Entwicklung der Gussstahlfabrik zu Essen.* Essen, 1889.

Berdrow, Wilhelm. *Die Familie Krupp in Essen von 1587 bis 1787.* Essen, 1931 K.

——— *Friedrich Krupp, Der Gruender der Gussstahlfabrik in Briefen und Urkunden.* Essen, 1915 K.

——— *Friedrich Krupp, Leben und Briefe.* Berlin, 1929 K.

——— *Alfred Krupps Briefe.* Berlin, 1928 K.

——— *Alfred Krupp.* Berlin, 1927 K.

——— *Alfred Krupp und sein, Geschlecht.* Berlin, 1937 K. Second (and changed) edition, Berlin, 1943 K.

Bernstein, Victor Heine. *Final Judgment.* New York, 1947.

Beusch, H. *Die Krupp-Wohnungen im 10 Jahre nach ihrer Zerstoerung.* Essen, 1955 K.

Borkin, Joseph, and Welsh, Charles A. *Germany's Mas-*

ter Plan. Introduction by Thurman Arnold. New York, 1943.

Boelcke, Willi, ed. *Krupp und die Hohenzollern; aus der Korrespondenz der Familie Krupp; Quellenveroeffentlichungen aus dem Deutschen Zentralarchiv Merseburg.* (East) Berlin, 1956.

Carnegie, Andrew. *Problems of Today.* New York, 1908.

——*Armaments and Their Results.* New York, 1909.

——*Autobiography of Andrew Carnegie.* Boston, 1920.

Class, Heinrich. *Wider den Strom.* Leipzig, 1932.

Clay, Lucius D. *Decisions in Germany.* New York, 1950.

Davidson, Eugene, *The Death and Life of Germany: An Account of the American Occupation.* New York, 1959.

Dicke, H. W., and Lenz, W. *Essen in Geschichte und Sage.* Essen, 1930.

Douglas, Norman. *Looking Back, An Autobiographical Excursion.* New York, 1933.

——*Materials for a Description of Capri.* London and Napoli, 1904-1915.

Dulles, Allen Welsh. *Germany's Underground.* New York, 1947.

Düwell, Wilhelm. *Wohlfahrtsplage.* Dortmund, 1903.

Ehrenberg, Richard. *Grosse Vermoegen.* Jena, 1925.

Fischer, Ruth. *Stalin and German Communism.* Cambridge, 1948.

Fried, Ferdinand. *Krupp—Tradition und Aufgabe.* Godesberg, 1956.

Goerlitz, Walter. *History of the German General Staff.* New York, 1953.

Grimm, Friedrich. *Vom Ruhrkrieg zur Rheinlandraeumung.* Hamburg, 1930.

Hauenstein, Fritz. "Alfred Krupp," in: *Die Grossen Deutschen.* Berlin, s.d.

Herchenroeder, K. H., Schaefer Joh., and Zapp, Manfred. *Die Nachfolger der Ruhrkonzerne.* Düsseldorf, 1955.

Heuss, Theodor. "Alfred Krupp," in: *Deutsche Gestalten.* Tuebingen, 1947.

Heydecker, Joe J., and Leeb, Johannes. *Der Nuernberger Prozess.* Koeln, 1957.

Höss, Rudolf. *Kommandant in Auschwitz.* Stuttgart, 1958.

Horne, Alistaire. *Return to Power.* New York, 1956.

Hue, Otto. *Krupp und die Arbeiterklasse.* Essen, 1911.

Hime, H. W. L. *Gunpowder and Ammunition.* London, 1904.

Kellen, T. *Die Firma Krupp und ihre soziale Taetigkeit.* Hamm, 1903 *K.*

——*Friedrich Alfred Krupp und sein Werk.* Braunschweig, 1904 *K.*

Klass, Gert von. *Die Drei Ringe.* Tuebingen, s.d., *K.*

Knieriem, August von. *The Nuremberg Trials.* Preface by Max Rheinstein. Chicago, 1959.

Krupp, Fried. A. G. *Krupp 1812-1912.* Jena, 1912 K.

—— *Die Krupps.* Essen, 1912 *K.*

Krupp, Alfred. *Ein Wort an die Angehoerigen meiner gewerblichen Betriebe.* Essen, 187?.

——*Generalregulativ (Vorbemerkungen und Kommentar von Ernst Schroeder), in Tradition: Zeitschrift fuer Firmengeschichte und Unternehmerbiographie.* October, 1956 *K.*

Krupp. *Cast Steel Manufactury near Essen, Germany; Philadelphia Exhibition.* Essen, 1876 *K.*

—— *Catalogue of the Exhibits sent to the Paris Exhibition of 1876,* by the manufacturers of cast steel works of Krupp in Essen. London 1876 *K.*

—— Exhibition Catalogue of the Cast Steel Works of Fried. Krupp, Essen on the Ruhr (Rhenish Prussia;) World's Columbian Exposition, Chicago 1893. *K.*

—— *Wohlfahrtseinrichtungen der Kruppschen Gussstahlfabrik zum Besten ihrer Arbeiter und Beamten.* Essen, 1883 *K.*

Krupp, Friedrich. *Erzeugnisse und Leistungen A–Z.* Essen, 1957 *K.*

—— *Krupp im Dienste des Technischen Fortschritts.* Essen, 1958 *K.*

—— *Titanium, The New Metal.* Essen, s.d. *K.*

Krupp, Gustav von Bohlen und Halbach, in Fritzsche Rolf. *Aufbau der deutschen Wirtschaft.* Berlin, 1934.

—— in: *Das neue Deutschland gruesst die auslands-deutschen Nationalsozialisten.* Erlangen, 1936.

Kuerenberg, Joachim von. *Krupp, Kampf um Stahl.* Berlin, 1935.

Leber, Annedore. *Conscience in Revolt.* Westport, Conn., s.d. (1958).

Lochner, Louis P. *Tycoons and Tyrant; German Industry from Hitler to Adenauer.* Chicago, 1954.

Maschke, Hermann. *Das Krupp-Urteil und das Problem der "Pluenderung."* Goettingen, 1951 *K.*

Menne, Bernhard. *Krupp, Deutschlands Kanonenkoenige.* Zurich, 1937.

Morgenthau, Henry, Jr. *Germany Is Our Problem.* New York, 1945.

Monthaye, E. *Krupp et De Bange.* Bruxelles, 1887.

Mühlon, Wilhelm. *Memoranda and Letters.* New York, 1918.

——*Revelations by an Ex-director of Krupp's.* New York, 1918.

—— (pseud. "A German") *J'Accuse.* New York, 1915.

Mueller, Gen.-Lieut. H. *Die Entwicklung der Feldartillerie von 1815 bis 1870.* Berlin, 1893.

Nizer, Louis. *What To Do with Germany.* Chicago, 1944.

Omann, Sir Charles W. *History of the Art of War in the Middle Ages.* London, 1924.

Peyrefitte, Roger. *L'Exilé de Capri.* Paris, 1959.

Ritter, Gerhard. *Carl Goerdeler und die deutsche Widerstandsbewegung.* Stuttgart, 1954.

Rothfels, Hans. *The German Opposition to Hitler.* Hinsdale, Ill., 1948.

Roosevelt, Elliot. *As He Saw It.* New York, 1946.

Schacht, Hjalmar. *76 Jahre meines Lebens.* Bad Woerishofen, s.d. (1953).

Schroeder, Ernst. *Krupp, Geschichte einer Unternehmerfamilie.* Goettingen, 1957 *K.*

Schwerin von Krosigk, Lutz, Graf. *Die Grosse Zeit des Feuers.* Tuebingen, 1957.

Seiss, J. A., D. D. *Remarks Made at the Funeral of Henry Bohlen, Brigadier-General U.S. Army.* Philadelphia, 1862.

Steiler, Konrad. *Rourkela, Eine neue indische Stadt.* Essen, 1958 *K.*

Strieder, Jakob. *Alfred Krupp.* Luebeck, 1942.

Taylor, Telford. *Nuremberg Trials.* New York, 1947.

Thayer, Charles. *The Unquiet Germans.* New York, 1957.

Thyssen, Fritz. *I Paid Hitler.* New York, 1941.

Tresckow, Hans von. *Von Fürsten und andern Sterblichen,* Berlin, 1922.

U.S. Government Printing Office. *Trials of War Criminals Before the Nuernberg Military Tribunals.* Vol. IX, Alfried Krupp, et al. (Krupp Case)

—— Vol. VI, Friedrich Flick, et al. (Flick Case)

—— Vols. VII and VIII, Carl Krauch, et al. (I. G. Farben Case)

—— *Der Prozess gegen die Hauptkriegsverbrecher vor dem Internationalen Militaergerichtshof.* 42 vols.

U.S. Strategic Bombing Survey, Reports, European War:
#73, *Fried. Krupp Borbeck plant;*
#108, *Fried. Krupp Gussstahlfabrik, Munitions Division;*
#69, *Friedrich-Alfred-Huette Rheinhausen, Munitions Division;*
102, *Fried. Krupp Grusonwerke Magdeburg, Ordnance Branch.*

United Nations War Crimes Commission, Law Reports of Trials of War Criminals, 15 Vols., London, 1947.

Utley, Freda. *The High Cost of Vengeance.* Chicago, 1949.

Wecker, Ernst. *Krupp; Berliner Volksbuch der nationalsozialistischen Kulturgemeinschaft.* s.d.

Weymar, Paul. *Adenauer.* New York, 1957.

Wiedfeld, Otto. *Friedrich Krupp als Stadtrat in Essen.* Essen, 1902.

Wilmowsky, Thilo Freiherr von. *Warum wurde Krupp verurteilt?* Stuttgart, s.d. (1950) *K.*

Woischnik, Bernhard. *Alfred Krupp, Meister des Stahls.* Godesberg, 1957.

Information from the following periodicals has been used:

Events before 1945: *Frankfurter Zeitung, Koelnische Zeitung, Koelnische Volkszeitung, Vorwaerts.*
Events after 1945: New York *Times;* New York *Herald Tribune; Time; Fortune; Financial Times,* London; *Steel Review,* London; *Krupp-Nachrichten,* Essen; *Der Spiegel, Die Zeit,* Hamburg; *Die Weltwoche,* Zurich; *Archiv der Gegenwart,* Bonn.

For the sake of bibliographical comprehensiveness, rather than to document my story, fictional accounts of— or inspired by—the Krupps may be added:

Friedrich Krupp is the hero of a dramatic play: *Friedrich Krupp, der ewige Deutsche,* by Hermann Hagedorn, Essen, 1936.
The figure of Alfred Krupp in Villa Hügel has inspired German novelists: Rudolf Herzog, *Die vom Niederrhein,* a devoutly hero-worshipping novel; and Heinrich Mann, *Die Armen,* a bitter novel of social criticism.
The Capri affair of Fritz Krupp is the subject of the recent novel *L'Exilé de Capri,* by Roger Peyrefitte, with a foreword by Jean Cocteau. One of the few brilliant social satires of German fiction, Otto Julius Bierbaum's *Prinz Kuckuck,* is also in parts inspired by the case.
The post-World War I dealings of the House of Krupp are the subject of Erik Reger's novel of Left-wing social protest, *Union der festen Hand.*

Index

Index